PARADOXES OF CONSCIENCE
IN THE HIGH MIDDLE AGES

The autobiographical and confessional writings of Abelard, Heloise, and the Archpoet were concerned with religious authenticity, spiritual sincerity, and their opposite – *fictio*, a composite of hypocrisy and dissimulation, lying and irony. How and why moral identity could be feigned or falsified were seen as issues of primary importance, and Peter Godman here restores them to the prominence they once occupied in twelfth-century thought.

This is a new account of the relationship between ethics and literature in the work of the most famous authors of the Latin Middle Ages. Combining conceptual analysis with close attention to style and form, it offers a major contribution to the history of the medieval conscience.

PETER GODMAN is Distinguished Professor of the Intellectual History and Latin Literature of the Middle Ages, University of Rome (*La Sapienza*).

CAMBRIDGE STUDIES IN MEDIEVAL LITERATURE

General Editor
Alastair Minnis, *Ohio State University*

Editorial board
Zygmunt G. Barański, *University of Cambridge*
Christopher C. Baswell, *University of California, Los Angeles*
John Burrow, *University of Bristol*
Mary Carruthers, *New York University*
Rita Copeland, *University of Pennsylvania*
Simon Gaunt, *King's College, London*
Steven Kruger, *City University of New York*
Nigel Palmer, *University of Oxford*
Winthrop Wetherbee, *Cornell University*
Jocelyn Wogan-Browne, *Fordham University*

This series of critical books seeks to cover the whole area of literature written in the major medieval languages – the main European vernaculars, and medieval Latin and Greek – during the period c.1100–1500. Its chief aim is to publish and stimulate fresh scholarship and criticism on medieval literature, special emphasis being placed on understanding major works of poetry, prose, and drama in relation to the contemporary culture and learning which fostered them.

A complete list of titles in the series can be found at the end of the volume.

PARADOXES OF CONSCIENCE IN THE HIGH MIDDLE AGES

Abelard, Heloise, and the Archpoet

PETER GODMAN

CAMBRIDGE
UNIVERSITY PRESS

CAMBRIDGE UNIVERSITY PRESS
Cambridge, New York, Melbourne, Madrid, Cape Town, Singapore, São Paulo, Delhi

Cambridge University Press
The Edinburgh Building, Cambridge CB2 8RU, UK

Published in the United States of America by Cambridge University Press, New York

www.cambridge.org
Information on this title: www.cambridge.org/9780521519113

First published 2009

Printed in the United Kingdom at the University Press, Cambridge

A catalogue record for this publication is available from the British Library

Library of Congress Cataloguing in Publication data
Godman, Peter.
Paradoxes of conscience in the High Middle Ages :
Abelard, Heloise, and the archpoet / Peter Godman.
p.   cm. – (Cambridge studies in medieval literature)
Includes bibliographical references and index.
ISBN 978-0-521-51911-3 (hardback)
1. Conscience.   2. Conscience–Religious aspects–Catholic Church.
3. Christian ethics–History–Middle Ages, 600–1500   4. Abelard, Peter, 1079–1142.
5. Heloise, 1101–1164.   I. Title.   II. Series.
BJ1278.C66G64 2009
189´.4–dc22   2009002690

ISBN 978-0-521-51911-3 hardback

to
BILJANA

Je ne trouve aucune qualité si aysée à contrefaire que la devotion,
si on n'y conforme les meurs et la vie; son essence est abstruse et
occulte; les apparences, faciles et pompeuses.

Michel de Montaigne, *Essais* III. 2

Je mets Montaigne à la tête de ces faux sincères qui veulent
tromper en disant vrai.

Jean-Jacques Rousseau, *Les Confessions*
(intro.; 1764)

Könnte Einer nicht, um zu zeigen, daß er versteht was 'Verstellung'
ist, Geschichten erfinden, worin Verstellung vorkommt?
Um nun den Begriff der Verstellung zu entwickeln, erfindet
er immer kompliziertere Geschichten. Was z.B. wie ein Geständnis
ausschaut, ist nur eine weitere Verstellung; was wie die
Verstellung ausschaut, ist nur eine Front um die eigentliche
Verstellung zu verbergen; etc. etc. etc.

Der Begriff ist also in einer Art von Geschichten niedergelegt.
Und die Geschichten sind nach dem Prinzip konstituiert,
daß *alles* Verstellung sein kann.

Ludwig Wittgenstein, *Letzte Schriften über die
Philosophie der Psychologie* I, 268–9

Contents

Preface and acknowledgements

Outside the Vatican, where much of the research for this book was done, there stood, on almost every occasion I visited the papal library, a gentleman whose behaviour and appearance suggested that he had seen better days. His occupation was, to admonish passers-by. 'Andate a confessarvi!' (Go and confess!) he would bellow to impassive monsignori, indifferent tourists, and curious me. My curiosity was aroused less by what he repeated than by what he did not say. He did not say, for example: 'Pentitevi!' (Repent!), as an evangelical Protestant might have done. Instead he alluded to the redemptive power of a sacrament administered by the Roman Catholic Church.

That he had chosen the right place to do so, no one denied. Nor did anyone appear to pay the slightest attention. If I did, the reason was not only fellow-feeling with one of those whom others regard as cranks. As I worked on the feigning and mockery of confession which he advocated so solemnly, I imagined a dialogue with him on that subject which I did not muster the pluck to conduct in reality. And now it is too late, for, when my research drew to a close, its companion deserted his post near the Porta Sant'Anna. If it would be too much to claim that I miss him, I still hear the echo of his admonition with melancholy gratitude.

The gratitude derives from the stimulus he provided to look at larger questions which the myopia of specialisation may not see. One of them is, how much can we know about the consciences of men and women who lived a millennium ago? Less than is knowable about the period nine hundred years previous to us. Why then, in the *longue durée* of the European conscience, does a single century make a difference? Because that century was the twelfth, during which new issues were perceived and forgotten problems recalled to memory. An example, novel in the intensity with which it was discussed during that period, is *fictio*.

Fictio does not mean 'fiction'. Rather theological than literary, this term signifies feigning and falsification of conscience, particularly in penance.

ix

Penance was given the status of a sacrament during the twelfth century, and confession was regarded as a test of spiritual authenticity and religious sincerity. A travesty of both, at the moment when sinners were expected to be truest to God and to themselves, *fictio* challenged the ethical imagination of Latin Europe. That challenge found a response in the works of Abelard, Heloise, and the Archpoet. Usually considered separately from one another, in terms of such harmless but unhelpful anachronisms as 'individuality' or 'renaissance', all three of them reflected on issues of moral identity posed by feigning and falsification of conscience. Because the morality to which Abelard and Heloise subscribed was, or became, monastic, their reflection also led them to allied problems of lying, dissimulation, and hypocrisy in a religious context. In the very different context of a German schismatic's court, opposed to Rome and hostile to monks, the Archpoet took *fictio* to its limit. There the dividing-line between irony and blasphemy blurred. With a refined wit directed against ethical concerns of the previous generation, this feigned penitent, in his 'confession', created a new figure of spiritual sophistry.

Spiritual sophistry has no history. Nor does the medieval conscience before the thirteenth century. This book attempts to make a contribution to both. Tracing the development of *fictio* and its implications for concepts of sincerity, authenticity, and their opposites, it tries to show how, why, and when a change in the ethical imagination of the West occurred. This occurred earlier than was maintained by Lionel Trilling in a justly celebrated work quoted at the beginning of the first chapter, which introduces the phenomenon of *fictio* as it emerged and mutated during the second and third quarters of the twelfth century. The next two chapters outline the evolution of feigned penance and related ideas from late antiquity to the High Middle Ages. Attention is then paid to their presence in the writings of Abelard, Heloise, and the Archpoet. They raised questions which were not forgotten later, as an *envoi* indicates briefly.

The works of these three figures have a claim to attention, not least because their concerns remain ours, in other shapes and forms. It is the thought of Abelard, Heloise, and the Archpoet that stands at the centre of this book; and an effort is made to link conceptual analysis with the study of style and form. My hope is that this approach may serve to answer questions which have vexed medieval scholarship, although I am sure that my way of going about them will be regarded, in some quarters, as old-fashioned. I have relied on my imperfect memory and made no use of databases, because I am sceptical of the mechanical methods of Latin-less ingenuity. Successive computations of *cursus*, which rarely tally with one another and never illuminate a single thought, have not spared us prolonged and fruitless controversies about the authenticity of Abelard's and Heloise's epistolary exchange or the attribution to them of some thirteenth-century love-letters. If weariness and boredom at the first controversy appear to have produced a measure of agreement that their writings are indeed what they claim to be, ghosts of uncertainty continue to haunt us.

The most spectral, the least substantial of them is the notion – unsupported by textual history, reason, or common sense – that Abelard forged Heloise's letters. This book contends that the differences between their moral outlooks, directly but subtly reflected in the ways they wrote, were such as to make speculation about common authorship untenable. So too, by implication, is the attempt to foist on the famous couple works that are below their intellectual level, known by the title *epistolae duorum amantium* given them by their first and best editor, Ewald Könsgen. If I have refrained from labouring that implication for the second and no less sterile controversy that has attracted to the names of Abelard and Heloise, the ground is not only a wish to preserve the thematic unity of this book. Almost all that needs to be said about the date and character of the *epistolae duorum amantium* has been argued, with learning and lucidity, by Peter von Moos and others.

∽

In the pages below, I often refer to the publications of Peter von Moos, whose collected studies on these and other subjects (cf. *Abaelard und Heloise: Gesammelte Studien zum Mittelalter* I, ed. G. Melville, Geschichte: Forschung und Wissenschaft 14 (Münster, 2005) deserve more attention than they receive in the English-speaking world. Nor does my debt to him stop there. Since we first met, thirty years ago, when I was a mere beginner and he an established expert, Peter von Moos has never ceased to give me advice and encouragement, from which this book too has benefited. The first study preliminary to it appeared in a *Festschrift* for him ('Cain at Soissons' in *Norm und Krise von Kommunikation: Inszenierungen literarischer und sozialer Interaktion im Mittelalter. Für Peter von Moos* ed. A. Hahn *et al.* (Berlin, 2006) 329–53). Other studies written for friends and colleagues that are related to the subjects I treat here are: 'The Paradoxes of Heloise, I: The First Letter', *Critica del Testo* 8 (2005) 29–53 (for Burghart Wachinger); 'The Paradoxes of Heloise II: Sincere Hypocrisy' in *Impulse und Resonanzen: Tübinger mediävistische Beiträge zum 80. Geburtstag von W. Haug*, ed. G. Vollmann-Profe *et al.* (Tübingen, 2007) 35–44; and

'The Moral Moment' in *Miscellanea Mediaevalia* 34 (2008) 338–45 (for Andreas Speer). All of them have been expanded, modified, and corrected.

Because penance, as it was re-conceived in the twelfth century, appeals to what Martha Nussbaum calls 'the intelligence of the emotions', I should like to think that my subject has something in common with hers. Hers alone is the insight embodied in a splendid book (*Upheavals of Thought: The Intelligence of the Emotions* (Cambridge, 2001)), which is complemented by two excellent studies by Richard Sorabji (*Emotions and Peace of Mind: From Stoic Agitation to Christian Temptation* (Oxford, 2002)) and Simo Knuuttila (*Emotions in Ancient and Medieval Philosophy* (Oxford, 2004)). The approach represented, in different ways, by these historians of philosophy has made an impact on several branches of medieval studies, amply documented by Rüdiger Schnell (cf. 'Historische Emotionsforschung: Eine mediävistische Standortsbestimmung', *Frühmittelalterliche Studien* 38 (2006) 173–276). One of them is not the Latin philology of the Middle Ages. That classical Latin philology, in this respect as in others, fares better, has been demonstrated by Robert Kaster in his perceptive and stimulating *Emotion, Restraint, and Community in Ancient Rome* (Oxford, 2005). It does not detract from Kaster's achievement to say that the texts with which he deals have been read closely for two thousand years. Such is the secondary literature on the classics of the twelfth century that one may wonder whether some of them have ever been read closely, and that is what I have tried to do in this book.

It could hardly have been written without the help of kind friends. In matters of divinity, I have followed the example of John Paul II, and turned to the former theologian of the papal household. His Eminence Georges Cardinal Cottier OP gave me expert advice at the beginning of my research. Knowing the many demands on his time, even in retirement, I have not inflicted successive drafts on him, nor does this book bear the *imprimatur* of authority. It is, however, indebted to the helpfulness of Father William Sheehan and Dr Paolo Vian at the Vatican Library, a *locus amoenus* which, at the time of writing, has become inaccessible. All the more appreciated, in these trying circumstances, is the hospitality which I have enjoyed at the Angelicum in Rome. To Alastair Minnis, the general editor of Cambridge Studies in Medieval Literature, and to Linda Bree, the commissioning editor at the Press, I am grateful for their understanding, encouragement, and unfailing courtesy.

Four personal debts are acknowledged warmly. Reviving a dormant but deep friendship, John Marenbon read the entire typescript, corrected errors, made valuable suggestions, and gave me heart. I recall our conversations about Abelard and much more with keen pleasure. To the generosity of Candi Rudmose I owe the freedom from less agreeable tasks to write. What I wrote by hand was not only typed with patient intelligence by Rodney Lokaj, but has also profited from his pertinent comments. And, finally, affectionate thanks to my Serbian family – Živka, Ivana, Vladimir, and, above all, Biljana, to whom this book is dedicated.

P. G., Umbria, March, 2008

Abbreviations

AHDLMA	*Archives d'histoire doctrinale et littéraire du Moyen Âge*
BAV	Biblioteca Apostolica Vaticana (Vatican Library)
BGPTMA	Beiträge zur Geschichte der Philosophie und Theologie des Mittelalters
CCCM	Corpus Christianorum Continuatio Mediaevalis
CCSL	Corpus Christianorum Series Latina
CSEL	Corpus Scriptorum Ecclesiasticorum Latinorum
HC	*Historia Calamitatum*
Landgraf, *Dogmengeschichte*	A. Landgraf, *Dogmengeschichte der Frühscholastik* 8 vols. (Regensburg, 1952–1955).
MGH	Monumenta Germaniae Historica
MlJb	*Mittellateinisches Jahrbuch*
PL	Patrologia Latina
RLAC	*Reallexikon für Antike und Christentum*
RTAM	*Recherches de théologie ancienne et médiévale*
SC	Sources chrétiennes

CHAPTER I

Moral moments

'Now and then it is possible to observe the moral life in process of revising itself, perhaps by reducing the emphasis it formerly placed upon one or another of its elements, perhaps by inventing and adding to itself a new element, some mode of conduct or of feeling which hitherto it had not regarded as essential to virtue.'[1] Three such moments occurred between the second and the third quarters of the twelfth century. Each of them marked the emergence of a paradox of conscience unknown, or at least unrecorded, for more than half a millennium. Revived and refashioned in Latin, the ancient language of high culture, none of these paradoxes was tinged with the nostalgia of classicism. Expressions of a moral sensibility in the re-making, they served as barometers of change.

The change to which paradox pointed was both spiritual and intellectual. Accurately described as the reformation of the twelfth century,[2] its motive force was monastic. The attempt to re-establish, in its original strictness, the Rule of St Benedict; the efforts to restore the pristine purity of liturgical worship and prayer; the measurement of *authentica et proba* by the standards of an exemplary past:[3] these and other signs of concern with the genuine article were not accompanied by a decline in the production of forgeries.[4] Naturally enough. Compliments paid to others by admirers striving to surpass themselves, fakes represent the other side of authenticity's coin.[5] That side has more than one facet. Viewed in less literal terms than the falsification of documents, it can also be seen to comprise the *fictio* of faith.

---

[1] L. Trilling, *Sincerity and Authenticity*, (Cambridge, Mass., 1971) 1.

[2] G. Constable, *The Reformation of the Twelfth Century* (Cambridge, 1996).

[3] See *Renaissance and Renewal in the Twelfth Century*, ed. R. Benson and G. Constable (Oxford, 1982) and M. -D. Chenu, *La théologie au xiie siècle* (Paris, 1957).

[4] See *Fälschung im Mittelalter*, MGH Schriften 33, 1–6 (Hanover, 1988–1990).

[5] Cf. F. Troncarelli, 'L'attribuzione, il testo, il falso' in *Lo spazio letterario nel Medioevo: Il Medioevo Latino I: La produzione del testo* (Rome, 1993) 373–90, and A. Grafton, *Forgers and Critics: Creativity and Duplicity in Western Scholarship* (Princeton, 1990).

The *fictio* of faith is hardly mentioned in accounts of medieval theology, philosophy, and psychology.[6] Their portrayal of an age of belief, painted in the white of orthodoxy or the black of heresy, makes little room for subtler shades of grey. All seem to agree that the twelfth century made a cult of interiority, woke the conscience from its slumbers,[7] and redefined such sacraments as penance, in which authenticity is assumed as categorically as St Paul commands (I Timothy 1:5).[8] These broad brushstrokes leave few traces of ambiguity to linger within the frame. Next to no one appears to reckon with feigning on the part of those who confessed their sins.[9] One of the grounds for this omission is doctrinal. Sinners who accused themselves with the Biblical bitterness of remorse (Job 10:1) were thought to demonstrate spiritual sincerity, and still are.[10] Duplicity and deception are seldom admitted to the scene, despite the alertness of thinkers in the

---

[6] The exception is Landgraf, *Dogmengeschichte*, III, 2, 86–181, who deals chiefly with baptism. His learned and exact study is ignored by later writers on the subject. (Cf. P. Cramer, *Baptism and Change in the Early Middle Ages c.200–c.1150* (Cambridge, 1993)). Legal aspects of this problem are considered in the valuable study by Y. Thomas, '*Fictio legis*: L'empire de la fiction romaine et ses limites médiévales', *Droits: Revue française de théorie juridique* 21 (1995) 17–63.

[7] See M. -D. Chenu, *L'éveil de la conscience dans la civilisation médiévale*, Conférence Albert le Grand 1968 (Montreal, 1969) and L. Honnefelder, '*Conscientia sive ratio*: Thomas von Aquin und die Entwicklung des Gewissensbegriffs' in *Mittelalterliche Komponenten des europäischen Bewusstseins*, ed. J. Szövérffy (Berlin, 1983) 8–19. Cf. P. Delhaye, *Le problème de la conscience morale chez S. Bernard*, Analecta medievalia namurcensia 9 (Louvain, 1957) and E. Bertola, *Il problema della coscienza nella teologia monastica del XII secolo* (Milan, 1970).

[8] See P. Anciaux, *La théologie du sacrement de pénitence au xiie siècle* (Louvain, 1949) and M. Colish, *Peter Lombard* II (Leiden, 1994) 583ff. Cf. R. Rusconi, *L'ordine dei peccati: La confessione tra Medioevo ed età moderna* (Bologna, 2002) and A. Carpin, *La confessione tra il xii e il xiii secolo: Teologia e prassi nella legislazione canonica medievale* (Bologna, 2006).

[9] Nothing about this in *Faire croire: Modalités de la diffusion et de la réception des messages religieux du XIIe au XVe siècle*, Collection de l'Ecole Française de Rome 76 (Rome, 1981); *L'Aveu: Antiquité et Moyen Âge*, Collection de l'Ecole Française de Rome 88 (Rome, 1988); K. -J. Klär, *Das kirchliche Bußinstitut von den Anfängen bis zum Konzil von Trient* (Frankfurt, 1990); A. Murray 'Confession before 1215', *Transactions of the Royal Historical Society* 3 (1993) 51–81 and 'Confession as a Historical Source in the Thirteenth Century' in *The Writing of History in the Middle Ages: Essays Presented to R. Southern*, ed. R. Davis and M. Wallace Hadrill (Oxford, 1981) 275–322; M. Ohst, *Pflichtbeichte: Untersuchungen zum Bußwesen im hohen und späten Mittelalter*, Beiträge zur historischen Theologie 89 (Tübingen, 1995); or P. Biller and A. Minnis (eds.), *Handling Sin: Confession in the Middle Ages*, York Studies in Medieval Theology (York, 1998). The brief discussion of 'fictive penance' by H. Lea, *A History of Auricular Confession and Indulgences in the Latin Church* II (Philadelphia, 1896) 422ff. is based on modern sources, polemically interpreted.

[10] For the ancient tradition, see F. Dingjan, OSB, *Discretio: Les origines patristiques et monastiques de la doctrine sur la prudence de saint Thomas d'Aquin* (Assen, 1967). Typical of the reticence on the subject of *fictio* by recent moral and pastoral theology is B. Marliangeas, *Culpabilité, péché, pardon* (Paris, 2005). Related issues are, however, discussed by philosophical theologians. Cf. J. Milbank, *Being Reconciled: Ontology and Pardon* (London, 2003) 107ff. and 147ff.

Latin West to the (originally Greek) association of *hypocrisis* (ὑπόκρισις) with acting.[11] This has been ignored for another, less compelling, reason. Literalism, ingenuous or edifying, has relegated *fictio* to the wings. Made to appear more marginal than the sleepwalkers whose antics have been brought to the fore,[12] the feigned penitents of the twelfth century in fact raised issues which, for their amused or appalled contemporaries, stood at centre-stage. The drama turned on ethical identity. Motivation played a leading role. Its uprightness was no longer accepted on the assurance of words or deeds. And in the glare of attention paid to guilt,[13] it was recognised that intentions could be crooked, even when sinners were meant to bare the secrets of their hearts.

The secrets of the heart, the *arcana* or *occulta cordis*, were considered unfathomable.[14] Ecclesiastical courts did not claim to judge them; only the penitential tribunal, in which the confessor acquired his knowledge like God, might do so, to the extent that they were admitted freely. As the patron-saint of the Holy Office, Pope Pius V, was later to note ruefully, confessors were not inquisitors.[15] The priest who received penitents' avowals did not, or was not supposed to, ferret out their *arcana cordis* by verbal

[11] See Chapters 2 and 7, below. No comprehensive account of this theme exists, but there are valuable studies by K. Hoheisel, U. Wilckens, and A. Kehl, 'Heuchelei' in *RLAC* XIV, 215ff.; F. Amory, 'Whited Sepulchres: The Semantic History of Hypocrisy to the High Middle Ages', *RTAM* 53 (1986) 5–39; R. Newhauser, 'Zur Zweideutigkeit in der Moraltheologie: Als Tugenden verkleidete Laster' in *Der Fehltritt: Vergehen und Versehen in der Vormoderne*, ed. P. von Moos, Norm und Struktur (Cologne, 2001) 377–402 (with bibliography) and W. Speyer, 'Religiöse Betrüger: Falsche göttliche Menschen in Antike und Christentum' in *Fälschungen im Mittelalter* 5, 321–44.

[12] A. Boureau, 'La redécouverte de l'autonomie du corps: l'émergence du somnambule (XIIe–XIVe s.)', *Micrologus* 1 (1993) 27–42.

[13] Still classic is S. Kuttner, *Kanonistische Schuldlehre von Gratian bis auf die Dekretalen Gregors IX*, Studi e testi 64 (Vatican, 1935).

[14] See Kuttner, 'Ecclesia de occultis non iudicat. Problemata ex doctrina poenali canonistarum et decretalistarum a Gratiano usque ad Gregorium P. P. IX', *Acta congressus iuridici internationalis* III (Vatican, 1936) 225–46. Cf. P. von Moos, '"Herzensgeheimnisse" (*occulta cordis*). Selbstverwahrung und Selbstentblößung im Mittelalter' in *Öffentliches und Privates, Gemeinsames und Eigenes: Gesammelte Studien zum Mittelalter* III, ed. G. Melville Geschichte: Forschung und Wissenschaft 16 (Berlin, 2007) 5–28 (= '*Occulta cordis*: Controle de soi et confession au Moyen Âge', *Entre histoire et literature. Communication et culture au Moyen Âge* (Florence, 2005) 579–610); '"Öffentlich" und "Privat" im Mittelater: Zum Problem der historischen Begriffsbestimmung', *Heidelberger Akademie der Wissenschaften*, Philosophisch – historische Klasse 33 (2004) 97–8; and S. Vecchio, 'Segreti e bugie: I *peccata occulta*', *Micrologus* 14 (2006) 41–58.

[15] See the letter of 8 September 1563 quoted by A. Prosperi, *Tribunali della coscienza: Inquisitori, confessori, missionari* (Turin, 1996) 10–11 and cf. (more generally and tendentiously) E. Brambilla, *Alle origini del Sant'Uffizio: Penitenza, confessione, e giustizia spirituale dal medioevo al XVI* (Bologna, 2000) 21–137.

coercion or physical force. It is obvious that this made him vulnerable to feigners. Less obvious is, why they wished to misrepresent and falsify their consciences. *Fictio* was practised by a particular type – mostly, but not exclusively, monastic. Fundamental to the religious identity of the majority of them were mourning for their sins and humility, which were related in theory and practice.

Humility, a virtue perhaps original to Christian ethics and certainly essential to monasticism,[16] was exemplified by penance. Monks are enjoined in the forty-ninth chapter of the Benedictine Rule to live every day as if it were Lent. St Benedict's recommendation was enforced by the habit of regular confession to superiors whom he describes as vicars of Christ. Small wonder that some quailed at this relentless soul-searching which they regarded as an ordeal, and attempted to bend its rules of self-accusation with *fictio*. More remarkable, in view of the many cultures in which confession figures,[17] is the rarity of the phenomenon (or the failure to note it). No account of feigned penance appears now to be taken by the moral and pastoral theology of Catholicism,[18] nor is it registered in all periods of Western Christianity.[19] Its identification as a problem with wide-ranging implications is distinctive of the ethical sensibility refashioned in the twelfth century.

Throughout this golden age of dialectic, rules of inversion prevailed. From a monk's *fictio* of penitential humility was concluded his guilt of pride. How the conclusion was drawn, St Bernard of Clairvaux explains in a work which that master-dialectician of the conscience wrote *c.*1125:

---

[16] See A. Dihle, 'Demut', in *RLAC* III, 735–78; P. Adnès, 'L'humilité vertu spécifiquement chrétienne d'après saint Augustin', *Revue d'ascétique et de mystique* 28 (1952) 208–23, and A. de Vogüé, *La règle de saint Benoît* VII: *Commentaire doctrinal et spirituel* (Paris, 1977) 168–83, 357, 367, 375, 384, 387, 399–400, 433.

[17] See H. Jaeger, 'L'examen de conscience dans les religions non-chrétiennes et avant le christianisme', *Numen* 6 (1959) 176–233; R. Pettazzoni, 'La confession des péchés dans l'histoire générale des religions' in *Mélanges F. Cumont*, Annuaire de l'Institut de philologie et d'histoire orientales et slaves 4 (Brussels, 1936) 893–901; and A. Hahn and V. Kapp (eds.), *Selbstthematisierung und Selbstzeugnis: Bekenntnis und Geständnis* (Frankfurt, 1987).

[18] Cf. L. Vereecke, *De Guillaume d'Ockham à saint Alphonso de Liguori: études de la théologie morale moderne 1300–1787* (Rome, 1986) and T. Fleming, *The Second Vatican Council's Teaching on the Sacrament of Penance and the Communal Nature of the Sacrament* (Rome, 1981). Thanks are due for advice on this point to His Eminence Georges Cardinal Cottier, OP.

[19] Relevant though it is to the later phenomenon of 'Nicodemism' (which is not an invention of the early modern period), no attention is paid to earlier *fictio* by C. Ginzburg, *Il nicodemismo: Simulazione e dissimulazione religiose nell'Europa del '500* (Turin, 1970), or J. Delumeau, *Le péché et la peur* (Paris, 1983) and *L'aveu et le pardon* (Paris, 1990).

There are quite a few who, when they are accused of obvious faults, knowing that their self-defence will not be believed, make up a subtler argument to defend themselves and reply in the words of a crafty confession … Their faces bowed, their bodies prostrate, they wring forth a few tearlets, if they can, inter-rupting their speech with sighs and their words with groans. Not only do such types not seek to excuse the reproaches levelled at them, but they themselves even exaggerate their fault, with the effect that, while you hear them adding some impossible or unbelievable detail about their guilt from their own lips, you are led to disbelieve even what you thought certain and, on account of your confidence about the falsehood of what is being confessed, you lapse into doubt about what you deemed almost secure. As they affirm what they do not want to be believed, by confessing they defend their fault, and hide it while revealing it; and when confession resounds laudably on their lips, wickedness continues to lurk in their hearts…[20]

Such a style, such a tone had not been heard since St Jerome, Bernard's only equal as a Christian satirist in Latin prose,[21] lashed the failings of all and sundry – each of them named. Anonymous but vivid, a type, not an individual, of feigned penance makes his début in European literature here. Bernard's *De gradibus humilitatis et superbiae*, aptly characterised as an 'inverse commentary on the seventh chapter of the [Benedictine] Rule',[22] was composed by a seasoned confessor of monks who drew on his pastoral experience to show how the penitential obligation of sincerity might be turned on its head. Self-accusation as self-defence, revelation as concealment, multiplication and invention of faults in order to affirm a remorse that amounts to a composite of simulation and dissimulation: in

---

[20] 'Nonnulli enim, cum de apertioribus arguuntur, scientes, si se defenderent, quod sibi non cred-eretur, subtilius inveniunt argumentum defensionis, verba respondentes dolosae confessionis… Vultus demittitur, prosternitur corpus; aliquas sibi lacrimulas extorquent, si possunt; vocem suspiriis, verba gemitibus interrumpunt. Nec solum qui eius modi est obiecta non excusat, sed ipse quoque culpam exaggerat, ut dum impossibile aliquid aut incredibile culpae suae ore ipsius additum audis, etiam illud, quod ratum putabas, discredere possis, et ex eo quod falsum esse non dubitas, dum confitetur, in dubium veniat quod quasi certum tenebatur. Dumque affirmant quod credi nolunt, confitendo culpam defendunt et aperiendo tegunt, quando et confessio laudabiliter sonat in ore et adhuc iniquitas occultatur in corde … ' *De gradibus humilitatis et superbiae* XVIII.46 in *Sancti Bernardi Opera* III *Tractatus et opuscula*, ed. J. Leclercq and H. Rochais (Rome, 1963) 51, 12–52. All translations, here and elsewhere in this book, are my own.

[21] Cf. D. Wiesen, *St Jerome as a Satirist* (Berkeley, 1964).

[22] C. Walker Bynum, *Docere verbo et exemplo: An Aspect of Twelfth-Century Spirituality*, Harvard Theological Studies 31 (Missoula, 1979) 102. Recent discussions of the work include M. Pranger, *Bernard of Clairvaux and the Shape of Monastic Thought: Broken Dreams* (Leiden, 1994) 84–121 and J. Kitchen, 'Bernard of Clairvaux's *De gradibus humilitatis et superbiae* and the Postmodern Revisioning of Moral Philosophy' in *Virtue and Ethics in the Twelfth Century*, ed. I. Bejczy and R. Newhauser (Leiden, 2005) 95–118.

this *sic et non* of false assertions masking real denials, a paradox takes form. It is a paradox of *fictio* constructed by a spiritual sophist who, through his pyrotechnics of auto-execration, aims at a pre-eminence of humility.

Humility aimed at exaltation inverts the teaching of Jesus, on which the seventh chapter of the Benedictine Rule is based: *Qui se humiliaverit, exaltabitur* (Matthew 23:12; cf. Luke 18:14). The inversion, as Bernard observes it, is theatrical. Performed in a pantomime of the sacramental stage, this 'crafty confession' requires a spectator. His suspicions are aroused by the overacting, which makes him aware that the monastic mummer is not just feigning but also showing off. Ostentation of piety, undertaken less out of love for God than from craving for men's praise, is condemned by Christ as pharisaical at Matthew 23:25ff. It is a mark of Bernard's restraint that he does not spell out what a long tradition of exegesis made plain.[23] To note that feigned penance could be ranked as a sub-species of hypocrisy might have seemed to him obvious or trivial or both. But Bernard is keenly interested in terminology, especially of the affective kind; and the care with which he employs it is unprecedented.

'Crafty' (*dolosa*), for example, has semi-legal connotations of malicious intent. Coupled with 'confession', the adjective mediates the tension between the penitent's motives for feigning and the effect he sought to produce on his confessor. That confessor, accustomed to browbeating popes,[24] admits to being unsure in his judgement. With a lack of confidence seldom paralleled in his other writings, Bernard of Clairvaux wavers in his opinion ('you are led to disbelieve', 'you lapse into doubt'). Subjectivity is one issue; verifiability, another. Their conjunction in this passage represents a turning-point in the development of the medieval conscience. Only a confessor who drew inferences unattested in the earlier tradition of penitential thought was capable of detecting the tension Bernard felt so acutely. It could not be felt until the sinner was recognised as potentially more sophisticated and less amenable to instructions from above than the stereotypes of passivity who recur in the handbooks of the early Middle Ages.[25] Their assumption of authority, unargued and peremptory, is shaken

---

[23] See K. Pollmann, 'The Splitting of Morality in *Matthew* 23 and its Exegetical Consequences' in Pollmann (ed.), *Double Standards in the Ancient and Medieval World* (Göttingen, 2000) 263–86, and 'Hypocrisy and the History of Salvation: Medieval Interpretations of Matthew 23', *Wiener Studien* 114 (2001) 469–82. See further Chapter 2.

[24] Cf. P. Godman, *The Silent Masters: Latin Literature and its Censors in the High Middle Ages* (Princeton, 2000) 120ff.

[25] See Chapter 2.

by this spiritual sophist. He is able both to misrepresent his inner state and to unnerve his judge.

On the judge-cum-prosecutor is placed the burden of proof. This reversal of roles was unknown to the prescriptive moralism long dominant in Latin Europe. It measured atonement, and therefore sincerity, by penitential 'tarifs' meant to be proportionate to sinners' transgressions.[26] Neither 'proportionality' nor the other clap-trap of pseudo-objectivity common in the manuals has any place in Bernard's work. He portrays a form of interiority that is evasive of measure and elusive of control. A moral maze, like a hall of mirrors where each reflection evokes its opposite, this labyrinthine conscience resists description in ordinary language. Hence the use of paradox. Combinations of contraries, such as 'proud humility' and 'simulating dissimulation',[27] highlight change. The change wrought in *De gradibus humilitatis et superbiae* is a new perception of ethical ambiguity.

Ambiguous because anxious, this monk does not experience the same fear inculcated into sinners by the penitential handbooks. It is not simply foreboding of punishment which leads him to feign, but an inverted (or perverted) sense of obligation. Obliged by the seventh chapter of the Benedictine Rule to reveal evil thoughts and deeds to his abbot 'in humble confession', he resorts to making a crafty one, which piles on the pathos. That pathos, affected to create the impression of a refined and rigorous conscience, cannot be assessed with the 'exteriority of the early medieval penitential codes which took deeds at face-value with no account of intention'.[28] Although intention and motivation are among Bernard's chief concerns, he had no means of probing them other than words, vehicles of duplicity, and gestures, signs of the soul.[29]

This soul is sick. Its spiritual physician makes his diagnosis delicately. So delicately does Bernard write that modern readers insensitive to the nuances of his Latinity may miss its critical and comic implications. The monk, for instance, does not weep. He 'wrings forth a few tearlets' (*lacrimulas*). The diminutive is derisory, the straining for effect dismissed in the sarcasm: 'if he can'. The dubitative tone leaves no room for doubt. *Fictio* is cast as

[26] Ibid.
[27] *De gradibus humilitatis et superbiae* XVIII.47, ed. Leclercq and Rochais, 52, 12 and 20.
[28] Constable, *Reformation*, 266 but see too R. Kottje, 'Intentions – oder Tathaftung? Zum Verständnis der frühmittelalterlichen Bußbücher', *Zeitschrift der Savigny-Stiftung für Rechtsgeschichte* 122, Kanonistische Abteilung 91 (2005) 738–41.
[29] Cf. C. Casagrande and S. Vecchio, *I peccati della lingua: Disciplina ed etica della parola nella cultura medievale* (Rome, 1987) and J. -C. Schmitt, *La Raison des gestes dans l'Occident médiéval* (Paris, 1990).

a caricature of the theology of tears.[30] Meant to be in a state of lacrimose lamentation for his sins, this monastic impostor manages only to produce a trickle when he should gush in streams. And as pathos dwindles into bathos, his corporeal rhetoric of remorse – sighs and groans, crestfallenness and prostration – is exposed as sham.

There is nothing sham or sarcastic, however, about Bernard's twin theme of abbatial surveillance. Discipline and authority are treated by him with deadly seriousness. Neither discipline limited to following rules nor authority derived from rank concerns this grand inquisitor *avant la lettre*, so much as the inner qualities displayed in governance of one's self and of others. His work trespasses beyond the limits imposed on the confessor to write a chapter in the pre-history of the inquisitorial mentality. The cast of mind that led to the foundation of the Holy Office begins to take form in this tract; and if Pius V was likened to Bernard of Clairvaux,[31] that was for good reasons. The patron-saint of the Roman Inquisition had much to learn from *De gradibus humilitatis et superbiae*.

Consider the mentality that scrutinised those stoops and twitches which, on the part of Bernard's brethren, revealed a 'sickness of the soul' identified with curiosity;[32] or that eavesdropped on the cackle emitted by a monk who had pursed his lips and ground his teeth to suppress his laughter which escaped, like a snort or a snore, from his nostrils, even when he stuffed his fists into his mouth;[33] or that followed the gaze of a virtuoso of fasting as it travelled down the table, 'more concerned about forfeiting glory [for abstinence] than about feeling hungry', in order to see whether others were eating less…[34] An inquisitorial psychology of suspicion is adumbrated here. Voluntary or involuntary, conscious or unconscious, the slightest sign of deviance from Bernard's draconian standards of self-control is construed as self-betrayal.

The foundation on which his psychology of suspicion builds is less the traditional ideal of harmony between thought and action held to constitute sincerity,[35] than a novel sense of responsibility for detecting

---

[30] See P. Nagy, *Le don des larmes au Moyen Age: Un instrument spirituel en quête d'institution (Ve–XIIIe siècle)* (Paris, 2000) 267ff.

[31] G. Catena, *Vita del gloriosissimo papa Pio Quinto* (Rome, 1587) 4.

[32] *De gradibus humilitatis et superbiae* x.28, ed. Leclercq and Rochais, 38, 20ff.

[33] Ibid. xii.40; 47, 17–19.   [34] ibid. xiv.42; 49, 5–10.

[35] Best discussed by G. Constable, 'The Concern for Sincerity and Understanding in Liturgical Prayer, especially in the Twelfth Century' in *Classica et Mediaevalia: Studies in Honor of J. Szövérffy*, ed. I. Vaslef and H. Buschhausen (Washington, 1986) 17–30. For a general survey of the problem, cf. J. Martin, 'Inventing Sincerity, Refashioning Prudence: The Discovery of the Individual in Renaissance Europe', *The American Historical Review* 102 (1997) 1309–42.

the evasiveness (*tergiversatio*) of his charges.[36] Detection, needless to say, meant punishment. The Rule did not prescribe this degree of dragooning: it is the invention of Bernard's obsessiveness. And if he tempered the punitive spirit of *De gradibus humilitatis et superbiae* in other works, declaring that the will should not be coerced into obedience and distinguishing between *confessio* and *defensio*,[37] he still appears to assume a vocation of martyrdom, or masochism, on the part of those who submitted themselves to his surveillance. The result is both hilarious and horrifying. Under the eagle-eye of their abbot, life cannot have been easy for feigned penitents at Clairvaux, that penitentiary of the spirit.

At the Paraclete, founded by Abelard and headed by Heloise after its donation by him to her in 1129,[38] she addressed similar issues from a different point of view. An inquisitrix not of others' consciences but of her own, Heloise was concerned to maintain the compatibility of her multiple roles as wife, abbess, and author. A precarious balancing-act, undertaken without the support of tradition or the reassurance of sympathy from the husband to whom she addressed her letters. Abelard now insisted on assuming the part of Heloise's spiritual director,[39] in the most recent of his several attempts to re-create himself. A master driven from the Parisian schools by the consequences of his scandalous affair and disastrous marriage with her, a monk who made Saint-Denis too hot to hold him, a precocious Petrarch whose enemies hounded him even from the solace of learned anchoretism, he had fetched up in the backwater of his native Brittany where, as abbot of Saint-Gildas, he was exposed to attempts by his brethren to murder him.[40] A lesser man might have despaired of playing Proteus. With a determination often misinterpreted as arrogance, Abelard again transformed

---

[36] *De gradibus humilitatis et superbiae* XVIII.47; 52, II.

[37] *De praecepto et dispensatione* IV.10; V.11; XI.28 in *S. Bernardi Opera* III, ed. J. Leclercq and H. Rochais (Rome, 1963) 260, 15ff.; 261, 8ff.; 273, 11. Cf. J. Leclercq, *Recueil d'études sur saint Bernard et ses écrits* V, Storia e letteratura 182 (Rome, 1992) 171–80.

[38] Abelard, *HC* 46, ed. I. Pagani, *Epistolario di Abelardo ed Eloisa* (Turin, 2004) 214. (All references are to this edition which, although not the most critical, is at present the most convenient, because it prints in one place texts that have been published separately.) For background, cf. T. Waldmann, 'Abbot Suger and the Nuns of Argenteuil', *Traditio* 41 (1985) 239–72 and M. McLaughlin, 'Heloise the Abbess: The Expansion of the Paraclete' in *Listening to Heloise: The Voice of a Twelfth-Century Woman*, ed. B. Wheeler (London, 2000) 1–18.

[39] See Chapters 5–7 below.

[40] Abelard's role-playing is well studied by M. Clanchy, *Abelard: A Medieval Life* (Oxford, 1997).

himself from a failed reformer of male monasticism into a guide of the nuns at the Paraclete.[41]

Their abbess understood, not for the first time, that he had given little thought to the consequences of the scenario he was staging. Twice before – when he forced Heloise to commit matrimony and when he coerced her into taking the veil – Abelard had disregarded her will.[42] His imperiousness had been doubly dire, because it had condemned her to live what she regarded as a lie and because he declined to acknowledge the obligations she believed he had incurred. The wish of this determined man was no longer the command of this equally resolute woman. Once his pupil, she was now his peer in learning and letters. Through adversities hardly less painful than his, she had arrived at a firm, if anguished view of who she was and should be. Moral identity, present and future, is at issue in the correspondence of Abelard and Heloise; and the form in which she chose to present hers is confessional.

Confessional not in the literal sense of that term, restricted to verbal borrowings from St Augustine's masterpiece,[43] but in the spirit of ambivalence and self-division in which its first eight books were written,[44] Heloise's autobiographical letters are animated by the principle of self-knowledge with which Abelard entitled his ethical tract, *Scito te ipsum*. To read them as mere exercises in Ovidian imitation,[45] to strain from between their lines a manifesto of proto-feminism,[46] is to ignore the standards of the twelfth-century culture in which they were composed. Its prime value was truth; its hierarchy of knowledge stationed *grammatica* at the lowest rung.[47] This most modest of disciplines, not yet puffed by the hot air of

[41] Cf. P. De Santis (ed.), *I sermoni di Abelardo per le monache del Paracleto*, Mediaevalia Lovaniensia Series 1/Studia 31 (Louvain, 2002) and (with caution) J. Szövérffy (ed.), *Peter Abelard's Hymnarius Paraclitensis*, 2 vols. (Albany, N.Y; 1975).

[42] See Chapters 4 and 5.

[43] Cf. P. Courcelle, *Les Confessions de saint Augustin dans la tradition littéraire* (Paris, 1963) 11, 13.

[44] See Chapters 2 and 7 below.

[45] P. Dronke, *Women Writers of the Middle Ages: A Critical Study of Texts from Perpetua (†203) to Marguerite Porete (†1310)* (Cambridge, 1984) 107, 126–7; a similar line is followed by P. Brown and J. Pfeiffer III, 'Heloise, Dialectic, and the *Heroides*' in *Listening to Heloise*, ed. Wheeler, 143–60 with bibliography of more of the same.

[46] Proponents, conscious and unconscious, of this thesis are applauded by J. Marenbon in his bibliographical study 'Authenticity Revisited' in *Listening to Heloise*, ed. Wheeler, 27–31.

[47] See P. Delhaye, '*Grammatica* et *Ethica* au xiie siècle', *RTAM* 25 (1958) 59–110; P. von Moos, 'Was galt im lateinischen Mittelalter als das Literarische an der Literatur? Eine theologisch-rhetorische Antwort Abelards' in *Abaelard und Heloise*, 303ff., and F. Bezner, *Vela veritatis: Hermeneutik, Wissen und Sprache in der Intellectual History des 12. Jahrhunderts*, Studien und Texte zur Geistesgeschichte des Mittelalters 85 (Leiden, 2005) 14ff., 99ff., 341ff., 631ff.

'literary' pretensions, sought to link itself with the higher ones of theology and philosophy.[48] The natural and intelligent product of their liaison was subordination of writing about the self to ethics. And the ethical scrutiny of her experience which Heloise undertook in letters probably composed during the early 1130s raised questions of sincerity and authenticity which found a focus in penance.

Central to her concerns, penance has been treated as peripheral by her interpreters.[49] How could so austere, so antiquated a theme fit the image of an emancipated woman whom her admirers wish to place in the avant-garde? For some (largely but not exclusively female), Heloise is a victim of male repression.[50] For others (mostly members of the repressive sex), she is a Roman or Romantic heroine. Combining brains and beauty with that rarest of feminine qualities – obedience – she deserves better than Abelard, they appear to think; and the alternatives at whom they hint are themselves.[51] Ardour is admirable but love, like ideology,[52] can be blind. They fail to note the simple but significant fact that, at her profession,[53] Heloise had vowed herself to penance for life.

She had cause for remorse. First of all, as she looked back at the past, on account of her sexual sins. Almost nothing wins her more sympathy today – nothing, that is, except her moving declarations of unrequited love for Abelard. So moving are they, that the tears which come to the eyes of his retrospective rivals prevent them from seeing a parallel between Heloise and Bernard of Clairvaux's feigned penitent. That parallel emerges, by way of paradox, in perhaps the most famous lines she wrote:

God knows that I never sought anything in you but yourself, desiring you purely and not your things. I did not aspire to the bond of marriage or a dowry, nor indeed did I aim to satisfy my pleasures and desires but yours, as you know. And if the

---

[48] Cf. Godman, *The Silent Masters*, 149ff.

[49] Despite its promising title, the main issues are not covered in L. Hödl's study, 'Die Reue der ungereuten Sünde im Briefwechsel zwischen Heloise und Abelard' in *Omnia disce: Kunst und Geschichte als Erinnerung und Herausforderung. Festschrift W. Ekkert*, ed. W. Senner (Cologne, 1996) 142–52.

[50] See B. Newman, 'Authority, Authenticity, and the Repression of Heloise', *Journal of Medieval and Renaissance Studies* 22 (1992) 121–57, repr. in Newman, *From Virile Woman to Woman Christ: Studies in Medieval Religion and Literature* (Philadelphia, 1995) 46–75.

[51] See E. Gilson, *Heloïse et Abélard*, 3rd edn (Paris, 1964) 105ff. (who is not alone).

[52] Cf. P. von Moos, *Mittelalterforschung und Ideologiekritik: Der Gelehrtenstreit um Heloise* (Munich, 1974), supplemented by 'Abelard, Heloise und ihr Paraklet: ein Kloster nach Mass. Zugleich eine Streitschrift gegen die ewige Wiederkehr hermeneutischer Naivität' in *Abaelard und Heloise*, 233–302.

[53] See H. Lutterbach, *Monachus factus est: Die Mönchwerdung im frühen Mittelalter*, Beiträge zur Geschichte des alten Mönchtums und des Benediktinertums 44 (Münster, 1995).

name of wife seems more hallowed and respectable, the word 'girlfriend' has always been sweeter to my taste or, if you will forebear, those of concubine and whore, so that, by humbling myself more fully for your sake, I may acquire an ampler measure of your grace, and thus detract less from the glory of your excellence.[54]

A proclamation of free love for some, a defence of clerical concubinage for others, this passage deals not only with Heloise's emotions but also with her identity. It is multiple and ambiguous. Her alternatives 'girlfriend', 'concubine', and 'whore' are multiple because each one matters less than their cumulative effect, which is to assert her obedient humility. That assertion is ambiguous. Emphasising her self-abasement before Abelard, Heloise also lays implicit claim to a kind of primacy – a primacy of suffering on his behalf. Less submissive than a victim of male repression and subtler than a Roman or Romantic heroine, she aspires to a position which, hardly definable in social or sexual terms, sets her apart from the ordinary categories of female experience. Singularity is Heloise's subtext, which depends on an inversion of Christ's words parallel to that of Bernard's monk: *Qui se humiliaverit, exaltabitur.*

All of this poses the problem of her sincerity. It has never been doubted, ready though many have been to pour scorn on Abelard for what they consider his obsession with *fama* or reputation. But are the two so different in this respect? When she goes on to reminisce about the glory-days of her affair with him,[55] Heloise both extols Abelard's *fama* and regrets her own. Fantasies of the past alleviate the asperities of the present. The abbess of the Paraclete finds the cloister cramped. Nostalgia for a boundless *imperium* of youthful passion haunts her middle-aged memory. Then, celebrated in Abelard's lovesongs, she had been the envy of all the women in the world. Yet it is not with one of these women that Heloise compares herself, but with their imagined empress, whose crown she would have declined to remain her beloved's mistress. The grand gesture of turning Augustus down, the magniloquence, the melodrama: it is not only Abelard who is obsessed with *fama*.

Conscious of having been a celebrity and loath to relinquish that eminence, Heloise makes a further and no less ambiguous claim to fame in her second letter. It examines the discrepancy between her self-perception and how she is seen by others. Others (unspecified) view her as chaste: she denies being so,

---

[54] 'Nihil umquam, Deus scit, in te nisi te requisivi, te pure non tua concupiscens. Non matrimonii foedera, non dotes aliquas expectavi, non denique meas voluptates aut voluntates sed tuas, sicut ipse nosti, adimplere studui. Et si uxoris nomen sanctius ac validius videtur, dulcius mihi semper exstitit amicae vocabulum aut, si non indigneris, concubinae vel scorti ut, quo me videlicet pro te amplius humiliarem, ampliorem apud te consequerer gratiam et sic etiam excellentiae tuae gloriam minus laederem', *Ep.* ii.10, ed. Pagani, 244.

[55] *Ep.* ii.10, ed. Pagani, 244–6.

on the disarming grounds of her hypocrisy.[56] All she possesses is 'cleanliness of the flesh'. *Munditia carnis*, a relative virtue in previous Christian tradition, is brushed aside. There is no ethical relativism in this inquisitrix of her own conscience. The body, in Heloise's stern judgement, counts for nothing. Nor does the opinion of others. All moral merit is confined to the sphere of interiority. And there she effects a pyrotechnic of paradox more daring than any attempted by Bernard's monk. For the premise of Heloise's denunciation of her own hypocrisy is, or ought to be, sincerity.

Sincere hypocrisy is an intricate paradox, woven from a complex web of doctrines. Why is she, once so ambiguously humble, now so unequivocally adamant? Because Heloise stands on her right to exercise *discretio*, the discernment between virtue and vice prized by monasticism. Neither Abelard nor we can challenge her. The testimony of her conscience, St Paul teaches (I Corinthians 10:29), is irrefutable.[57] But that is not all. Asserting the priority of her inner truths over the misconceptions of men, she arrogates an authority that is exclusive and severe. Only the God 'who sees in the dark' (cf. Ezekiel 8:12) can know her heart, and it is with Him – rather the implacable deity of the Old Testament than the merciful saviour of the New – that she identifies. This identification of the conscience as prosecutor, bent on inculpating itself, leads us into another moral maze. Its entrance is formed by the doctrine that self-accusation demonstrates purity of heart.[58] Its exit is blocked by Heloise. Pure of heart and of flesh yet impure of mind, she raises, with an acuteness unmatched by any author of her generation, the problem of verifiability. How can we, how could her contemporaries tell whether Heloise means what she says?

That was the problem faced, and manipulated to his own ends, by the most jocular of writers about penance in the next generation. The truth-claims made of sinners by monastic theorists of that sacrament were, for the Archpoet, butts of mirth. How and why, are not easy questions to approach. Clichés of literary history clutter the path. For if it is partly true that few things are more tedious than explanations of jokes, it is wholly true

[56] 'Castam me praedicant qui non deprehendunt hypocritam; munditiam carnis conferunt in virtutem, cum non sit corporis sed animi virtus'. *Ep.* IV.10, ed. Pagani 284 with n. 41. See further Chapter 7.
[57] See A. Dihle, *The Theory of the Will in Classical Antiquity*, Sather Classical Lectures 48 (Berkeley, 1982) 81; Dingjan, *Discretio* 18ff.; and W. Düring, 'Discretio' in *RLAC* III, 1230–45.
[58] See Dingjan, *Discretio*, 19ff. and J. Guillet, G. Bardy, and F. Vandenbroucke, 'Discernement des esprits' in *Dictionnaire de spiritualité* 3, 1222–57.

that nothing is more boring than reduction of this sophisticated author's tour de force to the banalities of 'goliardic' parody or satire.[59] Neither satirical nor parodic, the Archpoet's 'confession' in verse derived point and piquancy from the milieu in which it was composed.

He was employed, as a notary, in the imperial chancery of Frederick Barbarossa who, shortly before this 'confession' was written, issued an edict against the Cistercian order until recently dragooned by Bernard of Clairvaux (†1153).[60] The moment, in the early 1160s, was ripe for a reaction against the inquisitions of the conscience that had gathered momentum since he had written *De gradibus humilitatis et superbiae* four decades earlier. But the moment, fraught with tension between the empire and the papacy, required a catalyser. He was at once an arch-chancellor cherished by the emperor and an archbishop-elect of Cologne condemned as schismatic by the pope: Rainald of Dassel, then the most controversial and least conventional patron of letters in Latin Europe.[61]

Notorious for scoffing and scorning, Rainald mocked the solemnity with which Bernard advocated reform of the Church. More than a reactionary, he was a cosmopolitan intellectual and an unscrupulous politician. Prepared to sponsor the canonisation of the improbable Saint Charlemagne, Rainald also used his trilinguism in the interests of the Reich. Deliberately mistranslating a papal bull from the learned language into the vernacular at Besançon in 1157, he provoked a diplomatic incident that nearly led to the lynching of his future enemy, Alexander III, then a legate on mission to the emperor.[62] To address a 'confession' to this flamboyant figure took pluck. That pluck was mustered by a writer who, like his patron, moved with effortless ease between the clerical and secular worlds, flaunting what the reformers considered the worst abuses of both. Despite the fascination he has exercised, we cannot be sure of his name and wander in the shifting sands of pseudonyms.[63] But if poets are liars, what is an Archpoet … ?

[59]   On the term and its abuse, see G. Rigg, 'Golias and Other Pseudonyms', *Studi Medievali*, 3rd Ser., 18 (1977) 65–105.

[60]   Cf. R. Schieffer, 'Bleibt der Archipoeta anonym? ', *Mitteilungen des Instituts für österreichische Geschichtsforschung* 98 (1990) 59–79; J. Fried, 'Der Archipoeta: ein Kölner Scholaster? ' in *Ex ipsis rerum documentis: Beiträge zur Mediävistik. Festschrift H. Zimmermann*, ed. K. Herbers (Sigmaringen, 1991) 85–90, and P. Dronke in *Hugh Primas and the Archpoet*, ed. and trans. F. Adcock, Cambridge Medieval Classics 4 (Cambridge, 1994) xx–xxii, and see Chapter 8.

[61]   On Rainald, cf. Godman, *The Silent Masters*, 190ff. (with bibliography) and Chapter 8.

[62]   See W. Ullmann, 'Cardinal Roland and the Incident at Besançon', *Miscellanea Historiae Pontificiae* 18 (1954) 107–25.

[63]   The best study of this problem remains Rigg, 'Golias'. Little light is cast by P. Schmidt, 'Perché tanti anonimi nel medioevo? Il problema della personalità dell'autore nella filologia mediolatina', *Filologia mediolatina* 6–7 (1999–2000) 1–8.

A consummate liar or an ironist, a spiritual sophist or a blasphemer: each of these categories was available in twelfth-century culture, which applied itself to rethinking them.[64] How they might overlap, was a conundrum which the Archpoet did nothing to simplify. Not only were his subject and style unfamiliar, but even his form. Confessions in verse are uncommon in the Latin literature of the Middle Ages; and the most notable instance before his (which did not serve as its model) was written more than three hundred years earlier.[65] No one knew what to expect when, before the entourage of the archbishop-elect, he stood up to confess his sins. The factor of surprise was crucial. Bigots and boneheads – among them colleagues harping on his faults – had to be outflanked. The habit of self-accusation established in penance needed to be overturned. Battles were raging over the concepts of intention and motivation, and the target of each campaign was clarity. Obfuscation therefore occurred to the dialectical mind of the Archpoet, a zone of uncertainty where his self-appointed censors would feel just as nonplussed as Bernard confronted with his feigned penitent. How could they assess the motives of a professed sinner if he extolled his transgressions as the mainsprings of his art?[66]

Self-accusation served as self-commendation to Rainald of Dassel in a *fictio* whose inverted structure had been familiar to Bernard of Clairvaux. But there the precedent reached its limit, and a deep difference emerged. It lay in the complicity between the feigner and his judge, celebrated in this strophe:

> It is my intention to die in a pub,
> to have wines in reach at my last gasp.
> Then angelic choirs shall sing jubilantly:
> 'May God take mercy on this drinker!'[67]

> Meum est propositum in taberna mori,
> ut sint vina proxima morientis ori.
> Tunc cantabunt letius angelorum chori:
> 'Sit Deus propitius huic potatori!'

These verses were not written for laymen, ignorant of Latin. Recited before a circle of *clerici* fluent in the learned language, they were

---

[64] See the excellent analysis of M. Colish, 'Rethinking Lying in the Twelfth Century' in *Virtue and Ethics in the Twelfth Century*, ed. I. Bejczy and R. Newhauser (Leiden, 2005) 155–74.

[65] Cf. P. von Moos, 'Gottschalks *O mi custos* – eine *Confessio*', *Frühmittelalterliche Studien* 4 (1970) 210ff.; ibid. 5 (1971) 317ff.

[66] See Chapter 8 below.

[67] *Carm.* x.12 in *Die Gedichte des Archipoeta*, ed. H. Watenphul and H. Krefeld (Heidelberg, 1958) 75.

intended to silence the Archpoet's critics and to cement his bond with the archbishop-elect. Audacity, comic and calculated, linked author and patron. Each of them was responsive to the humour latent in *fictio*; each delighted in standing convention on its head.

If penitents were meant to confess their sins with the bitterness of remorse, the Archpoet extols his drinking with the sweetness of intoxication. Intoxicating in its headiness is his play, in the last verse above, on an apostle's prayer for divine mercy (*Deus propitius esto mihi peccatori*, Luke 18:13). Not mercy but indulgence and more are requested, or presupposed, from the dignitary to whom the pun *peccatori/potatori* is addressed. Rainald of Dassel could be trusted to spot the allusion and to smile at the joke. A smile at this spoof of the Bible on the pursed lips of Bernard of Clairvaux, who regarded mirth and merriment as sins, would have been less likely than an anathema for blasphemy, had he lived to hear such a 'confession'.[68] Yet Bernard should have grasped, no less firmly than Rainald, his polar opposite in the ecclesiastical hierarchy, why the Archpoet's play on words was not simply verbal. Irony, here as elsewhere in his writings, is used to thwart any attempt to penetrate the *arcana cordis*. The motives of this spiritual sophist resist inquisition. His conscience is as inscrutable as his appeal is urbane. And the appeal to complicity serves to enlist his judge as an ally. If Rainald cannot be entirely sure of his partner in a compact of *fictio*, he understands that neither sincerity nor authenticity is the issue. The issue posed by the Archpoet's feigning of penance is, how knowingly to smile.

The Archpoet, Heloise, and Bernard of Clairvaux: an unusual trio, seldom brought together. From different milieux and opposed perspectives – monastic and anti-monastic, male and female, in earnest and in jest – they converged on *fictio*, because it raised questions fundamental to their rapidly changing culture. Its reverence for truth, conceived primarily in religious terms, and its zest for dialectic led all three of them to reflect on falsification of moral identity in what was being redefined as the sacrament of penance. When sinners were meant to be most sincere, why were they moved to feign? In the space of two generations and over the course of some forty years, from *c.*1125 to 1163, this problem was identified and elaborated, but not solved. Yet that brief interval in the *longue durée* of the conscience was sufficient to enable Bernard, Heloise, and the Archpoet to

[68] Cf. I. Resnick, '*Risus monasticus*: Laughter and Medieval Monastic Culture', *Revue bénédictine* 97 (1987) 90–100.

convey how and why the ethical imagination of Latin Europe was being transformed.

When that transformation could not be grasped in conventional categories of analysis and expression, they and others resorted to paradoxes, which sustain a delicate equilibrium between originality and tradition. Tradition being regarded as a high road to the truth, deviances from it were suspect. Suspicion might be allayed by casting innovation (*novitas*) as a return to the ideals of the past. But which past? was the question that twelfth-century reformers and their opponents asked themselves as they surveyed the discontinuous development of penance. It resembled less a seamless garment than a worn patchwork. Pieces of prescriptive moralism frayed during the early Middle Ages were discarded, to be replaced by others from the patristic period, over which loomed the towering figure of Augustine. Yet even that colossus creaked. The saint too had his critics, some of whom, such as John Cassian, were far from being intellectual dwarves.[69] There, in the discord between contending arbiters of orthodoxy, were perceived opportunities for a different pattern of faith to be re-formed.

Reformation entailed making positive and negative choices from the legacy of a plural past. They are the subjects of the next two chapters.[70] Prolegomena to the unwritten history of the medieval conscience,[71] they trace the routes followed in quest of *fictio* and the paths which were not pursued. The crossroads which presented themselves to those searching for this concept led in more than one direction towards a goal that may now seem elusive. Did not the wisest and wittiest of philosophers, contemplating the proposition that God alone sees the most secret thoughts,

---

[69] See Chapter 2.

[70] The aim of the following two chapters is not to provide a survey of the theory and practice of penance from late antiquity to the twelfth century, since excellent accounts are available. (Cf. H. Vorgrimler, *Buße und Krankensalbung* Handbuch der Dogmengeschichte IV, 3 (Freiburg, 1978), and C. Vogel, *Le péché et la pénitence: Aperçu sur l'évolution historique de la discipline pénitentielle dans l'Eglise latine*, Bibliothèque de théologie II, Théologie morale 8, *Pastorale du Péché*, ed. P. Delhaye *et al.* (Tournai, 1961) 147–235, and see the notes to Chapters 2 and 3). Their purpose is to distinguish those aspects of penitential tradition which influenced twelfth-century thinkers, or against which they reacted, with special reference to *fictio*.

[71] Valuable material is assembled in articles on the conscience in religious encyclopaedias and handbooks, none of which is better than H. Chadwick's 'Gewissen' in *RLAC* X (1978) 1025–1107. Among theoretical treatments of this subject, outstanding, in complementary ways, are J. Cardinal Ratzinger (Benedict XVI), 'Conscience and Truth' in *Benedict XVI and Cardinal Newman* (Oxford, 2005) 41–52 and H. Arendt, 'Some Questions of Moral Philosophy' in *Responsibility and Judgment*, ed. J. Kohn (New York, 2003) 49–146. More confined to German evidence than its title suggests, but insightful, is H. Kittsteiner, *Die Entstehung des modernen Gewissens* (Frankfurt, 1992).

wonder whether they are all that important?[72] But no one in the twelfth century shared Wittgenstein's scepticism or caution, and if everybody paid lip-service to the doctrine that motivation is unfathomable, it did nothing to hinder attempts to prise the enigma apart. To the instruments employed in this perhaps quixotic undertaking it is time to turn.

---

[72] L. Wittgenstein, *Zettel*, 2nd edn ed. G. Anscombe and G. von Wright, trans. G. Anscombe (Oxford, 1981) no. 560, 97. An implicit answer to Wittgenstein's question is provided by B. Williams, *Truth and Truthfulness: An Essay in Genealogy* (Princeton, 2002) 104.

CHAPTER 2

The neurotic and the penitent

The instruments of ethical analysis with which thinkers of the twelfth century probed *fictio* were bequeathed to them by their Christian heritage. Although sharpened and polished over the centuries, they appear blunt to sensibilities refined by the elegance of Greek religion. Their distaste for what is taken to be the smut of medieval superstition can be projected backwards and forwards, without regard to time or place, onto almost any work. One of them is the delightful *De superstitione* which that 'Greek gentleman', Plutarch, wrote probably between AD 95 and 115.[1] A Middle Platonist prepared to concede the validity of faith in supernatural truth, he drew the line at certain forms of credulity.[2] That line ruled out a case of 'neurosis' whom some call the penitent and others describe, 'very roughly', as 'medieval man'.[3]

Rough indeed is this image of a premature neurotic bursting onto the scene centuries before the curtain went up on the Middle Ages. Chronology swept aside by rhetoric, metaphor runs rampant. So it is that 'medieval man' can be defined as one 'with a sense of sin, who walks in the Valley of the Shadow of Death'. 'Fear of freedom' is the motive for this lugubrious promenade, leading down to depths from which there is no ascent: 'for the refusal of personal responsibility in any sphere, there is always a price to be paid, usually in the form of neurosis'.[4] Such are the conclusions drawn from Plutarch's account (*De superstitione* VII.168C) of that figure of fun

---

[1] Cf. C. Jones, 'Towards a Chronology of Plutarch's Work', *Journal of Roman Studies* 56 (1966) 61–74.

[2] M. Baldassarri, 'Inquadramento filosofico del *De superstitione* plutarcheo' in *Plutarco e la religione*, Atti del vi convegno plutarcheo (Ravello, 29–31 May 1995), ed. I. Gallo (Naples, 1996) 373–87.

[3] E. R. Dodds, 'The Portrait of a Greek Gentleman', *Greece and Rome* 2 (1933) 101ff. The term 'neurosis' is cited from Dodds' discussion of Plutarch's *De superstitione* in *The Greeks and the Irrational* (Berkeley, 1971) 252–3, which draws on his former study.

[4] Dodds, *The Greeks and the Irrational*, 252.

who 'sits in a public place clad in sackcloth or filthy rags or wallows naked in the mire proclaiming what he calls his sins.'[5]

'What he calls his sins': the disdainful phrase sums up Plutarch's scepticism towards these uncouth manifestations of anxiety. Anxiety and guilt-feelings are linked, in the neurotic's mind, by a bond of irrationality. Dogma, condensed from philosophical speculation, provides him an 'unchanging rule of life' that offers him refuge from his confusion.[6] Sackcloth, rags, and mire are chosen by the superstitious because, protecting them from the horrors of free choice, these accoutrements of penance mirror their state of moral abjectness. That is what Plutarch means by the paradoxes 'filthy purifications and unclean godliness' (*De superstitione* XII.171B). They provide a measure of the perversion which stems from the failure to see that, in following our reason, we are following God.

The God of the Latin Fathers, who exercised a more direct influence on 'medieval man' than Plutarch,[7] took a different view of the same phenomenon. He approved of it, especially when penance was performed by members of a social class that had no less of a claim to superiority than this Greek gentleman. Some three centuries after Plutarch, in AD 399, St Jerome composed a famous obituary, in the form of a letter, on the Roman noblewoman Fabiola.[8] She had divorced her dissipated husband and remarried, unaware of the Gospel's prohibition of a second spouse during the lifetime of the first. For this inadvertent sin, Fabiola put on sackcloth and exposed her 'dishevelled hair, wan face, soiled hands, and dust-stained neck' to the gaze of the entire city of Rome.[9] We know how Plutarch would have viewed this spectacle of penance. He would have recoiled not only at the surrender to what he despised as irrationality, but also at the affront to his genteel sensibility.

Jerome was not a gentleman. He was an ascetic and a saint. For him, the public display of penance amounted to a guarantee of its religious authenticity. Confirmed by Fabiola's maintenance of a mortifying régime, her actions were not betrayals of neurosis but proofs of courage. That courage was enhanced by her noble status. Defying an aristocratic code of conduct,

[5] Ed. E. Lozza (Milan, 1980) 50 with 115–16.

[6] Dodds, *The Greeks and the Irrational*, 252–3. Cf. J. Caro Baroja, *De la superstición al ateismo* (Madrid, 1974) 152ff.

[7] Cf. H. Betz, *Plutarch's Ethical Writings and Early Christian Literature* (Leiden, 1978).

[8] Prosopography summarised in A. Fürst, *Hieronymus: Askese und Wissenschaft in der Spätantike* (Freiburg im Br., 2003) 178 (Fabiola I).

[9] Jerome, *Ep.* 77.4, ed. J. Hilberg, CSEL 55 (Vienna, 1912) 40, 16–17, with A. de Vogüé, *Histoire littéraire du mouvement monastique dans l'antiquité* I (Paris, 1996) 126–34.

she demonstrated a humility that, among the virtues arguably original to Christianity, took first place. The morality that exalted the humble and abased the proud had no time for the scoffing of sceptics. In its apparent vulgarity and seeming folly resided the subversive force of penance. Capable of reducing to rubble the standards of ancient elegance, it erected a different ideal of responsibility in their place. Responsibility towards God, evinced before the faithful, entailed the paradox of self-affirmation in self-abasement. Where Plutarch whiffed the reek of superstition, Jerome scented the odour of sanctity.

The symptoms of a malady for the Middle Platonist were the signs of a therapy for the Christian. That therapy did not prescribe retreat into an inner sphere of neurosis. Both public and private, it was undertaken by the spiritual patient before a congregation of fellow-sinners assisted by his doctor of the soul. This medical metaphor, derived from the Bible, was applied to the priest who, as healer and comforter, acted *in persona Christi*.[10] Christ the redeemer was his model and authority in a salvific mission that, during late antiquity, could be undertaken only twice. Baptism was the first 'plank of salvation' offered by the Church to mankind shipwrecked on the ocean of sin, and penance was the second.[11] The toughest test, after baptism, of religious authenticity, penance demanded truth not to one's former self but to a new one redeemed from sin by this unrepeatable sacrament. Many hesitated to take a step from which there was no going back, deferring it to their death-beds. Others were not permitted even to make the attempt. Whole categories of persons, such as the young and the married, were debarred from performing penance earlier, because the demands it made on them to reform their conduct were thought incompatible with their age, their status, or their occupations. Realism mingled with radicalism in this ordeal of spiritual sincerity. At issue was not 'fear of freedom' but the daunting consequences of assuming a different identity. Self-transformation was the aim of the penitential therapy prescribed, for selected patients, by their doctors of the soul.

As a doctor of the soul, St Jerome was not inhibited by false (or genuine) modesty. He recommended that others learn from him a 'holy arrogance'.[12]

---

[10] Luke 5:31ff. is cited in Pope John Paul II's Apostolic Exhortation (Advent, 1984) *Reconciliatio et poenitentia*, 29. See E. Sauer, 'Christus medicus: Christus als Arzt und seine Nachfolger im frühen Christentum', *Trierer Theologische Zeitschrift* 101 (1992) 101–23 and J. McNeill, 'Medicine for Sin as Prescribed in the Penitentials', *Church History* I (1932) 14–26.

[11] See H. Rahner, *Symbole der Kirche: Die Ekklesiologie der Väter* (Salzburg, 1964) 432–72.

[12] Splendidly studied by P. Brown, *The Body and Society: Men, Women, and Sexual Renunciation in Early Christianity* (London, 1989) 366ff.

Yet for all his exigency about being sincere, he was not insensitive to the paradoxical forms which feigning could take. 'Do not desire to appear highly religious', he cautioned Julia Eustochium, 'nor more humble than need be, lest you seek glory while fleeing it.'[13] Insightful words, to which Abelard recurred when confronted with the paradoxes of Heloise.[14] She, unlike her husband, who revered Jerome as a role-model,[15] was more in tune with St Ambrose. The preference is significant, because it indicates a different moral sensibility. Less polemical and more discerning than Jerome, Ambrose looked further behind the façade of penance and tested the foundations on which it rested. Alert to the ambivalence of the emotions provoked by the sacrament, he enquired how deeply they appreciated the purpose to which they were directed. Faces lined with tears or pale with fasting; bodies emaciated, prostrate, trampled by passers-by[16] – such displays of sorrow were of little value, unless accompanied by understanding of the gentleness of a God disposed to forgive.

In the cognitive capacity of the emotions aroused by penance, St Ambrose identified the essence of the sacrament. 'Wallowing in the mire', as Plutarch derided it, was not the point. The point was an affective intelligence that transfigured sinners and enabled them to persevere in their resolution to reform. How fragile that resolution could be, Ambrose was aware. Eschewing the verbosity of late antique mannerists, he expressed this awareness in paradoxes – pithy, pungent, and enlivened by black humour. The one thing that penitents should not do is, to repent repenting.[17] That is equivalent to 'seeking penance for bad deeds and performing it for good ones'.[18] Which emotions led to spiritual regress, which hindered religious advance? Above all, those complex feelings were summed up by St Ambrose in the term *erubescentia* which, as he uses it, combines the social and contextual meaning of embarrassment with the private sense

---

[13] 'Ne satis religiosa velis videri nec plus humilis quam necesse est, ne gloriam fugiendo quaeras', *Ep.* 22.27, ed. Hilberg, CSEL 54 (Vienna, 1910) 183, 5–7.

[14] See Chapter 7 below.

[15] See Chapter 5 and cf. C. Mews, 'Un lecteur de Jérôme au douzième siècle' in *Jérôme entre l'Occident et l'Orient*, ed. Y.-M. Duval (Paris, 1988) 31–44.

[16] *De paenitentia* 1.16 (90), ed. R. Gryson, *Ambrose de Milan, La Pénitence*, SC 179 (Paris, 1971) 126, 37–40, and cf. J. Romer, *Die Theologie der Sünde und der Buße beim heiligen Ambrosius* (St Gallen, 1968).

[17] 'Sed eos qui paenitentiam agunt, hoc solum paenitere non debe[n]t, ne ipsius paenitentiae agant paenitentiam', *De poenitentia* II.9 (86), ed. Gryson, 186, 36–8. The joke was not new. Cf. Pliny, *Ep.* x.7 and Tertullian, *De paenitentia* v.9, ed. C. Munier, SC 316 (Paris, 1984) 162.

[18] 'Hi videntur malorum petisse paenitentiam, agere bonorum' Ambrose, *De poenitentia* II.9 (86), ed. Gryson, 186, 41–2.

of shame or humiliation.[19] An audience is not needed, he argues, in order to employ *erubescentia* to liberating effect. Why blush to confess to God things that you do not hesitate to admit to a man?[20] Condemnation of one's faults frees one from them, providing nothing less than a 'training in innocence'.[21] Self-education through self-censure achieves a state of cathartic purity. It was not that Ambrose deluded himself about the obstacles to be surmounted before reaching this goal. In a disarming declaration, echoed centuries later by Heloise, he admitted: 'In my experience it is easier to find people who have preserved their innocence than those who have performed penance appropriately.'[22]

Appropriateness was to be taught by a penitential pedagogy of the emotions. Encompassing both the private and the public roles of the individual, it set standards measured by the example of Christ. These standards had nothing in common with post-modern ideas of authenticity as a product of significant symbols and meaningful metaphors or as an entity of limited autonomy and multiple centres that finds such cohesiveness as it can in dialogue with others.[23] Implying a relative or a complete arbitrariness, these attenuated senses of the self leave us with nothing much to which we can, or should, be true; and it is probable that Ambrose, had he known the word, would have dismissed them as neurotic (or worse). Neurosis, as he might have conceived it, was failure to recognise that truth was neither relative nor multiple but single and indivisible. Focused on God, authenticity was proved by obedience to divine will and sincerity was demonstrated by auto-accusation. The sense of the self expressed in penance was defined by guilt, admission of which should be preceded by contrition and followed by atonement. Equal weight not being attached to each of these parts of the model, priority was assigned to self-knowledge, expressed in the exhortation: 'Anticipate your accuser!',[24] which ruled out private avowals and secret sanctions.

Hence the importance of confession, frank and complete. When sinners admitted their faults, there was no room for dissimulation. As naked as

---

[19] Cf. R. Kaster, *Emotion, Restraint, and Community in Ancient Rome* (Oxford, 2005) 13ff. and M. Nussbaum, *Hiding from Humanity: Disgust, Shame and Law* (Princeton, 2004) 31, 205.

[20] *De poenitentia* II.10 (91), ed. Gryson, 188, 1–4.

[21] 'Fit quaedam de condemnatione culpae disciplina innocentiae' *De poenitentia* II.10 (92), ibid., 190, 24–6.

[22] 'Facilius autem inveni qui innocentiam servaverint, quam qui congrue egerint paenitentiam', *De poenitentia* II.10 (96), ibid., 192, 43–4. For Heloise, see Chapter 7 below.

[23] Cf. R. Rorty, *Contingency, Irony and Solidarity* (Cambridge, 1989); L. Guignon, *On Being Authentic* (London, 2004) and the critique by Williams, *Truth and Truthfulness*.

[24] *De poenitentia* II.7 (53), ed. Gryson, 166, 14ff.

Adam before his judge in the Garden of Eden,[25] they had no alternative but to answer honestly God's 'heart-rending' question (Genesis 3:9): 'Where are you?' That sinners might not be able to answer, because their wills were incapable of following the dictates of their consciences, is a possibility recognised but hardly developed by St Ambrose. Concerned to overcome *erubescentia* and to examine the cognitive potential of the emotions associated with penance, his moral imagination seldom ventured outside these self-imposed boundaries. Yet beyond them lay the divided will described by St Paul. In the exploration of that uncharted territory, the pioneer was not Ambrose but Augustine.

His division of will before conversion to Christianity is St Augustine's subject at *Confessions* VIII.5.10ff.,[26] his stated model, the Apostle's account of the struggle between the spirit and the flesh at Galatians 5:17 and Romans 7:14ff.[27] These texts are not easy to interpret, or to weave into the fabric of another life. Is Paul's description of a moral agent unable to follow the consequences of his better judgement informed by criteria of what Aristotle called ἀκρασία (*Nicomachean Ethics* VII.1.2ff.; 1145 b 1ff.)? Or does the Apostle simply refer to a state of paralysis caused by compulsive behaviour?[28] Neither of these definitions fits Augustine's case which, in the eighth book of the *Confessions*, is recounted in a negative dialectic of self-analysis.

His identity thrown into crisis by the conflict between two warring parts of himself, Augustine's authenticity consisted in a precarious balance of nuances: 'I was more in that which I approved of in myself than in that of which I disapproved' (*ego quidem … magis in eo, quod in me approbabam, quam in eo, quod in me improbabam, Confessions* VIII.5.11). Nuance takes on a tone of paradox in what he implies but does not say. For where was that preponderant part of his ego to which Augustine so enigmatically refers? In great part where he unwillingly suffered what he willingly did (*ex magna parte id patiebar invitus quam faciebam volens*, ibid.). A further party to this struggle, distinct from the two warring wills, is evoked. That

---

[25] 'culpa … apud Deum nuda', *De poenitentia* II.II (103), ibid., 196, 42–4.

[26] All references are to J. O'Donnell, *Augustine, Confessions* I: *Introduction and Text* (Oxford, 1992) 92ff.

[27] Literature on this subject is surveyed by F. Asiedu, 'Paul and Augustine's Retrospective Self: The Relevance of *Epistola* XXII', *Revue d' études augustiniennes* 47 (2000) 145ff.

[28] For bibliography, cf. R. Saarinen, *Weakness of the Will in Medieval Thought from Augustine to Buridan*, Studien und Texte zur Geistesgeschichte des Mittelalters 44 (Leiden, 1994) 8ff.

party is not identical with what St Paul describes at Romans 7:20. There the Apostle denies agency (*non ego operor illud*) and attributes to 'the sin that dwelleth in me' those actions he wishes not to perform. Independence of his will ascribed to that *peccatum*, Paul invites his readers to identify with his plight, which is theirs as well, and to apply his adverse judgement on it to themselves. Augustine presents the problem less directly and more subtly.

Led through the labyrinth of his warring wills, we are allowed to witness their aggressiveness, generated from and against himself. But we are not permitted to interpret. Hermeneutical priority is reserved to our guide. He forestalls our reactions in a question about his own sufferings that leaves us in no doubt about who is in control: 'By what right could anyone gainsay (*quis iure contradiceret*), since a just punishment pursued the sinner?' (*Confessions* VIII.5.11). Forensic in tone, this question evokes the courtroom, where the verdict is pronounced by God and the role of prosecutor is played by Augustine's third party: the conscience. Bidden as spectators, not participants, to his trial of the heart,[29] readers of the *Confessions* are forbidden to comment on its course. The right to define the degree of his identification with good or ill is reserved to the author. His is the obligation to declare the punishment deserved, because his hermeneutical priority is based on submission to the will of God.

That submission is not simply 'God-directed';[30] it is also intended to be exemplary for Augustine's readers. They are taught a lesson in the meaning and motives of confession. Even more incisively than Ambrose, Augustine offers a model of the conscience overcoming its struggle by a renunciation of self-will that leads, in a natural progression, from *accusatio sui* to praise of God.[31] That progression is achieved through humility which, in his view, amounted to both a foundation of self-knowledge and a guarantee of authenticity.[32] Writing the *Confessions*, Augustine also elucidated the principles according to which penance should be performed. At one with Ambrose in acknowledging the difficulties raised by that sacrament, he delved deeper into the forms of alienation to which the sinner is subject. Multiple are the analogies employed to convey that tormented state – torpor,

---

[29] On the metaphors of the tribunal and the heart, see J. Stelzenberger, *Conscientia bei Augustinus: Studie zur Geschichte der Moraltheologie* (Paderborn, 1959) 44ff.
[30] Guignon, *On Being Authentic*, 15.
[31] See J. Ratzinger, 'Originalität und Überlieferung in Augustinus Begriff der *Confessio*', *Revue des études augustiniennes* 3 (1957) 375–92.
[32] *In Johannis Evangelium Tractatus* XXV.16, ed. R. Willems, CCSL 36 (Turnhout, 1954) 257, 16–33.

ugliness (VIII.7.16), and the 'violence of habit' (VIII.5.12), culminating in a 'monstrosity' defined, successively, as an 'illness of the spirit' and as 'two wills' (VIII.9.21). Products of a 'big brawl within his interior house', they were nonetheless unable to wreak more than limited damage. From this scrap within himself, Augustine's will – no longer plural, but singular – emerged not even 'semi-scathed' (*semisaucia*, VIII.8.19).

The delicacy of that neologism, in the midst of images of violence and deformity, serves less to forestall a 'possible Manichean interpretation' of his self-division,[33] than to underscore his vulnerability. Vulnerable through a human nature corrupted by the Fall, Augustine shares in the punishment that makes Adam's descendants capable of involuntary sin.[34] But he does not subscribe wholly to St Paul's position, which he repeats while qualifying it. Despite the battle that he dramatises, Augustine maintains his identity intact. *Ego, ego eram* (VIII.10.22) – the affirmation stands in contrast to the Apostle's denial: *non ego*. The blows dealt to Augustine's self by its division are not fatal because, in that 'tribunal of the mind' where the conscience remains vigilant,[35] his authenticity, battered yet unbroken, is preserved. It establishes the validity of the spirit in which baptism and penance are performed;[36] it represents the agency of the heart whose truth to itself and to God is repeatedly defined in terms of I Timothy 1:5 'faith unfeigned'.[37] By no means the first Latin Father to employ the expression *fides non ficta*, Augustine was among the most forthright in acknowledging the existence of its double: *fictio*, by which he meant spiritual insincerity.[38]

This spectre haunted the saint. He linked *fictio* with the vice of hypocrisy, against which his polemic stands out, for its vehemence, in the abundant patristic literature on that subject. And not only for its vehemence. Augustine established the proximity of the terms 'hypocrisy', 'simulation',

---

[33] A. van Hoof, '*Confessiones* 8: Die Dialektik der Umkehr' in *Die Confessiones des Augustinus von Hippo: Einführung und Interpretationen zu den dreizehn Büchern*, ed. N. Fischer and C. Mayer (Freiburg, 1998) 270.

[34] Cf. M. Alflatt, 'The Development of the Idea of Involuntary Sin in St. Augustine', *Revue des études augustiniennes* 20 (1974) 113–34.

[35] See O'Donnell, *Augustine, Confessions* II: *Commentary*, 42–3.

[36] Augustine's views on penance are assembled by B. Poschmann, *S. A. Augustini textus selecti de paenitentia*, Florilegium Patristicum 38 (Bonn, 1934) and studied by A.-M. La Bonnardière, 'Pénitence et réconciliation des pénitents d'après saint Augustin', *Revue des études augustiniennes* 13 (1967) 31–53, 249–83; ibid. 14 (1968) 181–204.

[37] Cf. Stelzenberger, *Conscientia bei Augustinus*, 78ff.

[38] Cf. *Enarratio in Psalmum* 70, *Sermo* 2.1 *S. Aurelii Augustini Enarrationes in Psalmos LI–C*, ed. E. Dekkers and I. Fraipont, CCSL 39 (Turnhout, 1956) 959, 14–15.

and 'feigning' with an authority that remained uncontested for centuries.[39] Not until the twelfth did distinctions begin to be drawn, gradually and uncertainly, between *fictio* as an inversion of penance, attested in confession, and vices which, during late antiquity and the early Middle Ages, were considered to differ from one another less in kind than in degree. The degree of vice or sin attributed to feigning, simulation, and hypocrisy was as flexible as other issues in moral thought. Did not everyone agree with Augustine that pride was the root of all evil?[40] No, they did not; nor did the saint always adhere to his own line. He considered simulated humility worse than pride,[41] which could be construed as a form of sincerity. The simulated humility of the Pelagians was also a target of St Jerome's satire;[42] but he was more than satirical when, in a passage of his commentary on Isaiah which Heloise read as a condemnation of her own sins, he inveighed against that form of 'feigned sanctity' which consisted in pretending to be chaste despite an impure conscience.[43] Jerome's distinction between the less grievous, because 'open', evil and its severer, because 'hidden', version found general assent; Augustine was not alone in identifying and condemning such travesties of the Christian virtues of sincerity and authenticity.

His alone was the insistence that feigning and the family of vices to which it was related amounted to subversion, plotted by traitors to the City of God, who menaced its foundations.[44] Those foundations were the sacraments. When *ficti* undertook the formalities of baptism without the substance of faith, argued Augustine in a polemic against the Donatists which would influence theologians in the twelfth century, the sacrament remained valid, but only became effective after repentance had been

---

[39] E.g. 'sunt enim hypocritae simulatores mali adiungentes se ficta caritate', *Enarratio in Psalmum* 40:8, *S. Aurelii Augustini Enarrationes in Psalmos I–L*, ed. Dekkers and Fraipont, CCSL 38 (Turnhout, 1956) 454, 14–15.

[40] *In Johannis Evangelium Tractatus* xxv.16, ed. Willems, 256, 1ff.

[41] 'simulatio humilitatis maior superbia est', *De sancta virginitate* xliii. 44, ed. J. Zycha, CSEL 41 (Vienna, 1900) 289, 1–2.

[42] *Dialogus contra Pelagianos* 1.28, PL 23, 546A–B.

[43] 'Si castam me simulo et aliud est in conscientia mea, habeo … supplicia peccatoris … levius malum est aperte peccare quam simulare et fingere sanctitatem', *In Esaiam* xvi.14 in *S. Hieronymi Presbyteri Opera* I, 2, ed. M. Adriaen, CCSL 63 (Turnhout, 1963) 260, 41–5. On Heloise's use of this commentary, see Chapter 7.

[44] *De civitate Dei* I.35, *S. Aurelii Augustini De civitate Dei libri I–X*, ed. B. Dombart and A. Kalb, CCSL 47, 33ff.; xx.19, ibid., CCSL 48, 732, 72ff. For the link between *fictio* and pride, see *Enarratio in Psalmum* 121:8, *S. Aurelii Augustini Enarrationes in Psalmos CI–CL*, ed. Dekkers and Fraipont, CCSL 40 (Turnhout, 1956) 1808, 29–30.

evinced in 'true confession'.[45] Truth, as he conceived of it in this setting, not only demanded spiritual reparation for *fictio*; it also required actions. The instances Augustine gives of actions which prove that penance is authentic are concrete. One of them, which Abelard and others would cite, is that of the rich who rob the poor and fail to repay what they have stolen. Moans and groans for their misdeeds amount to nothing. Without restitution of ill-gotten goods, 'penance is not performed but feigned'.[46] The most literal definition of *fictio* by Augustine was also the one most frequently repeated.

His ideas, on this issue as on others, were far-sighted. They superseded the partial vision of his predecessors. *Fictio*, only glimpsed as a danger for penitents by earlier writers such as 'Hermas' in his *Pastor*,[47] is brought into focus by the saint when he writes of the threats faced by monks. If a brother declined to have a haircut, did that signify that he was humbling his pride in his appearance? Or that he was feigning humility by the ostentation of 'hairy holiness'?[48] These questions touched on more than fads and fashion. Breaching conformity of discipline in their hirsute individuality, long locks raised a problem to which a barber could provide no more than a superficial solution. They counted as outward symptoms of an inner malaise by which these perpetual penitents were afflicted.

As clear-cut about such manifestations of *fictio* as he is speculative about their causes, Augustine sets out the no-nonsense criteria by which they should be assessed in his exegesis of the Sermon on the Mount. Feigners, hypocrites, and simulators contrive to appear what they are not.[49] The negation is categorical, without qualification or nuance. Veracity, stark and simple, provides the measure of motivation. Human ability to fathom it is limited. Men should leave the secrets of the heart to divine judgement and stick to external facts.[50] Their potential conflict with moral agents' perception of inward truths is ignored in this work, although no one

---

[45] *De baptismo contra Donatistas* XII.18, ed. M. Petschenig, CSEL 51 (Vienna, 1908) 162ff., 10ff. For the influence of this discussion in the twelfth century, see Landgraf, *Dogmengeschichte* III, 2, 88ff.

[46] 'non agitur paenitentia, sed fingitur', *Ep.* 153.20, ed. A. Goldbacher, *S. Aurelii Augustini Hipponensis episcopi epistulae*, CSEL 44 (Vienna, 1904) 419, 6–7. For Abelard, see Chapters 3, 5, and 7.

[47] *Vis.* III.6.1 and *Sim.* VIII.6.2, ed. R. Joly, SC 53, 114 and 274 with N. Brox, *Der Hirt des Hermas* (Göttingen, 1991) 134ff. and 368. Cf. A. Schneider, '*Propter sanctam ecclesiam suam*': *Die Kirche als Geschöpf, Frau und Bau im Bußunterricht des Pastor Hermas*, Studia Ephemeridis 'Augustinianum' 67 (Rome, 1999) 67ff.

[48] *S. Augustini de opere monachorum*, 31, ed. J. Zycha, CSEL 41 (Vienna, 1900) 590, 23–591, 23.

[49] *De sermone Domini in monte* II.1; 2.5; 19.64, ed. A. Mutzenbecher, CCSL 35 (Turnhout, 1967) 92, 27ff.; 95, 87ff.; 160, 1454ff.

[50] *De sermone Domini in monte* II.18.60, ibid., 156, 1375ff., especially 1389–92.

analysed that dilemma more acutely than the author of the *Confessions*. Written during the same period as his exegesis of the Sermon on the Mount, they represent the subtler side of Augustine's ethical diptych.

His insistence on veracity was naturally accompanied by hostility to lies.[51] Their affinity with hellebore, which cures the terminally ill but kills the healthy, never occurred to Augustine. That likeness was drawn by 'Abbot Joseph' in the seventeenth of the *Conferences* by John Cassian,[52] a pupil of the master of monastic thought-control in the Greek East, Evagrius of Pontus.[53] His oriental subtlety left its mark on Cassian's work, which proposes an ethic of holy utilitarianism with panache. Pure ends justify impure means, he contends. Deception (*fallacia*) is permissible when a moral goal cannot be reached by truthfulness. False and misleading statements were employed by the saints and the patriarchs 'usefully' (*utiliter*).[54] Jacob, for example, wrapping himself in skins to look like his hairy brother, gained more merit by this 'artificial simulation' than by innate love of the truth.[55]

Truth, unvarnished and uncompromising in Augustine's exegesis of the Sermon on the Mount, performs so many masquerades in Cassian's *Conferences* that it is hardly distinguishable from simulation. Not content with being artificial, *simulatio* also assumes the guises of piety and religiosity.[56] All depends on motivation. Undertaken on the altruistic grounds commended by the Apostle (I Corinthians 10:33), simulation deserves praise. From there, by the same short-cut of others' interests, it is but a step to approving of lies told under such conditions as an 'indubitable necessity'.[57] The sleight of hand with which Cassian elides simulation and mendacity amounts to a slap in the face of Augustine's ethic of truthfulness; and this sparring with the saint is not easy to reconcile with the notion of monastic 'primitivism'.[58] If Bernard of Clairvaux adumbrates

[51] See M. Colish, 'St. Augustine's Rhetoric of Silence Revisited', *Augustinian Studies* 9 (1978) 15–18 and 'The Stoic Theory of Lies and False Statements from Antiquity to Anselm' in *Archéologie du signe*, ed. L. Brind'Amour and E. Vance (Toronto, 1982) 17–38.

[52] *Collationes* xvII.17, ed. E. Pichery, SC 54 (Paris, 1958) 260.

[53] See *Evagre le Pontique: Sur les pensées*, ed. P. Géhin, C. Guillaumont, and A. Guillaumont, SC 438 (Paris, 1998) with the excellent analysis of this and other works by R. Sorabji, *Emotion and Peace of Mind: From Stoic Agitation to Christian Temptation* (Oxford, 2000) 357–71.

[54] *Collationes* xvII.17, ed. Pichery, 260–1.

[55] *Collationes* xvII. 18, ibid., 262. For St Ambrose's position, see Colish, 'Rethinking Lying', 163ff., with valuable remarks on the anti-Augustinian tradition.

[56] *Collationes* xvII.19, ed. Pichery, 264–5.   [57] *Collationes*, ibid., 265.

[58] O. Chadwick, *John Cassian: A Study in Primitive Monasticism* (Cambridge, 1958). See now R. Goodrich, *Contextualising Cassian: Aristocrats, Asceticism and Reformation in Fifth-Century Gaul* (Oxford, 2007) and A. Casiday, *Tradition and Theology in St. John Cassian* (Oxford, 2006).

the psychology of the Roman Inquisition, John Cassian anticipates the casuistry of the Company of Jesus.[59]

Jesuit casuists, however, were more alert than Cassian to the consequences of blurring ethical borderlines. After the controversies provoked by his writings were stilled by St Benedict's recommendation of them to monastic readers in the forty-second and seventy-third chapters of the Rule, there remained, unsolved, the issue of how to distinguish between one man's virtue and another's vice. On the stylish but indistinct criteria of the *Conferences*, it is difficult to tell pious simulating or useful lying apart from wicked *fictio*. This problem was compounded by the habits, natural but confusing, of description by synonymity and of definition by antithesis that were widespread both in the Latin West and in the Greek East. Dorotheus of Gaza, for instance, identified feigned humility with vainglory; Rufinus did the same when he labelled it *iactantia*;[60] and others followed suit.[61] Their suit of moral opposites, constantly tending to paradox, was circular. At its centre stood the conscience, which alone was deemed capable of fathoming the secrets of the heart. On the margins languished the external judge, who might be suspicious but could not be exact. He had no means of scrutinising motivation, other than words and deeds. Yet the ambiguity of words and the duplicity of deeds were the premises on which his suspicion was based. Unable to convict on such shifty evidence, he had to rely on the testimony of the inner watchman. And who was to guard this guard? An answer to that vexing question was attempted by the first monk to become pope.

∽

St Gregory the Great, in his widely read *Moralia in Iob*,[62] provided more than a synthesis of these themes of late antique moral theology. No less

---

[59] Cf. P. Godman, *The Saint as Censor: Robert Bellarmine between Inquisition and Index*, Studies in Medieval and Reformation Thought 80 (Leiden, 2000).

[60] Dorotheus, *Instructions* II.32, ed. L. Regnault and J. De Preville, SC 92 (Paris, 1963) 194; Rufinus, *Historia monachorum* I, PL 21, 395D–396A.

[61] E.g. *Verba seniorum* xv.88, PL 73, 968A–969A.

[62] See C. Dagens, *Saint Grégoire le Grand. Culture et experience chrétiennes* (Paris, 1977) 133ff. For the influence of the *Moralia*, see R. Wasselnyck, 'Les compilations des *Moralia in Iob* du VIIe au XIIe siècle', *RTAM* 29 (1962) 5–32; Wasselnyck, 'L'influence de l'exégèse de saint Grégoire le Grand sur les commentaires bibliques médiévaux (VIIe–XIIe siècles)', *RTAM* 32 (1965) 157–204; Wasselnyck, 'La présence de saint Grégoire le Grand dans les ouvrages de morale du XIIe siècle' *RTAM* 35 (1968) 197–240; J. Gaudemet, 'L'héritage de Grégoire le Grand chez les canonistes médiévaux' in *Gregorio Magno e il suo tempo* II, Studia ephemeridis 'Augustinianum' (Rome, 1991) 199–221; E. Matter, 'Gregory the Great in the Twelfth Century: the *Glossa ordinaria*' in *Gregory the Great: A Symposium*, ed. J. Cavadini, Notre Dame Studies

alert than Augustine, his mentor and model, to the differences between ethical appearance and reality, he discussed penance with an insight that sharpened the perceptions of Bernard of Clairvaux.[63] Both of them shared a monkish disdain for the external world; both conceived of its relationship to the inner life as a radical opposition.[64] Interiority, pure and serene, had been the condition of mankind before the Fall, argues Gregory; the miseries of its post-lapsarian state are punishments for original sin. Pardon is possible and renewal can be achieved in confession motivated by genuine grief. Declarations count for nothing, unless this criterion is satisfied; and its satisfaction is knowable only to three parties, two of whom are the sinner and God. The third is the confessor, intermediary between the guilty penitent and the divine tribunal. His prime quality is *discretio* – discernment, prudence, sense of measure.[65] Yet the confessor is subordinate to the 'inner judge' (*iudex internus*) whom Gregory identifies with the conscience. Its pivotal part is travestied by those feigners and hypocrites whom he likens to the ostriches of Isaiah 34:13. They, 'in their perverse minds [where] the dragon reclines and the ostrich pastures', keep their 'underlying malice hidden shrewdly, while their simulation of goodness is paraded before the gaze of beholders'.[66]

Beholders of this parade through a scene set by the Gospel of St Matthew are invited to regard hypocrisy, simulation, and feigning as members of a trio:

Often hypocrites afflict themselves with extraordinary abstinence, wearing away all their bodily strength and virtually eliminating the complete life of the flesh while living it; and so near do they draw to death by abstinence that their daily life is led practically at death's door. But they seek to attract men's attention to this, craving the glory of being admired, as the Truth attests: *They disfigure their faces, that they may appear to men to fast* [Matthew 6:16]. For their faces grow pale, their bodies tremble with weakness, their chests are shaken by convulsive sighs. Yet,

---

in Theology 2 (Notre Dame, 1995) 216–26; and *Peter of Waltham, Remediarium Conversorum: A Synthesis in Latin of the Moralia in Job by Gregory the Great*, ed. J. Gildea, OSA (London, 1984).

[63] See B. Judiç, 'Confession chez Grégoire le Grand, entre l'intériorité et l'extériorité: l'aveu de l'âme et l'aveu du corps' in *L'Aveu*, 169–190, M. Cristiani, '*Ars artium*: La psicologia di Gregorio Magno' in *Le trasformazioni della cultura nella tarda antichità*, Atti del convegno tenuto a Catania 22 Sept.–2 Oct. 1982 (Rome, 1988) 309–31 and C. Straw, *Gregory the Great: Perfection in Imperfection* (Berkeley, 1988) 212ff. Still valuable is E. Göller, 'Die Sündenbekenntnis bei Gregor dem Grossen', *Oberrheinisches Pastoralblatt* 15 (1928) 1–25. On Bernard and Gregory, see below.

[64] Dagens, *Saint Grégoire* 168ff.   [65] Ibid. 117ff.

[66] 'latens malitia callide tegitur et intuentium oculis simulatio bonitatis antefertur'. *Moralia in Iob* VII.28.36, ed. M. Adriaen, *S. Gregorii Magni Moralia in Iob libri I–X*, CCSL 103 (Turnhout, 1979) 360, 99–101.

while this is going on, they seek admiring words from their neighbours and think of nothing, when they make such efforts, but the esteem of men.[67]

What concerns Gregory here is, the deceit that lies behind feigned penance. If *fictio*, the term which the twelfth century would attach to the phenomenon, is not used, elements constitutive of it are present in the saint's series of inversions. Life as death, physical mortification as spiritual ostentation, asceticism as humbug: the same pattern reappears in *De gradibus humilitatis et superbiae*. There, in his description of monastic feigning analysed in Chapter 1, Bernard develops a hint at the spurious 'habit of sanctity' given by Gregory later in the same book of the *Moralia*:

> There are a large number of persons who, abandoning the paths of open depravity, often put on the habit of sanctity; and, as soon as they reach the first step on the threshold of the virtuous life, forget who they have been and have no desire to suffer in penance for the acts of wickedness they have performed. They long to be praised for the righteousness on which they have embarked and hanker after precedence over others, even over those who are better than they are. When, in general, good fortune attends them for the moment as they wish, they become much worse than they were previously on account of their habit of sanctity. For, absorbed and confused by many kinds of busyness, they not only fail utterly to deplore what they have perpetrated, but go on piling up deplorable actions.[68]

In this labyrinth of inwardness, where the appearance of virtue augments vice, no outsider dares to tread. But Gregory does not baulk the problem of verifiability, which he attempts to resolve in terms of verdicts delivered by the conscience. From them, appeal to human witnesses is ruled out.[69] Manipulators of the truth become victims of their own ruses. Sterner in

---

[67] 'Plerumque hypocritae mira se abstinentia affligunt, omne robur corporis atterunt et quasi carnis vitam funditus in carne viventes extinguunt, sicque per abstinentiam morti appropriant, ut paene cotidie morientes vivant. Sed ad haec humanos oculos quaerunt, admirationis gloriam expetunt, Veritate attestante, qui ait: *Exterminant facies suas ut appareant hominibus ieiunantes*. Nam ora pallescunt, corpus debilitate quatitur, pectus interrumpentibus suspiriis urguetur. Sed inter haec ab ore proximorum sermo admirationis quaeritur nihilque tanto labore aliud, nisi aestimatio humana cogitatur.' *Moralia in Iob*, VIII.44.72, ed. Adriaen, ibid. 438, 28–38.

[68] 'Saepe namque nonnulli apertae pravitatis vias deserunt, sanctitatis habitum sumunt; moxque ut prima limina bene vivendi contigerint, obliti qui fuerint, affligi iam per paenitentiam de consummatis nequitiis nolunt; laudari autem de inchoata iustitia appetunt; praeesse ceteris etiam melioribus concupiscunt. Quos plerumque dum iuxta votum praesens prosperitas sequitur, multo quam prius fuerant de sanctitatis habitu peiores fiunt. Nam rebus multiplicibus occupati atque ipsa occupatione confusi, *non solum perpetrata minime deplorant, sed adhuc quae deplorentur exaggerant*.' *Moralia in Job*, VIII.47.77, ed. Adriaen, ibid., 442, 17–27. With the italicised phrases, cf. Bernard of Clairvaux, *De gradibus humilitatis et superbiae* XVIII: '*non solum* eiusmodi est non excusare, *sed* ipse quoque culpam *exaggerat*'. (See further Gregory, *In librum I Regum* VI.22, ed. P. Verbraken, CCSL 144 (Turnhout, 1972) 56, 441ff.).

[69] *Moralia in Iob* VIII.44.73, ed. Adriaen, ibid. 439, 61–5.

respect of veracity even than Augustine, Gregory goes on to argue for the existence of a 'hidden justice' which equates deceit with self-deception.[70] Because the operations of the conscience are involuntary and irresistible, an alternative to self-condemnation does not exist.

If he draws here on a *topos* of Roman rhetoric – attested, for example, in Cicero's invective against Catiline (III.27) – Gregory owes nothing to that rarefied concern with the self which classical Latin authors meant by *paenitentia*.[71] Penance, in the *Moralia*, is conceived more stringently. Only the bitterness of sincere remorse described in the Book of Job (10:1) can cure these sicknesses of the soul. The soul which Job addresses is his own, and the soliloquy is conducted with what Gregory the Great defines as penitential authenticity of *amaritudo*. It speaks the language of loathing: 'He who articulates abhorrence for his faults has no option but to declare them in the bitterness of his soul, so that every accusation made by the tongue, on the basis of mental judgement, be punished by the self-same bitterness.'[72] Yet Gregory is no naïve optimist. Even as he stresses the inexorability of the conscience, he acknowledges the persistence of what would later be called *fictio*: 'There are quite a few people who admit their faults openly, but do not know how to groan in confession and declare with joy what they should mourn.'[73] There, in perplexity at the substitution of jests for mourning, the first monk to become pope leaves open an issue which no theory of the conscience formulated in late antiquity succeeded in closing. Gregory the Great did not envisage an author like the Archpoet who, in order to amuse his anti-papal and anti-monastic patron, would turn these words on their head and make them into a motto of comedy.[74]

There is nothing comic about the moral ideas of that dull if diligent compiler, Isidore of Seville.[75] Nor is there much that is original. No ripple

---

[70] 'Occulta cum eis iustitia agitur, ut quo nituntur foras alios fallere, eo de se intus etiam ipsi fallantur.' *Moralia in Iob* XXVI.33.61, ed. Adriaen, CCSL 143 B 1312, 34–5.

[71] Kaster, *Emotion, Restraint, and Community*, 81–2.

[72] 'Qui culpas suas detestans loquitur, restat necesse est, ut has in amaritudine animae loquatur, ut haec ipsa amaritudo puniat quidquid lingua per mentis iudicium accusat.' *Moralia in Iob* IX.44.67, ed. Adriaen, CCSL 143, 504, 2–4.

[73] 'sunt nonnulli qui apertis verbis culpas fatentur, sed tamen in confessione gemere nesciunt et lugenda gaudentes dicunt.' *Moralia in Iob* IX.43.66, ed. Adriaen, ibid. 504, 12–14. The thought is indebted to Augustine, *Enarratio in Psalmum* 138:26, *S. Aurelii Augustini Enarrationes in Psalmos CI–CL*, eds. Dekkers and Fraipont, CCSL 40 2008, 14.

[74] See Chapter 8.

[75] P. Delhaye, 'Les idées morales de saint Isidore de Séville' *RTAM* 36 (1959) 17–49.

of ambiguity, no wave of complexity troubles the stagnant surface of his ethical commonplaces. Derived from others, they are transmitted in the familiar form of antithesis. Peccant thoughts, for example, are likened in Isidore's *Sententiae* to a viper lacerated by the offspring in its womb.[76] As an antidote to their 'viperous poison', he recommends purity of prayer.[77] Maladies, *fictio* among them, are promptly matched by cures. Recognising that there are those who accuse themselves in order to acquire the status of sanctity, he recommends that their 'feigned humility in confession' be countered by that sincerity which springs from 'compunction of heart'.[78] No one applied the principle of healing by contraries more literally, more mechanically than this doctor of the soul. Indeed Isidore was less a physician than a technician, who regarded the conscience as a machine to be maintained in working order by conventional lubricants of penance.[79]

How conventional and, at times, how coarse this simplifier of a complex tradition of moral thought could be, is indicated by his treatment of a theme that would play a role in twelfth-century representations of *fictio*. Feigners of penance, Bernard of Clairvaux and others recognised, were like actors. And acting, classical usage taught, was etymologically related to hypocrisy. This relationship is spelt out in a compilation of Isidore's that offered the High Middle Ages an approach to the problem of *fictio*:

Hypocrite in Greek is translated into Latin as feigner. He who is bad inside presents a good appearance to the outside world. 'γπό means false, κρίσις judgement. The name 'hypocrite' derives from the types who appear in theatrical performances with their appearance disguised, painting their faces with sky-blue or bright red and other pigments, putting on face-masks made of plastered linen and marked out with different colours, frequently anointing their necks and hands with clay to convey the look of a character and deceive the people while they perform, now taking the part of a man or a woman or of one who had had a haircut or one who is hairy, of an old and a young woman and other types, of various ages and sexes [in order to deceive the people, while they perform.] This type of analogy is applied to those who make their entrance under a false appearance and feign to be what they are not.[80]

---

[76] *Sententiae* II.25.4, ed. P. Cazier, *Isidorus Hispalensis Sententiae*, CCSL III (Turnhout, 1998) 143, 14–17.

[77] *Sententiae*, VII.7–8, ibid. 222, 35–44.   [78] *Sententiae* II.12.8, ibid. 119, 34–7.

[79] On the derivative character of Isidore's penitential doctrine, see E. Göller, 'Das spanisch – westgotische Bußwesen vom 6. bis 8. Jahrhundert', *Römische Quartalschrift* 37 (1929) 255–77. Cf. J. Fontaine, 'Pénitence publique et conversion personnelle: l'apport d'Isidore de Séville à l' évolution médiévale de la pénitence', *Revue de droit canonique* 28 (1978) 141–56.

[80] 'Hypocrita Greco sermone in Latino simulator interpretatur. Qui dum intus malus sit, bonum se palam ostendit. 'γπὸ enim falsum, κρίσις iudicium interpretatur. Nomen autem hypocritae tractum est ab specie eorum, qui in spectaculis contecta facie incedunt, distinguentes

Cobbled together from late antique clichés of suspicion towards the stage,[81] this rough image of hypocrisy, the twin of *fictio*, is noteworthy less for what it represents than for what it ignores. There is no trace, here or in Isidore's other writings, of Aristotle's comparison between the actor and that involuntary performer, the acratic (*Nicomachean Ethics* VII.4.2.2; 1147a 24). The brilliance of that perception was beyond the compiler's ken; and it remained beyond that of others until, circumventing the limits of this sorry stuff, Heloise re-created the Aristotelian insight without reference to the philosopher's works.[82] Isidore and the literalism typified by him inhibited many from attempting her feat of ethical imagination. Even so gifted a poet as Theodulf of Orléans, writing in the eighth century about the same themes, was incapable of lending *fictio* or its synonyms any meaning less pedestrian than outward deception.[83] The context had changed. Measurable standards of actions, not unquantifiable ideals of interiority, governed a system of penance that became repeatable. For the terse paradoxes of late antiquity were substituted long lists of 'tarifs' regulated by ecclesiastical accountants of the conscience.

∾

The 'tarifs' or sanctions for misconduct, both moral and criminal, exacted by the penitential handbooks that held sway in Western Europe from the late sixth to the eleventh centuries and beyond are sometimes called 'objective'. Never has a term been more pompous or less apt. This criticism was voiced in the early Middle Ages. The erratic imposition of penalties, without the

---

vultum caeruleo minioque colore et ceteris pigmentis, habentes simulacra oris lintea gipsata et vario colore distincta, nonnumquam et colla et manus creta perungentes, ut ad personae colorem pervenirent et populum, dum [in] ludis agerent, fallerent; modo in specie viri, modo in feminae, modo tonsi, modo criniti, anuli et virginali ceteraque specie, aetate sexuque diverso, [ut fallunt populum, dum in ludis agunt.] quae species argumenti translata est in his, qui falso vultu incedunt et simulant quod non sunt.' *Etymologiae* x.118–20, ed. W. M. Lindsay I (Oxford, 1911) (unpaginated). (The passage in square brackets seems to me to stretch beyond even Isidore's elastic limits his sense of tautology; and I suspect interpolation.) On Greek usage, see K. Hoheisel, 'Schauspielerei und Heuchelei in antiken Beurteilungen' in *Secrecy and Concealment: Studies in the History of Mediterranean and Near Eastern Religions*, ed. H. Kippenberg and G. Stroumsa (Leiden, 1995) 177–90.

[81] See H. Jürgens, *Pompa diaboli: Die lateinischen Kirchenväter und das antike Theater* (Stuttgart, 1972) 220ff. Cf. J. Suchomski, '*Delectatio*' und '*Utilitas*': ein Beitrag zum Verständnis mittelalterlicher komischer Literatur (Berne, 1975) 24ff.

[82] See Chapter 7.

[83] Theodulf, *Carm.* XVII, 1–8, 31, in *MGH Poetae Latini Ævi Carolini* I, ed. E. Dümmler (Berlin, 1881) 472–3.

authority of a bishop or synod,[84] was deplored from the Carolingian age onwards.[85] Lacking any unifying principle, the penitentials varied, from region to region and century to century, in the sanctions they prescribed for the same sin or crime. Criminality was hardly distinguished from sinfulness by the judges of the Church who filled the vacuum left by their secular forebears. If their harsh verdicts were informed by any common factor, it was belief in the necessity of atonement. Atonement, for them, was not a metaphysical concept. Penance meant, in the first place, fasting – the number of days, strictly yet arbitrarily calculated, during which meat was not to be eaten nor alcohol consumed.[86] Unlike the 'canonical' penance of the early Church, such 'tarifs' might be paid or performed time and again.

The rigours of self-reformation demanded by the doctrine of an Ambrose or an Augustine were alleviated and later abrogated. In their place emerged a contextual analysis that made allowance for the 'circumstances' (*circumstantiae*) – the age and sex, rank and profession, education, wealth or poverty – of those seeking forgiveness.[87] Questions were asked by confessors who did not neglect the temporal, spatial, and social factors that might be constitutive of, or mitigate, sin. Nor was the patristic emphasis on intention forgotten by prescriptive moralists with little taste, or capacity, for abstraction.[88] Lacking a clear concept of equity, some of them drew up lists of criteria for matching sanctions to sins evaluated in terms of these *circumstantiae*. An example is offered by the prologue to pseudo-Egbert's penitential (second half of the eighth century, possibly from the circle of St Boniface, with a rich manuscript tradition), which enjoins the priest not to 'weigh all cases in one and the same scale'.[89] The desire to discriminate

---

[84] See R. Kottje, 'Bußbücher' in *Lexikon des Mittelalters* II (1983) 1119 and cf. Kottje, *Die Bußbücher Halitgars von Cambrai und des Hrabanus Maurus: Ihre Überlieferung und ihre Quellen* (Berlin, 1980).

[85] H. Schmitz, *Die Bußbücher und die Bußdisziplin der Kirche: Nach handschriftlichen Quellen dargelegt* I (reprint Graz, 1958) 163.

[86] Cf. A. Angenendt, *Geschichte der Religiosität im Mittelalter* (Darmstadt, 2000) 632–6 and H. Lutterbach, 'Die Fastenbüße im Mittelalter' in *Frömmigkeit im Mittelalter: Politisch-soziale Kontexte, visuelle Praxis, körperliche Ausdrucksformen*, ed. K. Schreiner (Munich, 2002) 399–437.

[87] J. Gründel, *Die Lehre von den Umständen der menschlichen Handlung im Mittelalter*, BGPTMA 39, 5 (Münster, 1963) 67ff. and see Chapter 7 below.

[88] See Kottje, 'Intentions – oder Tathaftung?', criticising H. Lutterbach, 'Intentions – oder Tathaftung? Zum Bußverständnis in den frühmittelalterlichen Bußbüchern', *Frühmittelalterliche Studien* 29 (1995) 120–43.

[89] 'Non omnibus ergo in una eademque libra pensandum est, licet in uno constringantur vitio, sed discretio sit ...' Schmitz, *Bußbücher* I, 574. I thank Professor L. Körntgen (Tübingen) for advice on this work.

and do justice, however inarticulate, has been established beyond doubt.[90] Doubt accrues to the methods employed, for justice was done on the evidence of confession.

Confessio, by the eighth century, was synonymous with *paenitentia*.[91] So essential had confession become that, in the absence or unavailability of a priest, it was possible to avow one's sins to a layman.[92] The degree of faith (not always distinguishable from credulity) attached to the efficacy of *confessio* may be gauged by the practice of making it, in cases of isolation and emergency, to a cow, a horse, or a sword.[93] The knight repenting his violence to his weapon is emblematic of a mentality. The early medieval mentality, capable of confessing to an animal or an inanimate object, voiced a faith that was premised on literalism. And literal faith in a sacrament performed under such circumstances excluded most forms of *fictio*. It presupposes an inclination to abuse that faculty of ethical choice which the penitential handbooks, with their interminable questions posed from the outside, ignored or eliminated. If, at the beginning or at the end of such works, a genuflection was made towards the ideal of motivation, the actual space allotted to the moral agent was always far inferior to that devoted to his misdeeds.

Even in the theology of the Carolingian age, which did not fail to evoke the criterion of sincerity,[94] its links with the inner life were seldom probed, because the individual conscience was no longer a significant theme of ethical discourse. Sincerity was assumed on the basis of conduct. The *internus iudex*, so central and so eloquent for Gregory the Great, was consigned to muteness on the margins of this tradition of external judgement. And while 'public' and 'private' penance co-existed side by side,[95] in the awkward symbiosis of these two versions of the sacrament, the leading part

---

[90] See R. Kottje, 'Buße oder Strafe?' Zur 'iustitia' in den Libri Poenitentiales' in *La giustizia nell'Alto Medioevo*, Settimane del Centro Italiano di Studi sull'alto medioevo 44, 2 (Spoleto, 1997) 443–74, especially 446–8.

[91] B. Poschmann, *Die abendländischen Kirchenbüße im Frühmittelater* (Breslau, 1930) 168ff.

[92] A. Teetaert, *La confession aux laïques dans l'Eglise latine depuis le VIIIe jusqu'au XIVe siècle* (Bruges, 1926).

[93] Cf. Vogel, *Le péché et la pénitence*, 81 and 'La discipline pénitentielle en Gaule des origines jusqu'au IXe siècle', *Revue de sciences religeuses* 30 (1956) 1–26, 157–86.

[94] Alcuin, *De virtutibus et vitiis* XII, PL 101 622C (cf. M. Driscoll, *Alcuin et la pénitence à l'époque carolingienne* (Münster, 1999)) and Hincmar of Reims, *De cavendis vitiis et virtutibus exercendis* II.1.4, ed. D. Nachtmann, MGH Quellen zur Geistesgeschichte des Mittelalters 16 (Munich, 1998) 175–77, 196–7.

[95] See Poschmann, *Die abendländische Kirchenbüße* 92 ff., 168ff., M. Mansfield, *The Humiliation of Sinners. Public Penance in Thirteenth-Century France* (Ithaca, 1995) 21–34; and M. De Jong, 'What was *Public* about Public Penance? *Paenitentia Publica* and Justice in the Carolingian World' in *La giustizia nell'alto medioevo* 2, 863–902.

was taken not by sinners interrogating themselves, but by their confessors, whose absolution was obtainable only after what were taken to be truthful answers to the arsenal of questions with which they were equipped. Here lies one of the contributions made by the penitentials to the intellectual history of the Latin West: in the impulse, rude yet robust, which they provided to the growth of casuistry, as ancestors of the manuals for confessors that became an established genre in the thirteenth century.[96] Yet the casuistical methods employed in these handbooks were one-sided. Sinners were cross-examined. They were hardly expected to question themselves. Anticipated by a figure who was a cross between prosecutor and judge, their answers expressed a constrained and limited sense of responsibility. Responsibility, in its full and active meaning, was attributed to the confessor. His initiative, not their avowals, lent penance its structure.

The part of the *iudex internus* was now played by this ecclesiastical accountant. His task was computational. To each 'case' of sin or transgression was matched a proportionate 'tarif' – 'proportionality' meaning a fast or a fine determined by the author of the manual, not a penalty inflicted by the conscience on itself.[97] What the handbooks taught instead was, an itemised sense of guilt. Guilt is distinct from neurosis. Penitents were not inhibited by 'fear of freedom', but discouraged from reflection by a system that substituted commands for thought in a manner calculated to exact obedience. Told how and when they had erred, they were not invited to ponder why. Reliant on their confessors, whose judgements were pronounced after consulting, or memorising, a handbook (two were seeds of discord), these often illiterate recipients of authoritarian lore were given no incentive to reason about wrong-doings as seemingly unavoidable as they were apparently endless.

Small wonder if they learnt to feel the pangs of remorse without the consolation of understanding. Understanding entails an ability to think which, in this large, informative, but dispiriting literature, is regularly subordinated to the authority of the confessor. The *libri paenitentiales* did their considerable best to discredit, near its medieval origins, what the later history of moral casuistry attempted to prove: that rules of law and principles of ethics are compatible.[98] That was one of the reasons why, in the self-critical

[96] On the genre, see P. Michaud-Quantin, *Sommes de casuistique et manuels de confession au Moyen Âge* (Louvain, 1962).
[97] See Chapter 8.
[98] Cf. A. Jonsen and S. Toulmin, *The Abuse of Casuistry: A History of Moral Reasoning* (Berkeley, 1988).

age of twelfth-century reform, comparatively few of them were produced.[99] For the summit (or nadir) of this historically complex and ethically crude tradition had been reached, in 1008–1012, by an author who illustrates its strengths and weaknesses, Burchard of Worms. In the *Medicus sive Corrector* which forms the nineteenth book of his influential *Decretum*, Burchard draws on a variety of sources, some of them patristic.[100] He had not lost contact with the interiority of the Latin Fathers, nor was his approach solely negative. What counts, he asserts on the authority of St. Jerome,[101] is rather mortification of vice than abstention from food. More important than the time taken to perform penance is the depth of the grief that it evokes. So much for the rhetoric of motivation with which the *Medicus* opens and closes. In between stretch long lists of questions dealing, often in minute detail, with sinful behaviour and its sanctions. Nowhere is Burchard more meticulous than on the subject of sex, which is why his *Medicus* sheds light on the erotic practices of the early Middle Ages.[102] And the work also illuminates, at times with inadvertent humour, the mentality that the confessor was expected to acquire from reading such lists.

A sense of humour is not the most salient quality of those who composed early medieval penitentials, nor does a feeling for *fictio* appear to have been a notable attribute of that disciplinarian, Burchard of Worms.[103] None the less, his combination of strictness and suspicion that penitents

---

[99] See M. Muzzarelli, 'Teorie e forme di penitenza in fase di transizione' in *Dalla penitenza all'ascolto delle confessioni: il ruolo dei frati mendicanti*, Atti del XXIII convegno internazionale, Assisi, 12–14 Oct. 1995 (Spoleto, 1996) 33–58.

[100] PL 140, 949ff. A translation, with introduction and notes, is offered by G. Ricasso, G. Piana, and G. Motta, *Pane e acqua: Peccati e penitenza nel Medioevo. Il penitenziale di Burcardo di Worms* (Novara, 1986). The best study of Burchard's sources is L. Körntgen, 'Fortschreibung frühmittelalterlicher Bußpraxis: Burchards "Liber corrector" und seine Quellen' in *Bischof Burchard von Worms 1000–1025*, ed. W. Hartmann (Mainz, 2000) 198–226. Cf. G. Austin, 'Jurisprudence in the Service of Pastoral Care: The *Decretum* of Burchard of Worms', *Speculum* 79 (2004) 929–59. On the influence of the *Decretum*, see P. Fournier, 'Le Décret de Burckhardt de Worms, son caractère et son influence', *Revue d'histoire ecclésiastique* 12 (1911) 451–79, 670–701 and Fournier, 'Études critiques sur le Décret de Burchard de Worms', *Revue d'histoire de droit français et étranger* 24 (1910) 40–112, 213–21, 289–331, 564–84; O. Meyer, 'Überlieferung und Verbreitung des Dekrets des Bischof Burkhardt von Worms', *Zeitschrift der Savigny – Stiftung. Kan. Abt.* 24 (1935) 141–83, and G. Theverkauf, 'Burchard von Worms und die Rechtskunde seiner Zeit', *Frühmittelalterliche Studien* 2 (1968) 141–61. Fundamental is the work of H. Hartmann and R. Pokorny, *Das Dekret des Bischof Burchard von Worms. Textstufen. Frühe Verbreitung. Vorlagen*, MGH Hilfsmittel 12 (Berlin, 1991).

[101] *Medicus* 31, PL 140, 985D.

[102] H. Lutterbach, *Sexualität im Mittelalter: eine Kulturstudie anhand von Bußbüchern des 6. bis 12. Jahrhunderts* (Cologne, 1999).

[103] Cf. S. Haarländer, 'Die *Vita Burchardi* im Rahmen der Bischofsviten seiner Zeit' in *Bischof Burchard von Worms*, ed. Hartmann, 129–60. See further Chapters 3 and 4.

might pretend to be sincere but fail to be frank about their sexual conduct may explain why the *summae confessorum* of the thirteenth century advised against making too many demands about these matters, in order to avoid putting ideas into sinners' head. How, is suggested by the following question:

Have you done what some women are accustomed to do with a device or instrument in the shape of male sexual organ made to the measure of your taste, and tied it with straps to your *pudenda* or those of another woman in order to fornicate with other wenches … ?[104]

Imagine the position of the priest trained by the *Medicus* to interrogate in so delicate a manner. With a muster of material furnished by Burchard of Worms, he was to become a vicarious expert on sexual deviances which he was prohibited to know at first hand. Obliged to anticipate what he could not be sure that sinners would be willing to admit, this accountant of the conscience then set off in search of the balance-sheet of penance. Sowing from his baggage of erotic demands the seeds of misconduct in all too receptive minds, he pursued a goal that could lead in comic directions, although its starting point was serious. For the confessor, as depicted in Burchard's *Medicus* and similar sources, departed from the complementary premises of *fictio*, in the form of penitents' readiness to misrepresent themselves as innocent by remaining silent, and of measureless mistrust.

Measureless because as protean as human ingenuity or natural embarrassment, mistrust of sinners' willingness to avow their transgressions was accompanied by severity in judging them. Five years of penance were prescribed for the lesbian antics above, besides the sanctions for bestiality, incest, and abortion. The varieties of sin envisaged by Burchard are numerous, and sometimes stretch the elastic limits of fantasy. What, for example, is to be made of the medieval women who – according to him – placed a live fish in their vaginas, waited until it died, and then cooked it, serving it to their husbands as an aphrodisiac? (To say nothing of the bread prepared on their naked backsides, when prostrate, and then cooked for the same purpose – presumably not in the same place.)[105] Here as elsewhere, one hopes that Burchard has made the case up; and fears that he has not.

---

[104] 'Fecisti quod quaedam mulieres facere solent, ut faceres quoddam molimen aut machinamentum in modum virilis membri ad mensuram tuae voluntatis et illud loco verendorum tuorum aut alterius cum aliquibus ligaturis colligeres et fornicationem faceres cum aliis mulierculis … ?' *Medicus* 5, PL 140, 971D–972A.

[105] Ibid. 974A.

Never hesitant to match the penalty to the transgression (two years of penance, in this instance), Burchard of Worms, like others, draws no distinction between moral and criminal justice. Accidental infanticide committed by a mother was a case, regularly cited in early medieval penitentials,[106] that might have posed this problem; and its difficulty was compounded when the child died unbaptised. Religious observance versus human compassion, extenuating circumstances combined with degrees of knowledge and forms of responsibility: all these issues were raised by accidental infanticide; and Burchard deals with them briskly. After touching on similar instances of death by fire or boiling water, he focuses on the example of a suffocated baby.[107] Its mother did not intend to murder it, nor did it perish under the weight of her clothes. Motivation disposed of, attention is directed to the issue of whether the infant had been baptised. If so, fasting is imposed for forty days, together with abstention from marital sex. This régime was to be followed, during Lent and on other occasions, over a period of three further years. Two years more are added for a mother who had failed to have her smothered child baptised. So it was that, in this rudimentary arithmetic of retribution, the ancient link between the sacraments of baptism and penance was affirmed. Failure to secure the first lengthened the second.

Exemplary punishment is inflicted on a double negligence, fatal to the body and to the soul; yet the degree of culpability is left to be inferred at this point. Inferred, not explained, because the doctor of the soul in Burchard's *Medicus* is instructed to apply purgatives and effect excisions, but given no guidance on how to account for his tough treatment of the spiritual patient. Of a pedagogy of the emotions, so prominent in the works of Ambrose and Augustine, there are few traces in the penitential literature of the early Middle Ages. And yet, as if unsettled by the pathos of the problem with which he has dealt summarily, Burchard continues to worry at it, adding the figure of a father to the *dramatis personae* of this domestic tragedy. Neither the man nor his wife knows which of them might have suffocated the baby when it lay between them in bed; the death could even be ascribed to natural causes. In these cases, 'much allowance

[106] See F. Wasserschleben, *Die Bußordnungen der abendländischen Kirche* (reprint Graz, 1958) 172, 200, 239, 255–6, 313, 358, 380, 413, 507, 530, 558; and cf. Ivo of Chartres, *Decretum* xv, 164, PL 161 893C–894D. For context, see E. R. Coleman, 'L'infanticide dans le Haut Moyen Âge', *Annales* ESC 29 (1974) 235–335 and G. Schmitz, 'Schuld und Strafe: Eine unbekannte Stellungnahme das Rathramnus von Corbie zur Kindestötung', *Deutsches Archiv* 38 (1982) 363–87.
[107] PL 140, 975A–975C.

should be made for compassion' (*in his magna consideratio debet esse pieta-tis*), and forty days on bread and water are prescribed for non-culpable ignorance. Culpable ignorance, by contrast, carries a penalty of three years' penance. Guilt and punishment augment in proportion to knowledge. Yet knowledge of sin and its difference from crime are not enhanced a whit by this instance of penitential discipline. It teaches a blunt lesson of prudence: that it is imperative to have your baby baptised, and advisable to acquire a cot.

That there is, or may be, a distinction between exemplary justice and moral equity never appears to have entered Burchard's mind; nor was it perceived clearly by others until Abelard, in tacit polemic against the *Medicus* and the penitential tradition, refashioned the same example in his ethical tract.[108] He reacted against an approach which, however didactic and edifying its intentions,[109] taught what was, in effect if not in name, a pastoral of punishment. The formalism of early medieval thought on this subject is summed up in a declaration by Bonizo of Sutri, a canonist and writer on penance linked with the circle of Pope Gregory VII:

> What is assigned to the penitent according to the canons in the way of fasting, mortification of the flesh, distribution of alms, and assiduous prayer are the fruits of true penance which we demand from the penitent. *There is no other way of knowing whether he is a true penitent or not.*[110]

Implicitly conceding, by antithesis to 'true penance', the possibility of *fictio*, Bonizo frankly admits his inability to deal with it. In what amounts to a variant on the canonists' theme of 'the Church does not judge the secrets of the heart', he acknowledges that actions or conduct provide his sole standards of penitential truth. But the examples of atonement which Bonizo cites as proving sincerity and authenticity are the same ones that Gregory the Great had employed to illustrate feigning, hypocrisy, and simulation. Missing from Bonizo's list are the criteria of interiority portrayed by the *Moralia in Iob* as fundamental. They depended on an ethic of personal responsibility which the mentality of the 'tarifs' rejected as

---

[108] See Chapter 7.
[109] Cf. Austin, 'Jurisprudence' and Kottje, 'Buße oder Strafe?'.
[110] 'Quod autem secundum canones ieiunium et carnis maceratio et helemosinarum distribu-tio et assidua oratio penitenti indicitur, fructus enim sunt vere penitentie, quos a penitente requirimus. *Non aliter enim potest cognosci verusne esset penitens necne.*' Bonizo of Sutri, *Liber de vita christiana* IX.2, ed. F. Perels, Texte zur Geschichte des römischen und kanonischen Rechts im Mittelalter I (Berlin, 1930) 277–8. Cf. W. Berschin, *Bonizone de Sutri: La vita e le opere* (Spoleto, 1992) 73ff. and 211–17.

immeasurable and therefore 'subjective'. Yet between its pseudo-objectivity and arbitrariness, the dividing-line was often so slight as to be invisible; and even as Bonizo formulated this view, traditional in the eleventh century, it was beginning to be criticised by an anonymous writer who sought cover behind the *magnum nomen* of St Augustine.

CHAPTER 3

True, false, and feigned penance

Two, not three, types of penance exercised the moral imagination of the early Middle Ages. For feigning in this context there was, or ought to have been, no place. Truth versus falsehood, white against black, with scarcely a hue of ethical indeterminacy between them: such were the categories in which the penitential 'tarifs' were computed. Dispensed from burdening their brains with vexing questions of personal responsibility, sinners fasted, paid fines, and abstained from sex. Sex representing the major exception to these rules of literalism, *fictio* was suspected in the limited form of reticence. It was overcome by confessors in ever longer lists of questions that anticipated what partial penitents might be unwilling to admit. Failure to respond or to accept the sanctions imposed was taken to demonstrate falsehood. So too was an ingenious resort of embarrassment, cunning, or subterfuge: dividing up one's accumulated transgressions, and confessing some to one priest and others to another. For the Church, this amounted to the dirt of disavowal.

That dirt could be cleansed only by unabridged candour. Official pronouncements on the subject remained within the confines of the black-and-white mentality well into the second quarter of the twelfth century. 'True and false penance', for example, was dealt with at the second Lateran Council which opened, on 3 April 1139, with a speech by Innocent II, now uncontested as pope after the death of his rival Anacletus II and the resignation of Victor IV. The tone was upbeat. The reform legislation of previous decades had to be consolidated in a spirit of severity; monastic discipline was to be toughened and clerical concubinage suppressed. There followed, in the twenty-second canon promulgated by the council, a mixed bag of offences deemed 'particularly disturbing to the Church'.[1]

---

[1] *Sacrorum conciliorum nova et amplissima collectio* 21 ed. J. Mansi (Venice, 1726) 530–2 with R. Foreville, *Latran I, I, III e Latran IV* in *Histoire des conciles oecuméniques* (Paris, 1965) 92–3.

Incomplete confession was one of them. This abuse was set on the same level as a penitent's failure to resign an office that could not be exercised without committing sin, as nourishing hatred in his heart, as neither satisfying an offended person nor forgiving an offence, and as bearing arms 'contrary to justice'. The justice implied by this canon drew no distinction between public conduct and private motivation. Their conflation marked the distance that had been established, over centuries, from the self-critical spirituality of St Augustine and others. The legislation enacted by the second Lateran council is the most recent source quoted by Gratian in the earliest recension of his *Decretum*. Yet, in a lengthy section of that work dealing with penance (C.33, q.3),[2] he is also the first scholar to cite the contrary approach of a monastic thinker who, significantly, assumed Augustine's name.[3]

Augustine's name signified both a programme and an alternative. An alternative to the system of 'tarifs', with their unargued regulation of the external spheres of moral life, *De vera et falsa paenitentia*,[4] despite its traditional title, heralded a return to patristic interiority. More than that pseudo-Augustine did not effect. Neither a radical innovator nor a master of Latin prose, he plods with pedestrian caution where the saint soars. None the less his tract maintains an affinity of thought with Augustine's, especially that of *De libero arbitrio* and *De spiritu et littera*, which led *De vera et falsa paenitentia* to be accepted as authentic for centuries.[5] It is that affinity which sets this work apart from the handbooks of the early Middle Ages.

In the straightjacket of their prescriptive moralism, the expansive concept of free will was cramped by rules. The rules so arbitrarily prescribed by this tradition were not enough for pseudo-Augustine. He sought to identify the principles that did, or should, lie behind them. Locating the prime source of sin in abuse of free will,[6] his restatement of this ancient axiom, set against the claustrophobic context of the 'tarifs', inspires an air of freshness. That freshness derives from the attention paid by pseudo-Augustine

---

[2] See A. Winroth, *The Making of Gratian's Decretum*, Cambridge Studies in Medieval Life and Thought 49 (Cambridge, 2000) 7, 128, 193.
[3] Cf. L. Hödl, *Die Geschichte der scholastischen Literatur und der Theologie der Schlüsselgewalt* I, BGPTMA 38, 4 (Münster, 1960), 159ff.
[4] PL 40, 1113–1130.
[5] The otherwise valuable discussion by Ohst, *Pflichtbeichte* 50ff., is flawed by his presentation of *De vera et falsa paenitentia* 'unter der Herrschaft der Logik der Tarifbüße'. See further M. de Kroon, 'Pseudo-Augustin im Mittelalter', *Augustiniana* XXII (1972) 511–30; Teetaert, *La confession aux laïques*, 50–56; Poschmann, *Die abendländische Kirchenbüße*, 193ff. and J. Le Goff, *La naissance du Purgatoire* (Paris, 1981) 290ff.
[6] VIII.22; XVI.32; PL 40, 1120; 1126.

to the neglected problem of motivation. Faith is not assumed on the basis of obedience to punitive guidelines of conduct. Sincerity is sought. And in sincerity expressed through the assent of free will, he identifies a 'fundament of the faith'.[7] Conviction alone ensures that the sacrament is valid. In its absence, penance is emptied of content and reduced to a mere ritual which he dismisses as 'useless or sterile'.

Sterility and uselessness, not stark falsehood as opposed to absolute truth: these nuances of patristic origin are more than plays with words. What *De vera et falsa paenitentia* seeks to formulate is, a category of ethical censure that the manuals ignored. They ignored the inadequacy of an appearance of correctness; they failed to consider the possibility that regular fulfilment of obligations might be beside the point. The point of penance, as pseudo-Augustine regards it in the manner of his model, is established by the sinner's intentions. *Why* a full confession to a single priest should be made, is more important than *how* incompletely or selectively it may be performed. Formalism, for pseudo-Augustine, is inadequate. Emphasising the principle rather than the rule, he places at the centre of his tract the issue of spiritual authenticity.

That issue is linked by him to another, equally neglected by early medieval tradition: the affective implications of penance. The key term is *erubescentia*, which he restores to its former prominence. What could that combination of feelings which, as St Ambrose envisaged them, ranged from embarrassment to shame, have meant to confessors accustomed to asking women whether they had inserted live fish into their vaginas? The manuals did not train such enforcers of the Church's law to reflect on the cognitive capacity of the emotions that their demands might provoke in penitents. It is on the recipients of sanctions, rather than their imposers, that pseudo-Augustine focuses attention. He reverses the standpoint of the handbooks, urging the value of an emotion they had deprecated or ignored. No longer regarded negatively as a barrier to be overcome by invasive questioning, *erubescentia* is highlighted positively as a source of self-knowledge.[8]

Knowledge of the self was not a quality which early medieval writers on the same subject had attributed to, or encouraged in, penitents. Portrayed as capable of concealment but not of analysis by the manuals, they were treated like bondsmen of conscience. Pseudo-Augustine, by contrast, not only awaits a reaction but seeks to provoke it. Emphasising *erubescentia* as a form of self-chastisement, he defines it as the indispensable condition of

[7] II.3; ibid., 1113.   [8] X.25; ibid., 1122.

divine mercy. A dormant doctrine of personal responsibility is re-woken; and *De vera et falsa paenitentia* portrays the sinner as a moral agent free to move within limits which are defined clearly. Outside the Church, penance is invalid; inside, it is normally to be administered by a priest.[9] Exceptional circumstances permit a layman to receive avowals; but there is no hint of the literalism that believed in the efficacy of confession to a sword or a horse. The admission of sins takes second place and motivation the first, as the focus shifts from words and deeds to emotions and their cognitive qualities. Penance, reconceived in these terms, is implicitly acknowledged as a sacrament. That is why pseudo-Augustine asserts that '*erubescentia* contains, in itself, a part of the remission [of sins]'.[10] The teaching of his namesake had been absorbed by this intelligent author and re-applied to different circumstances, which include the form and manner in which admissions of sin are to be made. The Fathers' directive that they should be verbal is not merely repeated, but developed further: since orality is prescribed, it follows that written confession is prohibited.[11]

That prohibition points to the audience for which *De vera et falsa paenitentia* was intended: those monastic readers, capable of becoming scribes, whose daily life was compared by the Rule to a perpetual Lent. They would have recognised from the same source this variant on the theme of never-ending penance:

Let him [= the sinner] always grieve and rejoice in grief and ever grieve about the penance of grief, should it occur. And let it not suffice that he grieves, but let him grieve from faith, and grieve that he has not always grieved.[12]

That monkish mixture of remorse at wrongdoing and joy in atonement is premised on a sincerity that admitted no boundaries, affective or temporal. Penitential sorrow, profound and continuous, cannot be limited to acts of reparation. Pseudo-Augustine's lugubrious concept of authenticity encompasses the whole life and the entire personality.

The seemingly virtuous action of alms-giving provides an example of what is meant. Then it is 'not the quantity that should be considered, but the cast of mind, the feeling' (*qua mente, qua affectione*).[13] This emphasis on interiority, sustained throughout *De vera et falsa paenitentia*, marks its author's distance from the official line later taken at the second Lateran

---

[9] XII.27; ibid., 1127.   [10] X.25; ibid., 1122.   [11] Ibid.

[12] 'semper doleat et dolore gaudeat et de doloris paenitentia, si contingerit, semper doleat. Et non sit satis quod doleat, sed ex fede doleat, et non semper doluisse doleat', XIII.28; ibid., 1124.

[13] XV.30; ibid., 1125.

council. Addressing the same issue, defined in 1139 as 'false penance', pseudo-Augustine regards those who 'divide up confession within themselves', admitting different things to different priests, as guilty of self-praise.[14] If that was a category in which Innocent II and others thought, it was not one expressed in their twenty-second canon. They, not pseudo-Augustine, remained within what has been called the 'dominant logic of the 'tarifs'.[15] Ranging beyond these boundaries, he likens to hypocrisy the self-praise implicit in partial confession. And there, at the point of paradox where falsehood halts and *fictio* commences, *De vera et falsa paenitentia* transcends its title, in a first attempt to substitute for the stereotypes of the early Middle Ages an ethic of Augustinian restoration. That restoration was already in course when this author wrote. Its leading exponent was, like him, a monk.

St Anselm of Aosta and Canterbury was the most accomplished Augustinian since Gregory the Great. Never more faithful to his model than when he departed from it, he understood and applied Augustine's lesson of independence.[16] Others were less imaginative. One of them was Anselm's pupil, Guibert of Nogent, whose faltering attempt, in his *De vita sua, sive monodiae*, to copy the *Confessions* demonstrated no more than that they were not imitable by fidelity to the letter of the text.[17] Its spirit, bold and free, could only be recaptured through that emulation which the saint practised both in the tours de force of his *Prosologion* and *Monologion* and

[14] XV.31; ibid., 1125–26.   [15] Ohst, *Pflichtbeichte*, 54.

[16] On affinities between Augustine and Anselm, see R. Southern, *Saint Anselm: A Portrait in a Landscape* (Cambridge, 1991) 71ff.; F. van Fleteren, 'The Influence of Augustine's *De Trinitate* on Anselm's *Monologion*' in *Saint Anselm – A Thinker for Yesterday and Today: Anselm's Thought Viewed by His Contemporaries*, ed. C. Viola and F. van Fleteren (Lewinston, 2002) 421–43; K. Kienzler, 'Zur philosophisch-theologischen Denkform bei Augustinus und bei Anselm von Canterbury' in *Anselm Studies: An Occasional Journal* II, Proceedings of the Fifth International Conference: *St. Anselm and Augustine – Episcopi ad saecula*, ed. J. Sehnanbelt *et al.* (New York, 1988) 353–87; and T. Bestul, 'St. Augustine and the *Orationes sive Meditationes* of St. Anselm' ibid. 597–606.

[17] Edited and translated by E.-R. Labande, Guibert de Nogent, *Autobiographie*, Les classiques de l'histoire de France au Moyen Age (Paris, 1981). The translation by J. F. Benton, *Self and Society in Medieval France: The Memoirs of Abbot Guibert of Nogent* (New York, 1970) is more faithful, in the sense that, when the Latin is unintelligible, so is the English. (A new edition is needed.) Still the best study is by G. Misch, *Geschichte der Autobiographie* II, *Das Mittelalter* II: *Das Hochmittelalter im Anfang* (Frankfurt am Main, 1959) 108ff. and 266–7. Bibliography is assembled by W. Berschin, *Biographie und Epochenstil im lateinischen Mittelalter* IV, 2 *Ottonische Biographie. Das hohe Mittelalter 920–1120*, Quellen und Untersuchungen zur lateinischen Philologie des Mittelalters 12, 2 (Stuttgart, 2001) 341ff.

in less celebrated feats of introspective analysis, such as his letters and his table-talk. Oral sources for the history of the medieval conscience are few and far between, and Eadmer's account of Anselm's career at Bec gives us rare insight into how an abbot instructed his monks on the ethical issues raised by versions of *fictio*. The occasion was less formal than a sermon from the pulpit or a discussion in the chapter. The stiffness of hierarchy relaxed when Anselm talked and taught at meals. His conversation sparkled with aphorisms, parables, and paradoxes. We do not know how Burchard of Worms or Bonizo of Sutri spoke, but if their table-talk resembled their writings, it was less exhilarating, because they were accustomed to laying down the law.

What lay behind the law interested Anselm and made him fascinating to his hearers. His cast of mind was speculative. He searched for principles. Where others detected breaches of rules, he was sensitive to finer distinctions. That sensitivity was displayed in his emphasis, during conversations that ranged over such topics as humility, patience, and gentleness, on the theme of obedience. Anselm never doubted that obedience was a paramount necessity for monks. Nor was he content to equate it with outward correctness. Here the contrast between him and the likes of Burchard and Bonizo is striking. For them, a member of a religious order who sought and obtained permission to leave his monastery was straightforwardly in the right. Discussing this case,[18] Anselm argued that conformity to the letter of the Rule might be fulfilled in breach of its spirit. If the deed was excusable, the desire to commit it was not, unless the monk made good his inner violation of obedience by repenting.

Repentance, so conceived, was no longer located in the external sphere of action, where Burchard and Bonizo placed it, but in the conscience of the moral agent, where neither permission nor prohibition by a hierarchical superior mattered so much as the authority of what Gregory the Great had called the 'inner judge'. Both Gregorian and Augustinian in inspiration is Anselm's view of the will. Not that potential delinquent whom the penitentials curbed by threat of sanctions, the will, in Anselm's subtler opinion, is an inadvertent rebel, given to self-deception. Hence his terse but telling expression, 'willing against obedience' (*velle contra obedientiam*), which does not simply mean a breach of monastic discipline. It signals wrong, no less grave for being imperceptible to outside observers, done to the obligation of self-surrender. 'Unbridled will' (*illicita voluntas*), as he

---

[18] Eadmer, *Vita S. Anselmi* I.9, ed. R. Southern, *The Life of St. Anselm, Archbishop of Canterbury, by Eadmer* (London, 1962) 77.

redefines this source of sin in a parable related to his table-talk, represents
a form of servitude that is the opposite of the true freedom to be found in
conformity to God's commands.[19]

Paradox, distinctive of Anselm's thought,[20] permeates even his occasional works, including the letters which he wrote while abbot of Bec. Part
of their significance lies in the breach which they effect with the prescriptive moralism of the early Middle Ages and the return which they mark to
the questions of ethical appearance and reality that concerned Augustine
and Gregory. Replying to an enquiry about priests who had committed
unchaste acts put to him by Abbot William of Fécamp,[21] Anselm did not
answer with the toughness traditional in the penitential literature. If unre-
pentant sinners of this kind deserved to be deprived of office and to be
damned, those who showed heartfelt contrition in admitting their faults
merited forgiveness and should be re-instated. So far, so conventional. But
Anselm goes on to diverge from the standard line in adopting a Christian
Socratism. Since 'it is almost always hidden whose wicked deeds are remitted', he argues that it is safer – not obligatory – for an unchaste priest to
abstain from exercising his office, even after confessing his sins.

To the personal responsibility of the moral agent is conceded a choice
generally denied him by the penitentials. Augustine's stress, in his exegesis
of the Sermon on the Mount, on the inscrutability of divine judgement
becomes Anselm's reason for leaving to the sinner's conscience the decision
as to whether he should resume his sacerdotal functions. *Discretio* is the
criterion restored by Anselm to the pivotal position it once occupied, the
ethical discernment not imposed by ecclesiastical law but exercised freely
by the penitent in relation to God. Contrition defined as the paradox of
'trampling proud shame',[22] priority is given to remorse felt for the divine
judge, rather than to sanctions accepted from his human intermediary.

At the tribunal of interiority to which Anselm appeals, the testimony
that counts is provided by the emotions. Their cognitive capacity is emphasised by him, as by pseudo-Augustine, through a detour into the past that
bypasses the penitential tradition of the early Middle Ages. Shunning its

---

[19] Eadmer, *De S. Anselmi similitudinibus* 89, PL 159, 658C–659A, with R. Southern, *St. Anselm and his Biographer: A Study of Monastic Life and Thought 1059–c.1130* (Cambridge, 1966) 105, 221ff.

[20] See G. Evans, 'The Secure Technician': Varieties of Paradox in the Writings of St. Anselm', *Vivarium* 13 (1975) 1–21.

[21] *Ep.* LXV in *S. Anselmi Cantuariensis Archiepiscopi Opera omnia* III, ed. F. Schmitt OSB (Edinburgh, 1956) 181–5.

[22] *Ep.* LXV, ed. Schmitt, 184, 84–5.

literalism and tempering its severity, Anselm selects two authorities to support his distinction between God's verdict on acts of unchastity and public perception of them. One is Gregory the Great (†604), proponent of the inexorable conscience; the other is Calistus I (†222), advocate of reconciliation with sinners against Tertullian's intransigence. The teaching of these popes is adapted by a moral imagination inspired, but not limited, by its models. Anselm begins with the cautious wish to avoid scandal. In notorious cases of immorality, Gregory recommends that transgressors be forbidden to celebrate mass, but secret sinners are to be treated indulgently, 'lest the road of salutary confession be blocked for many'. On that road Anselm detects two obstacles, both of them paradoxical. If there is the 'proud shame' to be subdued by humble avowal, there is also the 'presumptuous obedience' expressed in eagerness to be restored to office. Such symmetries of *fictio*, present but underdeveloped in monastic literature before Anselm, are foreign to the mentality of the penitentials. Reviving ethical categories neglected by them, he was, in this sphere as in others, a harbinger of the twelfth-century reformation. Although Anselm's impact on his followers was swift and strong, they were not always equal to his lesson, as may be gauged from Guibert of Nogent's fumblings with similar issues.[23]

The issue of *fictio*, particularly in penance, which Anselm restored to the agenda of moral debate was taken further, although not deeper, along Augustinian lines by another Anselm at Laon. His approach was systematic. If order was to be re-established in the mixed and muddled heritage of thought bequeathed by previous generations, that entailed a return to basics – meaning, above all, the problem of original sin. All mankind is participant in Adam's fall, argues Anselm of Laon, but the repentance consequent on it is not only a human emotion. Even God repented when he saved those about to be damned. The mortal version of *paenitentia*, however, differs from the divine; and the difference is expressed in terms of 'filial fear'.[24] Anselm does not mean by that expression what it signified in the penitentials: trepidation at punishment felt by those bondsmen of the conscience whom he likens to slaves. It is the freedom of the sinner, viewed as a moral agent capable of choice, that is stressed. In a paradox which aligns his thought with that of pseudo-Augustine and St Anselm, he defines filial fear as liberty realised in the desire to obey God.

[23] E.g. *Autobiographie* I.12, ed. Labande, 82.
[24] *Anselms von Laon systematische Sentenzen* IV, VIII, ed. F. Bliemetzrieder, BGPTMA 18, 2–3 (Münster, 1919) 107–8, 121ff. Cf. Anciaux, *Théologie* 59ff.

This shift of emphasis, from outward sanctions to the exercise of free will, is reinforced by a scaling-down of the importance attributed, in the handbooks, to mortification. Hair-shirts, bare feet, heads sprinkled with ashes, expulsion from church – all these aspects of the ancient ritual of 'canonical' penance are treated, by Anselm of Laon, as formal features of the sacrament.[25] Its substance lies in the remission of sins, which depends on voluntary consent. Consent, active and aware, not simple submission is Anselm's point; and he underscores the trenchancy attributed to the will with a simile of the sword. Contrition is regarded by him as indispensable; and this 'inner penance' ought to precede the external version adminis-tered by the Church.

If the Church, as Anselm thought of its role in traditional terms, was incapable of judging the secrets of the heart,[26] it performed an essential role in reconciling the 'inner' and 'outer' forms of penance. They are com-plementary. 'Compunction of the heart' is insufficient without confession; the priesthood must administer a sacrament which, in his opinion, is unre-peatable. Thus far and no further Anselm ventures with an Augustinianism that never trespasses beyond the limits set by the saint. His timid follower recognises the existence of *fictio*, but cites only Augustine's most concrete definition of the phenomenon as failure to repay ill-gotten goods;[27] and it is perhaps this literalism which made Anselm's method seem so uninspired to his pupil Abelard.[28]

For Anselm's systematic accumulation and careful ordering of authori-ties, which he identified with theological renewal,[29] Abelard had neither time nor respect. Yet, despite his scorn, his own procedures, when dealing with *fictio* in *Sic et non* and in *Scito te ipsum*,[30] were little different. With the modest addition of a few passages from Jerome, the textual basis remains Augustinian; and if it is true that the first of those works is equally

[25] *Anselms von Laon systematische Sentenzen* VII, ed. Bliemetzrieder, 120.

[26] Ibid. VIII, ibid., 121–2.

[27] Ibid. VIII, ibid., 123, and see Bliemetzrieder, 'Trente-trois pièces inédites de l'œuvre théologique d'Anselme de Laon', *RTAM* 2 (1930) 64 (no. 24). Cf. Chapter 2 for Augustine's *Ep.* 153.

[28] See Chapter 4 below.

[29] See M. Colish, 'Systematic Theology and Theological Renewal in the Twelfth Century', *Journal of Mediaeval and Renaissance Studies* 18 (1988) 135–56 and Colish, 'Another Look at the School of Laon', *AHDLMA* 53 (1986) 7–22.

[30] *Sic et non* LXI, ed. B. Boyer and R. McKeon (Chicago, 1976) 363–6; *Peter Abelard's Ethics*, ed. D. Luscombe (Oxford, 1971) 78, 22ff. – 84, 20 and *Scito te ipsum* 1.53, ed. R. Ilgner, *Petri Abaelardi opera theologica* IV, CCCM 190 (Turnhout, 2001) 52, 1356ff. *Fictio* is not discussed at *Collationes* II. 209, ed. J. Marenbon and G. Orlandi, (Oxford, 2001) 208–10, nor does *Carmen ad Astrolabium* 373ff., especially 385–6, ed. J. Rubingh-Bosscher (Groningen, 1987) 127, shed light on this problem. See further Chapter 4.

concerned with baptism, the second, which deals more extensively with penance, adds to Anselm of Laon's quotation from the saint only a tirade against the folly of seeking forgiveness without reparation and against the cupidity of priests. Neither of these treatments of feigning contributes anything new, for Abelard depends more heavily on the master he pilloried than he cared to acknowledge. There are original insights in both *Sic et non* and *Scito te ipsum*, but their number does not include his derivative and diffuse remarks on *fictio*. Acknowledging a problem to which the two Anselms had directed his attention, Abelard left it to be redefined by Bernard of Clairvaux.

∾

Bernard, in his account of feigned penance analysed in the first chapter, considers not only monastic *fictio* but the linked issues of the abbot's authority and the confessor's role. That role was being addressed, during and after his lifetime, in terms that began by limiting the confessor's temporal jurisdiction and ended by enhancing his spiritual status. The starting point was, the inviolability of avowed secrets, a theme recurrent since Lanfranc of Bec.[31] A notable contribution was made in a work whose theological and ecclesiological significance may have been underestimated – the *Sententiae* by the first English cardinal, Robert Pullen. This protégé of Bernard and chancellor of the Roman Church likened the confessor hearing the *occulta cordis* to God.[32] His analogy was repeated in 1148, at the council of Reims, by a pope whom Pullen advised. Then Eugenius III forbade bishops to exclude from communion those whom they knew, through confession, to be guilty of crimes. His stated reason was that they had obtained their knowledge 'not like a judge but like God'.[33] The risk that such a likeness might lend itself to misrepresentation was understood. With an untypical touch of irony, Hugh of Saint-Victor added to his version of this doctrine the caveat that he did not wish to make priests into gods.[34] His misgivings

[31] *De celanda confessione*, PL 150, 625A–632C. Cf. L. Honoré, *Le secret de la confession: Étude historique-canonique* (Paris, 1924) 39ff.
[32] 'Sed quoniam *quasi Deo ita confiteris presbytero*, ideo occulta tua ita audit quasi non sibi sed Deo detecta fuissent', *Sententiae* VIII.6, PL 186, 898B. For context, cf. R. Southern, *Scholastic Humanism and the Unification of Europe* I: *Foundations* (Oxford, 1995) 176ff. and F. Courtney, *Robert Cardinal Pullen: An English Theologian of the 12th Century*, Analecta Gregoriana 64 (Rome, 1954).
[33] ' … non nominatim potest eum removere a comunione, licet sciat eum esse reum, *quia non ut iudex scit sed ut Deus*' in *Decreta Gregorii IX*, I, tit. xxxi. 2, ed. E. Friedberg, *Corpus Iuris Canonici* II (reprint Graz, 1959), 186–7.
[34] *De sacramentis* II.14.8, PL 176, 566A–566B.

were not shared by others. Peter the Chanter, for example, later amplified into *fortissimo* the original *piano* of Pullen's analogy.[35] In and beyond the circle of Bernard of Clairvaux, from a cardinal whom he patronised to a pope whom he hectored, the importance which he attached to the role of the confessor was taken with the utmost seriousness.[36]

Bernard fostered this process by the incisiveness with which he wrote. His is the most lucid analysis of the principles of confession made in the twelfth century.[37] Its basis, as defined in a *sermo* on the subject, was self-knowledge.[38] This central concern of Bernard's thought dominates his approach to the conscience. He did not believe that it was infallible, and recognised its susceptibility to error.[39] A safeguard against moral mistakes was provided, in his view, by critical enquiry of the self which led, in a natural and necessary progression, to repentance.[40] But Bernard recognised difficulties along the way. One of them was fear; another, simulation.[41] Hence his insistence on sincerity and his concern to eliminate *fictio*.[42] That term and its cognates, in Bernard's diction, are invariably negative. Yet his hostility did not extend to the entire spectrum of theatricality. He was capable of likening the ethical inversions performed by monks, who turned worldly values upside down, to the virtuosity of *jongleurs* or to dancers' acrobacy.[43] If somersaults could be regarded as commendable figures of spiritual renunciation, the monastic mummers who subverted penitential humility committed deadly sin. Bernard's caustic description of their feigning in *De gradibus humilitatis et superbiae* is complemented by this no less trenchant passage from his sixteenth interpretation of the Song of Songs:

---

[35] Peter the Chanter, *Summa de sacramentis et animae consiliis* II.3.5, ed. J.-A. Dugauquier, Analecta mediaevalia namurcensia 7 (Louvain, 1957) 434ff. Cf. Peter the Chanter, *Verbum abbreviatum*, 144 (PL 205, 344Bff.). For context, see J. Baldwin, *Masters, Princes, and Merchants: The Social Views of Peter the Chanter and his Circle* I (Princeton, 1970), 13, 24, 36, 50–6.

[36] Cf. S. Kramer, 'The Priest in the House of Conscience: Sins of Thought and the Twelfth-Century Schoolmen', *Viator* 37 (2006) 149–66.

[37] The subject is not exhausted by J. Leclercq, *Recueil*, v. 137–80. More penetrating, but silent on the subject of *fictio*, is Delhaye, *Le problème*.

[38] *Sermo* 11.3 in *S. Bernardi Opera* VI, 1, ed. J. Leclercq and H. Rochais (Rome, 1970) 236, 9–10. Cf. P. Courcelle, *Connais-toi toi-même: De Socrate à saint Bernard* I (Paris, 1974) 258ff.

[39] Constable, *Reformation*, 271 and nn. 61, 63.

[40] *Sermo* 11.4 in *S. Bernardi Opera* VI, 1, ed. Lerclercq and Rochais, 237, 3–4.

[41] *Sermo* 11.6, ibid; 239, 27 – 240, 2.

[42] *Sermo* 11.6, ibid. 240, 3–6 and cf. *Ep.* 18 in *S. Bernardi Opera* VII, ed. Leclercq and Rochais (Rome, 1974) 68, 15–16.

[43] *Ep.* 87 ibid. 231, 11ff. with Leclercq, *Recueil* V. 347–90.

We have often heard of a number of those who, despite their religious garb and monastic profession, recall and boast most shamelessly about their misdeeds in the past, such as, on occasion, a forceful performance in a fencing match or an eloquent one in a literary contest or another mark of success according to worldly vanity but harmful, pernicious, and damnable in terms of their salvation; this is the sign of a persistently secular mentality, and the humble habit worn by such people is not a distinction of holy renewal but a trifle of hoary decreptitude. A large number of them recall such things as if in grief and repentance yet, as their aim is to acquire glory, they do not atone for their transgressions but dupe themselves, for *God is not mocked* [Galatians 6:7]. The old rot is neither exposed nor cast out by confession, but set fast ... It is shameful to be put in mind of the immense insolence of some of them, such that they do not flinch from boasting with high spirits about what they should mourn – for example, even after donning the holy habit, their shrewd outwitting of someone and their pulling the wool over the eyes of a brother in an affair of business or their repaying an insult or a curse with an eye for an eye and a tooth for a tooth, that is matching evil to evil and curse to curse.[44]

The presence of Gregory the Great is palpable here. On the passages of his *Moralia in Job* cited in the second chapter Bernard has modelled his own account of *fictio*, from the symbolic detail of the monastic habit to laughing about what one should mourn and deceit being equivalent to self-deception. In the perverse logic of these feigners, confession becomes boasting. It is impossible to seem holy, notes Bernard satirically, unless you appear criminal.[45] What kind of offence does he understand by this *reductio ad absurdum* of penance? The worst. In a context that subordinates the sacred to the profane is evinced a vainglory that is less a provocation to human judgement than a sin against divine majesty. Why? Because the avowals of penitents are, or should be, made

---

[44] ' ... Et de his, qui religiose vestiti et professi sunt religionem, nonnumquam audivimus aliquos reminisci et iactitare impudentissime mala sua praeterita, quae, verbi gratia, aliquando vel fortiter gladiatorio vel argute litterario gessere conflictu, seu aliud quid secundum mundi quidem vanitatem favorabile vero salutem nocivum, perniciosum, damnosum; saecularis adhuc animi indicium est hoc et humilis habitus, qui gestatur a talibus, non sanctae novitatis est meritum, sed priscae vetustatis operculum. Nonnulli talia quasi dolendo et paenitendo rememorant; sed gloriam intentione captantes, commissa sua non diluunt, sed seipsos illudunt: nam *Deus non irridetur*. Non proditur aut proicitur vetus fermentum illud confessione, sed statuitur ... Pudet reminisci quorumdam tantam proterviam, ut non pudeat eos cum exsultatione lugenda iactitare, quod et post susceptum sanctum habitum callide quempiam supplantaverint et circumvenerint in negotio fratrem, aut quod talionem pro convicio vel maledicto, id est malum pro malo aut maledictum pro maledicto reddiderint', VI. 9, *S. Bernardi Opera* I, ed. Leclercq, Rochais, and C. Talbot (Rome, 1957); 94, 16ff. – 95, 3.

[45] 'Mirabile iactantiae genus, ut non possis putari sanctus, si non appareas sceleratus', ibid. VI.10; 95, 12.

to a confessor who is His intermediary. So it is that *fictio* amounts to mockery of God.

The mortal sin of blasphemy was the ancient category into which Bernard fitted his new perception of *fictio*;[46] and Cardinal Pullen, discussing mockery of the twin sacrament of baptism, promptly followed suit.[47] The rapidity of its reception is hardly less notable than the aptness of the idea. If it was not invented by Bernard, it was applied by him, with theological originality, to a problem which his contemporaries struggled to pin down.[48] Most of them lacked a working definition of *fictio*;[49] and his clarity served to supply the want. Yet this insight was anything but the product of systematic thought. With much intuition and no argument, Bernard imposed a label as arresting as it is unreasoned. His term might be copied, but his procedure was hardly imitable in an age of systematisation, during which penance was being recognised as a sacrament by less inspired theologians and more methodical canonists.[50]

Their activities, complementary and interdependent,[51] were not always easy to harmonise, as is illustrated by Gratian's treatment of *fictio* in the first book of his *Decretum*.[52] There, on the basis of one of the fullest citations of sources made in the twelfth century, he addresses the question of whether contrition, voiced by the sinner directly to God, made it superfluous to confess to a priest.[53] The sacerdotal power of the keys might have

[46] Cf. Isidore, *Sententiae* II.16.1–2, ed. Cazier, 128–9 with Landgraf, *Dogmengeschichte*, IV, 1, 15ff.; H. Merkel, 'Gotteslästerung' in *RLAC* XI, 1185–1201; W. Speyer, 'Fluch', *RLAC* VII, 1260–88, and see now D. Nash, *Blasphemy in the Christian World: A History* (Oxford, 2007).

[47] 'Si quis catholice per omnia baptizet, baptizandus autem irrisorio animo accedat, nonne *irrisio sicut fictio* rem sacramenti tollit … ? '*Sententiae* v.15, PL 186, 842A.

[48] Delhaye, *Le problème*, 111 denies originality to Bernard, perhaps because he never considers *fictio*.

[49] Landgraf, *Dogmengeschichte* III, 2, 110ff.

[50] An important study of the twelfth-century systematisation of the sacraments, with rich bibliography, is provided by Colish, *Peter Lombard* II, 516–697, especially 583ff. (on penance). See too D. van den Eyde, *Les définitions des sacraments pendant la première période de la théologie scholastique* (1050–1240) (Rome, 1950). Anciaux, *Théologie* offers a systematic rather than historical account, based on deep knowledge of the sources but with little capacity for analysis and no mention of *fictio*. Unreliable is J. Payen, 'La pénitence dans le contexte culturel des XIIe et XIIIe siècles: des doctrines contritionistes aux pénitentiels vernaculaires', *Revue des sciences philosophiques et théologiques* 61 (1977) 399–428. Landgraf, *Dogmengeschichte* III, 2, 86–181 provides essential background.

[51] N. Häring, 'The Interaction between Canon Law and Sacramental Theology in the Twelfth Century' in *Proceedings of the Fourth International Congress of Canon Law*, ed. S. Kuttner (Vatican, 1976) 483–93.

[52] Winroth, *The Making of Gratian's Decretum*, 44.

[53] For a lucid summary of discussions of this subject, see Colish, *Peter Lombard* II, 584ff. and 589ff. Cf. J. Gaudemet, 'Le débat sur la confession dans la Distinction I du "De penitentia"

been undermined by this hypothesis,[54] had Gratian advanced it, but he was neither so rash nor so clumsy. With stylish non-commitment at what seemed to him an insoluble problem, he threw up his hands at opinions that differed less in kind than in degree. Even the most vocal advocate of contrition, Peter Abelard, maintained the priority, not the predominance, of inner remorse over its outward expression, which he by no means belittled.[55] The issue was not whether confession might be dispensed with, but how its function should be understood. The debate focused less on the administration of the sacrament of penance than on the principles of religious authenticity and spiritual sincerity that should animate it. That was where, by antithesis, *fictio* came in.

Its entry into the *Decretum* is gauche. Gratian knew that he was dealing with an awkward concept. How awkward, Bernard had shown him, in an associative style that was difficult to transpose from theological to legal terms. If the phenomenon remained elusive, at least it was clear that *fictio* had nothing to do with contrition and everything to do with confession. Less clear was, how to classify a fundamentally verbal transgression. Gratian uses the term 'simulated confession' which, for him, springs from the same root as Bernard's 'crafty confession'.[56] An inversion of the penitential virtue of humility, it betrays pride. That is why the *Decretum* describes, in the manner of *De gradibus humilitatis et superbiae*, 'simulated confession' as 'evasiveness' (*tergiversatio*) 'of speech',[57] , undertaken in an effort to extenuate sins, like Adam and Eve, or to dissimulate them, like Cain.[58] The Old Testament sets the limits of Gratian's vision of this issue. No mention is made of Christ's condemnations of hypocrisy in the New, nor are other criteria of verifiability proposed. Everything else is left, by him as by Bernard, to the insight of the sacerdotal judge. God-like he needed to be, with so little human guidance; and as if to emphasis that the problem of *fictio* was not primarily legal, even if it had implications for canon law, Gratian cites Wisdom 1:5 on feigners being routed by the Holy Spirit.

(Décret de Gratian C.33, q.3)', *Zeitschrift der Savigny-Stiftung für Rechtsgeschichte* Kan. Abt. 71 (1985) 52–75 and A. Debal, 'La première distinction du *De poenitentia* de Gratian', *Revue d'histoire ecclésiastique* 15 (1914) 251–73, 442–55.

[54] Cf. Hödl, *Geschichte*, 155ff. [55] See Chapter 5 below.

[56] *Decretum* C.33.q.3.D.3, 35, ed. E. Friedberg, *Corpus Iuris Canonici* I (reprint Graz, 1959) 1222. (This and the following passages cited are contained in the first recension. See Winroth, *The Making*, 224–5.)

[57] *Decretum* C.33.q.3.D. 1, 87, ed. Friedberg, 1187.

[58] *Decretum* C.33.q.3.D. 1, 60 (iv), ibid. 1175. Cf. Peter Lombard, *Sententiae* IV.d.17.4 in *Sententiae in quattuor libros distinctae*, ed. I. Brady, II, Spicilegium Bonaventuranum 5 (Grottaferrata, 1981) 354.

The Holy Spirit remained deaf when the decretists, who made little use of the Roman concept of *fictio legis*,[59] implored His aid. Inspiration is not evident in the remarks of Rufinus on the category of simulated penance which he adapted from Gratian. Performed by clerics guilty of 'manifest crimes', it disqualifies them from office, he observes,[60] reverting to the legalism prevalent before St Anselm's treatment of the same problem. While the minutiae of measurable guilt did not interest Anselm, only they engaged the attention of Rufinus, who did no more than quote Augustine's definition of *fictio* as failure to restore ill-gotten goods.[61] He and other decretists lagged behind the theological systematisers of the sacraments, one of whom, writing during the late 1130s in Flanders, was the neglected but perceptive 'Master Simon'. Acquainted with Bernard of Clairvaux's views, he modified them. *Fictio*, in 'Master Simon's' discussion of penance, is no longer viewed exclusively from the standpoint of its judge:

Some undertake penance in a spirit of feigning, some truly, some with love. The act is feigned on the part of those who do not wish to give up their sins and, what is worse, desire to revert to the same or graver ones like dogs to vomit, and do this rather to show off than out of love for God. They receive no benefit whatever from this remedy but instead are burdened more heavily, which is worse, for this *would appear* not to be penance, but mockery of God. 'Truly' ie: not with simulation, one proceeds [to penance] when one wishes to confess and rectify one's sins, as *one may view* [them].[62]

If these ideas are basically Bernard's, they undergo a subtle change. 'Master Simon' couches his nuances in the hypothetical subjunctive of a passive verb, eschewing the hyper-active indicatives of the saint. *Fictio* and blasphemy are not equated, but 'would appear' to be the same; the capacity of the sinner to act in error, without ill-will, is conceded in the phrase 'as one may view [one's sins]'. *Videatur*, repeated in successive sentences,

[59] See Thomas, '*Fictio legis*'.
[60] Cited by Kuttner, 'Ecclesia de occultis non iudicat', 235, n. 13.
[61] Rufinus, C. XIV, q. 6, *Die Summa magistri Rufini*, ed. J. Schulte (Giessen, 1892) 305. Cf. ibid. C. XXXIII, 3; 438 and Peter Lombard, *Sententiae* IV.d.15.7 in *Sententiae* II, ed. Brady, 335.
[62] 'Ad penitentiam vero quidam ficte, quidam vere, quidam in caritate accedunt. Ficte agunt, qui voluntatem peccata dimittendi non habentes et, quod peius est, ad eadem sive ad deteriora tamquam canes ad vomitum reverti cupientes, magis ostentatione quam Dei dilectione hoc faciunt. Qui profecto hoc remedio nullatenus adiuvantur, immo vero, quod deterius est, magis gravantur, cum hoc non penitentia, sed irrisio quaedam Dei *videatur*. "Vere", id est non simulatorie, accedunt qui voluntatem peccata confitendi et emendandi, *ut eis videatur*, habent', *Maître Simon et son groupe 'De sacramentis': Textes inédits*, ed. H. Weisweiler, Spicilegium sacrum lovaniense 12 (Louvain, 1937) 214, 10–20.

marks 'Master Simon's' distance from Bernard's categorical manner. And that distance enables him to consider *fictio* from the perspective of moral agents not necessarily as malicious or calculating as the saint assumes. The disagreement, understated and tactful, demonstrates that there were other ways than Bernard's of thinking about *fictio*, while continuing to employ his terms. One of them that remains unchanged here, because so plainly pertinent, is, *ostentatio* or showing off.

Ostentatio and its synonyms recur in the *sententiae*-literature. The mental world of these compilations was not always limited by the school or the cloister. Some of them hint at irreverent milieux of performance beyond the monastery's walls and the ivory tower. One such collection was produced, in the second quarter of the twelfth century, at Sion, that crossroad of cultures (now in the Swiss Valais) between Rome, Northern France, and England.[63] What sets the *Sententiae Sidonis* apart from the reflection of monastic and scholastic theologians on *fictio* is, a readiness to link the phenomenon with popular entertainment:

We do not call confession any showing off of sin, because buffoons do this as well either joking or laughing or even with abuse.[64]

The translation 'buffoons' may err on the side of politeness. The term *leccatores* is unclassical and injurious. Duplicity is one of its connotations; lechery, another. Such ribald jesters enact a *propalatio peccati* which makes mockery of confession. Where and when did this spectacle occur? Probably in those 'Dionysia of the Catholic Church' that took place during the Feast of Fools.[65] Then the proprieties of ecclesiastical comportment were turned upside down. Hierarchical order reversed, a boy became bishop, the clergy was pilloried, lewd songs were sung, and – the prohibitions state indignantly – solemnities of the Church were profaned. Spoofs of the sacrament of baptism are recorded by members of the

[63] Cf. H. Cowdrey, 'Bishop Ermenfrid of Sion and the Penitential Ordinance following the Battle of Hastings', *Journal of Ecclesiastical History* 20 (1969) 225–42.
[64] 'Confessionem autem appellamus non quamlibet propalationem peccati, quia et leccatores sive iocando sive ridendo sive etiam improperando profitentur … ' *Sententiae Sidonis*, BAV. Vat. lat. 1343, 84*v*. (On the date and sources of this compilation, see D. van den Eyde, 'La *Summa Sententiarum*, source des *Sententiae Sidonis*', *RTAM* 27 (1966) 136–41.) Cf. Raoul Ardens, *Speculum universale*: 'sermo quippe irrisorius … qui, si frequenter et in consuetudinem vertatur, peccatum est criminale … damnosi sunt scurre et histriones … ' BAV. Vat. lat. 1175 (II) 321*ra*.
[65] Bibliography is assembled by P. Schmidt, 'The Quotation in Goliardic Poetry: The Feast of Fools and the Goliardic Strophe *cum auctoritate*' in *Latin Poetry and the Classical Tradition*, eds. P. Godman and O. Murray (Oxford, 1990) 43, n. 11.

school of Anselm of Laon;[66] and it was but a step from them to parodies of penance. This was the setting in which theatrical metaphors for *fictio* acquired concreteness.

The noun *propalatio* used by the author of the *Sententiae Sidonis* is uncommon, and it may indicate acquaintance with Hugh of Saint-Victor's discussion of this subject in his *De sacramentis*. Hugh employs the same word to refer dismissively to those who believed that a 'show of words' (*verborum propalatio*) would be enough to absolve them from sin.[67] Distinguishing between 'exterior' and 'interior' penance, defining the second as contrition of the heart and the first as affliction of the flesh, he dwells on the devaluation of sacral language which reduces it to the level of empty rhetoric.[68] That, with the welcome addition of details from *realia*, is essentially what the *Sententiae Sidonis* record. But Hugh is more concerned with motivation. Like Bernard of Clairvaux, he is inclined to regard it as evil. *Multa est malitia hominis* is the first phrase in the section of his treatise which deals with penance and confession;[69] and the opening sets the tone for his treatment of *fictio*. Perverse because premeditated, it is damned without appeal. No account is taken of the involuntary or unconscious feigning registered in 'Master Simon's' qualifications. They represent a tributary to the mainstream of censure; and it was not to flow further in the direction of ambiguity until Heloise, during the same decade in which 'Master Simon' composed his work, wrote her confessional letters.[70]

They cast the problem of *fictio* in a light which no male theologian of the twelfth century had eyes to see. Many of them wandered in the darkness of misplaced ingenuity or pedantic banality. A feigner or deceiver (*illusor*) could hardly be considered a penitent, asserted to his unsurprised readers Roland Bandinelli (the canonist who did not become Pope Alexander III, as was long believed), adding for those unaware of the commonplace that 'true' should be distinguished from 'empty' or 'insubstantial' forms of confession.[71] And if Abelard subsumed penance under *caritas*, denying it

[66] Landgraf, *Dogmengeschichte*, III, 1, 120ff.
[67] 'pro sola consuetudine explenda ad dicenda peccata sua se ingerunt, existimantes se propter solum *verborum propalationem* a debito peccatorum suorum absolvi', *De sacramentis* II.14.1, PL 176, 554C–D.
[68] 'Inveniuntur enim quaedam eiusmodi dicta ['lacrymae lavant delicta'] et rapiunt ea homines gaudentes, non quia veritatem quaerunt in eis, sed quia malitiam suam defendere volunt ex eis', *De sacramentis* II.15.1, PL 176, 549D.
[69] Ibid., II.14.1, PL 176, 549D.   [70] See Chapters 6 and 7.
[71] A. Gietl (ed.), *Die Sentenzen Rolands, nochmals Papstes Alexanders III* (Freiburg, 1891), 239–40.

independent status as a sacrament,[72] Omnibene, a member of his school, constructed on this slender basis a circular argument. The sins of a feigned penitent, according to Omnibene, are not remitted because, if they were, he would possess *caritas*, and if he possessed *caritas*, he would not be a feigner.[73] As dialectic severs its already tenuous links with reality, similar sophisms are recorded in the *summae* and in mystical theology.[74]

Sophistry of the spirit was, however, a key to unlocking the mysteries of *fictio*. It took time to be discovered. After Bernard of Clairvaux, his ally Pullen, and his modifier 'Master Simon', uncertainty characterised discussion up to the end of the twelfth century. Between 1193 and 1200 an expert on the sacraments, Raoul Ardens, drew up a comprehensive account of virtue – ethics in his *Speculum universale*. Comprehensiveness did not mean clarity. Raoul discriminates between 'bad, feigned, false, deficient, excessive, insufficient, and sufficient penance'.[75] He told *ficta* apart from the rest on the sole criterion of the hypocrisy it implies, which 'increases evil' (*malum auget*). The evil to which Raoul refers is presumably that of the feigner's motives; and the point is hardly different from Hugh of Saint-Victor's who detected, and execrated, in *fictio* a premeditated sin. Some elaboration, and no advance.

Not until the last years of the twelfth century was a term found to convey the distinctive nature of the phenomenon. And then it was discovered by Alan of Lille, shrewd observer of the 'pharasaical' misuse of Biblical quotations by monks.[76] 'Sophistical penance', Alan called it, ably summing up both the fallacious character of *fictio* and its cultural level.[77] For the feigners to whom he referred were not only those with religious experience but also beginners in the spiritual life. To them, in the same spirit, are directed Adam of Perseigne's strictures at the opening of his epistolary tract on the training of novices.[78] Their tendency

---

[72] See Chapter 5.
[73] Cited from Munich, Bayerische Staatsbibliothek, clm. 168, 47 (the tract is unpublished) by A. Landgraf, 'Grundlagen für ein Verständnis der Bußlehre der Frühscholastik', *Zeitschrift für katholische Theologie* 51 (1927) 174. For context, see D. Luscombe, *The School of Peter Abelard. The Influence of Abelard's Thought in the Early Scholastic Period* (Cambridge, 1969) 253ff.
[74] BAV, Barb. Lat. 484, 32*vb* and William of Saint-Thierry, *De natura et dignitate amoris*, ed. M.-M. Davy, *Guillaume de Saint-Thierry, Deux traités de l'amour de Dieu. De la contemplation de Dieu. De la nature et de la dignité de l'amour* (Paris, 1953) 246.
[75] BAV, Vat. Lat. 1175 (I), 133*v*.
[76] *Sermo de Trinitate*, ed. M.-T. D'Alverny, *Alain de Lille: Textes inédits* (Paris, 1965) 261.
[77] Alain of Lille, *Liber poenitentialis* xxviii, ed. J. Longère, II, Analecta mediaevalia namurcensia 18 (Louvain, 1965), 181. For the date of the longer version of this work, see I, 217ff.
[78] *Ep.* 11 PL 211, 620C–D. Cf. L. Merton, 'La formation monastique selon Adam de Perseigne' *Collectanea ordinis Cistercensium Reformatorum* XIX (1957) 1–17.

to become spiritual sophists is assumed from the outset. *Fictio*, they are warned, is a form of religious death. Cunning simulation is of no use. However ingenious the feigner, he will be caught out. The only remedy for this malaise is frank confession. The significance of this letter lies in the evidence it provides of how established the theological category of *fictio* had become, and how widespread the phenomenon was regarded as being, even at the stage of initiates and aspirants. But the category was reserved for particular types of person. To them, when confessing, Robert Grosseteste attributed the dubious distinction of that 'subtle form of hypocrisy [characteristic of] clerics and especially the religious'.[79]

&

'A subtle form of hypocrisy': Grosseteste's phrase, evocative yet vague, sums up the habits of description by synonymity and of definition by antithesis entrenched in the Latin West. They prevented a clear distinction being drawn between the concept of *fictio* and related ideas by thinkers before Bernard of Clairvaux. These difficulties were compounded by St Paul's doctrine of the irrefutable conscience, which was commonly held to entail reliance on the testimony of moral agents whose word there was reason to suspect. Suspicion accrued first to language, whose evasiveness both Bernard and Gratian called *tergiversatio*. Such metaphors of movement were cast in theatrical terms intended to raise doubts about these impostors of the conscience. The conscience stood at centre-stage, where pyrotechnics of paradox were enacted. If the leading role was not confined to monks, the importance attached by the Rule to humility and obedience often propelled them into the limelight. It shone brightest on scenes of confession, the prime locations of *fictio*. About this point, established by Bernard in Northern France, there was an agreement that reached from the schools of Paris, where Robert Pullen wrote his *Sententiae*, to the Flanders of 'Master Simon', and the Bologna of Gratian. In the second quarter of the twelfth century, theologians from the north to the south of Latin Europe began to engage with a problem of penance neglected by their early medieval predecessors.

If *fictio* was a problem that chiefly concerned the learned, some of them recognised its affinities with popular culture. Even the most monastic of writers were aware that jesters, *jongleurs*, and buffoons performed

---

[79] 'haec est subtilis hypocrisis, scilicet clericorum et maxime religiosorum', 'Robert Grosseteste's Treatise on Confession, "Deus est"', ed. S. Wenzel, *Franciscan Studies* 30 (1970) 269.

caricatures of confession and parodies of penance. Their antics were complemented by those of less amusing feigners who, in order to prey on the sympathies of the ingenuous, dressed up in penitential costumes.[80] Costumes have symbolic significance, as Bernard of Clairvaux learnt from Gregory the Great. So it was that the leading critic of *fictio* in the twelfth century inveighed against behaviour likely to lead to confusion between fraudulent sackcloth and the monastic habit. Members of the religious orders, Bernard and others believed, were, or ought to be, sharply distinct from the laity.[81] Feigners of penance profaned a hallowed vocation and committed blasphemy. That is why, in all Bernard's sternness on this subject, there is never a hint of humour. What we might be inclined to shrug off as a venial fault, he regarded as mortal sin. And if the saint did not reach the point of identifying *fictio* with heresy, he was well on the way. The way led to damnation.

The damnations of *fictio* prevalent in writing about this subject ought not to close our ears to the ribald laughter that, hundreds of years ago, accompanied its carnevalesque performances or hide from sight the wily grin on the lips of a sinner who had duped his confessor. These are the signs and the sounds of medieval feigning, public and private, which the sources do their considerable best to censure. What we hear, loud and clear, are the voices of the ecclesiastical authorities raised to deplore scandal. On no topic were they more stentorian than on that of penance, favourite theme of preachers in the Paris where Abelard taught and Heloise learnt.[82] The language chosen, in this and related contexts, could be rough. Vomit, salutary not sickly, was a common metaphor for confession;[83] and the men and women who undertook it were delicately described as: 'nothing but stinking sperm, a sack of filth, food for worms'.[84] *Contemptus mundi*, dismissive of human dignity, often lapsed into a vulgarity of vehemence.

---

[80] See H. Platelle, 'Le problème du scandale: les nouvelles modes masculines au XIe et au XIIe siècle', *Revue belge de philologie et d'histoire* LIII (1975) 1071–96, especially 1085.

[81] See Hugh of Saint-Victor, *De sacramentis* II. 3–4, PL 176 417B–418D and cf. L. Prosdocimi, 'Chierici e laici nella società occidentale nel secolo XII: A proposito di Decr. Grat. C. 12. q.1. c.7: "Duo sunt genera Christianorum"' in *Proceedings of the Second International Congress of Medieval Canon Law*, ed. S. Kuttner and J. Ryan, Monumenta Iuris Canonici, Series C, Subsidia 1 (Vatican, 1965) 105–22.

[82] See J. Longère, *Oeuvres oratoires de maîtres parisiens au XIIe siècle* I (Paris, 1975) 255ff.

[83] Cf. Peter of Celle, *De conscientia*, ed. J. Leclercq in *La spiritualité de Pierre de Celle* (Paris, 1946) 216, 1–5. On the antiquity of the metaphor, cf. Sorabji, *Emotion*, 297.

[84] 'sperma fetidum, saccus stercorum, cibus vermium', *Meditationes piissimae de cognitione humanae conditionis* III.8 (ps.-Bernard of Clairvaux), PL 184, 490A–B.

Feelings about *fictio* ran high because the menace which it posed was considered urgent. The sincerity and authenticity subverted by feigning, particularly in penance, were central to the twelfth century's understanding of itself. To address these questions in more moderate terms, with less condemnation and coarseness, was no simple task. It was performed, in unequal measure, by the abbot Abelard and the abbess Heloise in an exchange of epistolary treatises composed both for one another and for a wider readership from radically different standpoints.[85] They were poles apart on the subject of *fictio*, which figures in both their works. Heloise believed that she lived it, in a hypocritical charade of monasticism: Abelard was hardly disposed to take the notion seriously in her case. His own case was worse. In 1117 he had entered Saint-Denis with no conviction about becoming a monk. Better the purgatory of never-ending Lent, Abelard had reasoned – if reason can be attributed to him after his castration – than the infernal pangs of shame.[86] His profession, made without religious sincerity, rendered him vulnerable to a charge of *fictio* graver than exaggerating sins during confession. That charge was levelled by Bernard of Clairvaux who, choosing to ignore his own guilt on the same head,[87] accused Abelard of not being a true monk. The accusation begged a question. What did it mean, in the twelfth century, to be a true monk? It certainly did not mean feigning the penitential life, as Abelard intended to establish when he wrote the *HC*.

The *HC* is much concerned with religious authenticity, a quality notable for its absence from Abelard's youth and early manhood. Self-knowledge rather than self-description was his purpose in this autobiography, which represents an integral part of his project of ethical enquiry. Not confined to *Scito te ipsum*, the *Collationes*, the commentary on Romans, and the various versions of his theology, Abelard's moral thought was linked with his life. Experience, harsh and bitter, jolted him from his former position as a logician second to none and as bottom of the class in ethics. To ethics he brought the intensity of a late developer. Unlike Heloise who, on the evidence of her reported speech against matrimony in the *HC* and of letters that have been taken to reveal the secrets of her heart, seems to

---

[85] Cf. J. Marenbon, *The Philosophy of Peter Abelard* (Cambridge, 1997) 92. F. Troncarelli (review of I. Pagani *Abelardo ed Eloisa, Epistolario* in *MlJb* 41 (2006) 135ff.) has the merit of re-opening a question closed by weariness or boredom at the 'authenticity-debate'. The 'possibili rielaborazioni' of Abelard's and Heloise's letters about which he speaks (ibid. 136) are, however, distinct from the question of common authorship.

[86] See Chapter 4 below.

[87] Cf. Godman, *The Silent Masters*, 93ff.

have possessed moral insight from an early age, Abelard, as he describes himself during his prolonged adolescence, does not appear to have had much heart; nor did he excel at questions of conscience. How and why he first lacked, then acquired both qualities are the themes of the next two chapters.

CHAPTER 4

Fame without conscience

Fame and conscience are the categories, borrowed from St Augustine and employed by others, in which Abelard considers the most traumatic of his adversities in the *HC*.[1] In 1121 he was condemned – wrongly, as he saw it – by a council at Soissons. That event and its aftermath represent a turning-point in the narrative of his life. Previously measured by the standards of fame, Abelard's experiences in and after 1121 then begin to be analysed in terms of conscience. That distinction, fundamental to the *HC*, is made by an author who, as he portrays himself in youth, had strutted and struggled on the public stage almost as if there were no private one. Not until he began to exercise the cognitive capacities of his emotions in the sequel to Soissons was Abelard capable of making the choices needed to redefine his responsibility to himself and to others.[2] The moral maturity evinced at the end of the *HC* is far removed from the ethical adolescence described at its beginning.

Abelard's development is traced in an autobiographical work which is the natural and necessary complement to his *Scito te ipsum*. Self-knowledge and conscience had been linked by ancient philosophers,[3] and the link is maintained by this philosophical author in what is far more than a history of his calamities. That is why the traditional title, which rests on the fragile authority of a scribal rubric, is inadequate and misleading. It serves to reinforce the literalism with which Abelard's exercise in therapeutic writing has been read. The *HC* (we may fume against the misnomer, but it will not go away) is therapeutic in the classical sense of that term, maintained

[1] *HC*, ed. Pagani, 220. Abelard draws on Augustine, *Sermo* 335 in *Sermones selecti duodeviginti*, ed. C. Lambot, Stromata patristica et mediaevalia 1 (Utrecht, 1950) 124. C. Walker Bynum, *Jesus as Mother: Studies in the Spirituality of the High middle Ages* (Berkeley, 1982), 48–9, examines the use of these categories by regular canons. This passage is discussed in Chapter 5.

[2] On emotions and moral choice, see R. Solomon, *Not Passion's Slave: Emotions and Choice* (Oxford, 2003) especially 195–203.

[3] See A. Lloyd, 'Nosce te ipsum and Conscientia', *Archiv für Geschichte der Philosophie* 46 (1964) 188–200.

throughout the Middle Ages and beyond, of self-examination aimed at refashioning moral identity.[4] How that identity was refashioned can be understood in terms of the difference, elementary but important, between Abelard the subject and Abelard the narrator of the *HC*.

Their voices sing in discordant duet. The narrator's bass resounds with the tale of his transformation from a self-styled knight-errant of scholarship to a monk in more than habit and name. The subject's treble is shrill. It takes as its text an account of his experiences written with commata which, although inverted and invisible, are audible to those with an ear for tone. Literalism is tone-deaf. In the *HC* it hears only the assertive style, the aggressive manner, the crows of triumph and *Schadenfreude*. They have been construed, by a pop-psychology discredited elsewhere but still alive and kicking in medieval studies, as expressions of an outsized ego. That ego, wounded by blows of envy and malice, is said to have turned in on itself and presented to the world an aggrieved mask of the victim. The effect is, that Abelard, both before and after Soissons, can be regarded as essentially the same. Overweening in success or disconsolate in reversal, he is regarded as an incorrigible egotist whose self-awareness altered only in its degree of self-centredness.

All of this is crude, and none of it does justice to the simple but significant fact that the author of the *HC* was an abbot. Humility, for him and his monastic readers, was both a virtue and a duty. Currently considered one of the least likely pretenders to this title in the Middle Ages, Abelard does reveal himself as humble and capable of self-criticism in his role as narrator of the *HC*. And he does more, using the emotive language of penance to evoke what he, the arch-dialectician, could not define. This straining at the limits of Latinity is another of his subtleties, no less conceptual than stylistic, that has yet to receive its due. Too much has been written about the alleged arrogance of Peter Abelard; too little about his sense of humour and feel for nuance.

More than a nuance of thought lies behind his decision not to imitate the *Confessions* when writing about himself. The fact is obvious, but far from banal. A choice made against pursuing paths available can cast light on the route which an author took, and Abelard knew his way. Not put off by the awkward essay in Augustinian imitation by Guibert of Nogent, he thought

[4] Fundamental is P. Hadot, *Exercices spirituels et philosophie antique* (reprint Paris, 2002). See too P. Rabbow, *Seelenführung* (Munich, 1966).

seriously about the differences between his life and that of the saint. Initially a monk by convenience rather than conviction and later an abbot for want of better, Abelard realised that his story was not neatly divided by conversion in a garden at Milan or elsewhere. There is no scene of conversion in the *HC*. Instead there is a gradual development of vocation, directly proportionate to his acquisition of self-knowledge. It is acquired the hard way, through violent ruptures, laborious reconstructions, unending difficulties. And if, at the end of his work, Abelard approaches a degree of inner composure, it is far from the serenity of the saint.

That is why the *HC* represents a form of autobiographical literature related to, but distinct from, the hybrid genre of confession. The two differ in several respects, the first of which is, their addressee. Augustine's masterpiece is directed primarily to God; Abelard's tour de force is, formally, a letter to a friend. Its opening is modelled on the *Epistolae morales* of the influential Seneca,[5] who wrote them for Lucilius. Why is the addressee of the *HC* not named? Who is Abelard's friend, anonymous but male, as everyone has agreed since it was pointed out by Heloise, the earliest and best reader of this work?[6] Its evidence is plain. This mysterious *amicus*, about whom many have speculated, did not exist. There are no male friends in Abelard's narrative of affective isolation. Only pupils and partisans, allies and subordinates figure in the *HC*. All these roles and more besides were played by Heloise, but few will deny her femininity. None other than she came close to Abelard, on conditions that assured his dominance; and even she had to suffer before she disproved his rule. The rule of moral solipsism practised by him as a young man scarcely acknowledged others as persons in their own right.[7] After reducing his social and emotional environment to an arena in which combats were conducted in self-referential terms, what Abelard needed most was, a friend.

A friend was also needed to offset the rivals, detractors, and enemies who formed a cosmic conspiracy bent on doing him down (*quasi adversum me universus conspirasset mundus*).[8] Cardinals and prelates, 'new apostles' and old masters in the schools: each of them, in his envy, enmity, and obtuseness, serves to define antithetically the qualities of Abelard's 'friend'. He is intelligent, sympathetic, an eye-witness to victories won by this triumpher

---

[5] Cf. K.-D. Nothdurft, *Studien zum Einfluß Senecas auf die Philosophie und Theologie des zwölften Jahrhunderts* (Leiden, 1963).
[6] *Ep.* ii.i, ed. Pagani, 134.
[7] On moral solipsism and its consequences, see G. Taylor, *Deadly Vices* (Oxford, 2006) 127ff.
[8] *HC* 35, ed. Pagani, 194.

against the odds and to wrongs inflicted on this martyr of malice.[9] Above all, he possesses the signal advantage, which Heloise eventually forfeited, of not answering back. An ideal reader, in short, whose complicity Abelard courts. Such is the *amicus*, anonymous but not unidentifiable, on whose behalf the *HC* develops its therapy. This understanding individual, knowing whom the author casts as a means of knowing himself,[10] is none other than you or I.

We grasp, from its very first sentence, that his work offers a therapy of the emotions:

Often human feelings are either stirred or soothed more fully by examples than by words.[11]

Affectus, Abelard writes, not *animum*, *mentem*, or *ingenium*. Each of these alternatives would have been appropriate in context, and the third presently becomes a leitmotiv of the narrative. If Abelard singles out the affective, rather than the dispositional or intentional, senses of his chosen noun,[12] that is because he wishes to stress that the philosophy embodied in the *HC* works on, and through, the sentiments. Philosophical too is his next proposition, that he is offering comfort to a friend whose hardships dwindle into insignificance by comparison with his own adversities. Standard in paraenetic letters, such as Seneca's to Lucilius,[13] consolation offered an altruistic pretext for writing about the self. The tradition was already ancient in the twelfth century.[14]

Far from traditional is the description that follows of Abelard's early years.[15] About his childhood, untypically, we learn little. No anecdote of the boy's prowess foreshadowing feats of the man is recorded, in a departure from conventions long established in Latin biography and autobiography. Abelard's character, influenced by the factors of birthplace and of Breton

---

[9] *HC* 1, ibid., 104; 6, 120; 11, 130, 132; 14, 138; 55, 230. Each of these passages is discussed below.

[10] For the origins and development of this theory, see R. Sorabji, *Self: Ancient and Modern Insights about Individuality, Life, and Death* (Oxford, 2006) 230ff.

[11] 'Saepius humanos affectus aut provocant aut mitigant amplius exempla quam verba', *HC* 1, ed. Pagani, 104.

[12] Cf. Constable, *Reformation*, 16.

[13] See I. Hadot, *Seneca und die griechisch-römische Tradition der Seelenleitung* (Berlin, 1969) 8ff.

[14] See P. von Moos, *Consolatio: Studien zur mittellateinischen Trostliteratur über den Tod und zum Problem der christlichen Trauer*, 4 vols. (Munich, 1971–1972).

[15] *HC* 2, ed. Pagani, 106–8.

character, was formed by a single, dominant *affectus*: love. It is not love for his parents and siblings on which he dwells. His mother Lucia and his brothers and sister are not even mentioned, nor does he say anything about his feelings for his father. What mattered were, his father's feelings for Abelard. Although Berengar had only a smattering of education (*litteris aliquantulum imbutum*), he transmitted a passion for learning to his first-born son. The ardent terms in which Abelard describes it (*ardentius … adhaesi, tanto … amore inlectus*) are used, in the *HC*, only of this ideal, to which he always remained attached. Neither to God nor to Heloise was applied the immediate and constant devotion he reserved for scholarship. This was the affective bond which, despite other discontinuities, Abelard never severed with his past.

His past, as a child, was distinguished by easy and ample successes (*amplius et facilius … profeci*) which were denied to Abelard in the sequel. All his achievements, as a youth and a man, were hard won. His earliest experiences did not prepare him for resistance to his plans for conquest of the scholarly world, if plans so headstrong a figure may be imagined to have made. Abelard does not state but implies, by his self-heroising language in the first chapters of the *HC*, that, when he came to compose it, he was surprised to be unable to model his work on the epic deeds of Alexander the Great. That, or something very like it, was the measure of himself which he had been encouraged to take by paternal ambition and premature triumphs.

And that is why, when we observe what appears to be the magniloquence at the opening of the *HC*, it is worth remembering that it was written by an author who had reason to feel disappointed about his achievements. There is frustration in Abelard's autobiography, there is fear, but there is little bitterness. Looking back at his life from the standpoint of middle age, in the early 1130s, he did not view it as a history of calamities. He accepted the hardships and struggles, and acknowledged that he had inflicted some of them on himself. Abelard had learnt to consider critically his misguided exercises in self-will. Criticism of his own impetuousness is often expressed, in the *HC*, by irony, which is not just an ornamental device. Abelard uses irony as a means of establishing distance between himself as he was and the self which he became.

Distance is not a quality cultivated by the simple egotist who insists on the linearity of his character, because he is perturbed that his identity may be fragile. Nor was it a quality which Abelard possessed naturally; it had to be acquired with time and experience. The process of learning to transform himself began in early youth. It is expressed in the military metaphors which he transposes to the scholarly career he selected from the chivalric one he might have pursued. No one has failed to note the connotations of combativeness. Nor does anyone seem to have pondered the less obvious implications of Abelard's martial language. For, in the counter-productive violence it describes, it raises the question of whether he, during his prolonged adolescence, was a knight-errant or a wandering thug of scholarship.

∾

An answer is implied by the geography of the places in which Abelard first wielded his dialectical truncheon. They represent not a sequence of successes but, at best, a zig-zag of near-misses. Paris, Melun, Corbeil, Paris again, Melun revisited before a further assault on Paris: in each and every one of these battles or brawls the self-styled knight-errant of scholarship was dismounted from his high horse. Aware that his erratic combativeness might be interpreted as a compulsion to thuggery, Abelard concedes that he had no strategy in academic politics. What he describes, in the early chapters of the *HC*, is his inability to turn to his advantage a series of temporary gains. The repeated setbacks are framed in a symmetry between *fama* and *invidia*. Conscience is absent at this stage in Abelard's self-aware-ness. He sees himself as others view him, from the outside; and the per-spective is initially skewed towards fame, the target of his inaccurate aim. Envy is introduced when he falls short of the mark. Embellished with classical quotations as self-flattering as they are inept, the misprisions of the subject are treated by the narrator with a hint of humour. Tilting at the windmills of fame, young Abelard is made to resemble, if not a thug, then a Don Quixote of scholarship.

The humour derives from what he says. There is nothing funny about his silences. Some of them are embarrassed, and embarrassment may account for Abelard's omissions. They are evident in the chronology of the *HC*, which leaps from his birth in 1079 to *c.*1102, when he sat at the feet of William of Champeaux, before trampling them with his own. No word of Abelard's earlier studies with Roscelin at Loches. The memory had to be suppressed. In one of his earliest letters of *c.*1120, he had denounced his former master to the bishop of Paris,[16] before being trounced by Roscelin for this attempt to rake up controversies long settled.[17] The first, but not

---

[16] *Ep.* 14 in E. Smits (ed.), *Peter Abelard: Letters IX–XIV* (Groningen, 1983) 279–80.
[17] Ed. J. Reiners, *Der Nominalismus in der Frühscholastik: Ein Beitrag zur Geschichte der Universalienfrage im Mittelalter* (Münster, 1910) 62–80.

the last, of Abelard's selective silences draws a veil over the probable origins of this inglorious episode.

How glorious then were the successive episodes of struggle between *c.*1102 and *c.*1112? In that decade Abelard did not pass from early to mature adulthood but remained, on his own account, a brilliant bonehead incapable of profiting from his experiences. They form a pattern. First, recognition of a teacher's fame, intolerable when, as in the case of William of Champeaux, it was undeniable.[18] Next, an attack on this object of unstated but unmistakable envy, followed by ambiguous proclamations of victory.[19] Then, unless circumstances supervened – which they generally appear to have done as soon as the laurels of triumph began to wilt – a tactical withdrawal. And throughout this pattern recur, as inseparable as Tweedledum and Tweedledee, the paired abstractions of *fama* and *invidia*.[20] Never the one without the other.

Abelard declares that their relationship was symmetrical. No sooner had he conquered fame, than he was defeated by envy. If the symmetry is plain, the ways in which he slants it are complex. Abelard the narrator does not encourage us to accept Abelard the subject's version of events. The trajectory of what cannot be regarded as his ascent up the slippery pole poses the issue of why he slithered and stumbled. Did William of Champeaux impede his rise? Or were obstacles placed in his path by himself? These questions are answered with candour. All the blame is not laid at the door of *invidia*. Presumption too played a part. It was presumptuous, Abelard states, in one of his tender years to set up school at Melun;[21] and the same fault, repeated at Corbeil, was exacerbated there by misjudgement (*importunitas*), in the double sense of failure to assess the situation and to reckon with others.[22]

Others, again on his own account, did not always reckon with Abelard as he should have wished. To his first attacks on William of Champeaux replied not that master but his pupils, indignant about their seniority.[23] Perhaps piqued at his failure to draw the attention of this figure whom he both admired and envied, Abelard withdrew first to Melun, then to Corbeil, making mistakes on the way. How he made them, is implicit in the confusion he ascribes to the motives of others, in particular William of

---

[18] 'in hoc tunc magisterio *re et fama* praecipuum', *HC* 3, ed. Pagani, 110.

[19] E.g. 'ei … gravissimus extiti, cum nonnullas scilicet eius sententias refellere *conarer* et … nonnumquam superior in disputando *viderer*', *HC* 3, ibid., 110–12.

[20] On *invidia* cf. S. Spence, *Texts and the Self in the Twelfth Century* (Cambridge, 1996) 68ff.

[21] *HC* 4, ed. Pagani, 112.   [22] *HC* 4, ibid., 114.   [23] *HC* 4, ibid., 112

Champeaux. Although William's 'machinations' against Abelard at Melun were 'secret', his 'envy' was 'obvious'.[24] What does this mean? If the master's *invidia* was not known from his actions, what else betrayed it? The answer has less to do with William than with Abelard, on the principle that: 'When a man denominates another his *enemy*, his *rival*, his *antagonist*, his *adversary*, he is understood to speak the language of self-love.'[25]

The subject's language of self-love does not cohere with the language of causality which he misuses. As his fame grew, William's diminished. Far from explaining the master's envy, this gave rise (*hinc*) to his own presumption. An error is being noted. For, in what were or ought to have been Abelard's terms, the effects of William's *invidia* had not been unwelcome. They served to win the young man the support of 'very many', among whom were 'quite a few' local potentates who disliked his rival. It follows that envy is a double-edged weapon capable of wounding those who brandish it. And since it also follows that one scholar's enemies can become another's allies, an academic politician disposed to learn this lesson would have cultivated his connections and stayed put.

Abelard, driven by what he describes as presumption and misjudgement, moved on from Melun to Corbeil, which had the advantage of being nearer to Paris. The intellectual capital attracted, like a magnet, this provincial from Brittany. So strong was its pull that, after a long convalescence at home, he returned not to Corbeil but to Paris, there to resume his role as William of Champeaux's worst pupil. His subordinate status galled Abelard. It turned him against William who remained, irritatingly, the *magister*. Immutable in his authority, he had to be shown, or at least insinuated, to have changed. The change, of course, could not be for the better; and, having nothing to say against the intellectual abilities of his master, Abelard has to content himself with sarcasm at the expense of his character. The sarcasm is presented as gossip (*ut referebant*).[26] Doing William down, the subject does not raise his own voice. Others alleged that the master had become a regular canon in order to obtain promotion to the episcopate, and their prophecy was fulfilled when, in short order, he became bishop of Châlons. That success was won by the exercise of talents which Abelard did not possess. Shrewd at judging the right moment to move, William of Champeaux also knew when to stay put.

[24] *HC* 4, ibid., 114.
[25] D. Hume, *An Enquiry concerning the Principles of Morals* 9, 6 ed. T. Beauchamp (Oxford, 1998) 148.
[26] *HC* 5, ed. Pagani, 114.

Remaining in Paris and continuing to teach, the master represented a barrier to the triumphal march which his self-appointed rival longed to stage. Abelard overcame this obstacle by forcing (*compuli*) William to yield to his arguments about universals.[27] Not once but twice does he crow over this feat, repeating the same verb in a different mood (*coactus*). The repetition, deliberate on the part of a scrupulous stylist, betrays not only glee at what was to prove a short-lived victory but also relief at a breakthrough in what was beginning to look like an impasse. The path ahead, however, was tortuous and uncertain. If William's pupils flocked to Abelard and his chosen successor obligingly vacated his post for the better candidate, the master, undaunted by his philosophical mishap and uninhibited by his religious vows, bounced back. Ousting Abelard from his Parisian position, William forced him to beat a retreat to Melun.[28]

The cold comfort of a quotation from Ovid (*Remedia amoris* 369) about envy scaling the heights does not conceal its feebleness as an explanation for this reversal. In the academic politics of Paris, Abelard was plainly outflanked. Each of his proclamations of victory is a prelude to sounding the retreat and, no sooner has he withdrawn, than he is planning a comeback. The zig-zag of his wanderings to and fro begins to take the form of a question-mark about the intelligence of his designs. How intelligent was it, for example, then to move from Melun to Mont-Sainte-Geneviève in the hope of living in peace with William, who had left the city, while at the same time intending to 'lay siege' to what Abelard regarded as the 'occupation' of 'his' post?[29] If this is meant to be the language of a general planning a campaign, the battlefield selected was a twelfth-century Waterloo.

The errors of Abelard the subject are highlighted by his misapplication of moral categories. Shame is the category introduced at this point, up to which the subject has displayed nothing but barefaced ambition. When William of Champeaux is described as reappearing in Paris *impudenter*, the adverb invites emendation by the adjective *invictus*. Unbowed and unbeaten when he was on the scene, William could be outflanked only during a temporary absence. His 'shamelessness' consisted in his resistance to Abelard's assaults. If they fell flat, collateral damage was also done to William's most recent successor (the last one having been driven out for his imprudence in making over his post to the usurper), for whom crocodile-tears are shed. He was filched of his few and mediocre pupils (*aliquos habuit qualescumque discipulos*) who deserted his lectures on Priscian, although 'he was considered a high authority' (*plurimum valere credebatur*).

[27] *HC* 5, ibid., 116.   [28] *HC* 5, ibid., 118.   [29] *HC* 6, ibid., 118.

'He was considered', not 'he was': the professional sarcasm, as facile as the ethical slur on their common master, betrays doubt behind the show of assurance. Abelard tries to dispel that doubt about his dominance in an account of the 'war' that followed. But, as usual when he has something to hide, he protests too much. The struggle between his pupils and William's was won by his faction, he claims. Is that not obvious, although Abelard had been worsted in all of their previous conflicts? It is obvious because we, his readers, have learnt the lesson of a self-evident fact (*te quoque res ipsa edocuit*). The testimony appealed to here is not that of a fact but of an attitude – an attitude of benevolence, or gullibility, prepared to accept at face-value the terms in which the circular argument is constructed.

They are not even Abelard's own. He cites, with the 'moderate boldness' of oxymoron (*ut temperatius loquar, audacter proferam*), a line from Ovid's *Metamorphoses* (XIII.90), which ends: 'I was not beaten by him' (*non sum superatus ab illo*).[30] This does not necessarily mean what the cunning quoter wishes to insinuate. Taken out of context, the half-verse lacks the force of a double negative, and cannot be construed as a declaration of unconditional surrender on William's part. Acceptance of an armed truce or acknowledgment of a draw is the most favourable interpretation that can be put on this phrase, the allusiveness of which Abelard then proceeds to strain: 'Were I to be silent, the facts speak out for themselves, as does the issue of the event.' (*Quod si ego taceam, res ipsa clamat, et ipsius rei finis indicat.*) Repetitive in its insistence and evasive in its silences, it is rhetoric, not factuality, that speaks for itself and the subject. He insinuates what he purports to prove. His ideal reader is cast as an eye-witness not because he was present but because he is, or ought to be, partisan. Complicity becomes collusion in wishful thinking by this expert in what not to say.

Yet Abelard knows how and when to be specific, passing deftly from one theme to another. The 'war' was cut short by his being forced (*compulit*) to return to Brittany when his mother took the veil.[31] Was her vocation timely? Did it free him from the frustration of yet another impasse? We, long in possession of the facts (*te ... res ipsa dudum edocuit*), are not encouraged to indulge in such speculation. We are, however, invited to admire the symmetries of our friend's style. *Compulit* is the third person perfect of the same verb twice used by Abelard to describe William of Champeaux's being made to give way to his arguments on universals. If the rising star had to yield to the demands of filial piety, the falling one had been compelled to bow before the *force majeure* of a higher intellect.

---

[30] *HC* 6, ibid., 120.   [31] *HC* 7, ibid., 120.

The elegance, and the innuendo, are meant to be noted. They avert our amicable gaze from the sleights of hand.

⤳

These minor symmetries reinforce the major one between *fama* and *invidia*. Because the balance is now tilted towards envy – the chief, but not the sole, explanation given for Abelard's adversities – it is worth recalling some of the associations which this concept had for his readers. They were more attuned to edifying literature than we are. Hagiography offered one of their models for living;[32] and it is in relation to that exemplar, both moral and literary, that the *HC* would have been set by Abelard's audience. Its monastic and clerical members encountered *invidia* especially in biographies of saints and of their likes. A representative example is the Life of an eleventh-century bishop who has figured in these pages – Burchard of Worms, described by his anonymous admirer as *quasi sanctus*.[33] Envy looms large in this work. It is ascribed by the author to his critics, to the devil, and to Burchard's detractors.[34] Whited sepulchres who carp at achievements of which they are incapable, they bear the brunt of his criticisms, as was conventional in biographies of holy men.

Their writers, since late antiquity, had accustomed readers to third-person polemic against the envy suffered by the subjects of their works. The scope given to this rhetoric of defence and recrimination could be ample. Far more restricted was the space allowed to first-person protests against *invidia*. At variance with the modesty which authors were expected to cultivate, or affect, they were usually confined to apotropaeic gestures in prologues, where a biographer might speak not only of his subject but of himself. Less binding than a rule but no less effective as a curb, this decorum of restraint was generally maintained by autobiographers in the Latin West. The exception is, Abelard. He dwells on the *invidia* which he claims to have endured at a length and with a frequency to which his readers were used only in third-person accounts of the exemplary lives of others. The narrator notes this recurrent tune in an ill-chosen key, and marks distance between himself and the subject of the *HC*. Abelard the subject, loud in his first-person lamentations about *invidia*, jarred with the expectations of twelfth-century readers.

---

[32] In the vast literature on this subject, one of the most perceptive contributions remains W. von den Steinen's account of saints as hagiographers in *Menschen in Mittelalter: Gesammelte Forschungen, Betrachtungen, Bilder*, ed. P. von Moos (Berne, 1967) 7–31.

[33] *Vita Burchardi episcopi* III, ed. G. Waitz, MGH *Scriptores* IV (Hanover, 1841) 833, 37.

[34] *Prol.* ibid. 831, 9ff.; 832, 35ff.; 15 ibid. 839, 28ff.; 24 ibid. 846, 6ff.

What they expected of a holy man is not provided here, in the account of his youth, but later in the work, where the benevolent hand of providence is detected in even the harshest of adversities. Of providence and benevolence no sign is registered in the *HC* up to and including the point at which Abelard describes his encounter with Anselm of Laon. There he is said to rise to heights of virtuosity. But the level of writing is low. And it is meant to be seen as such, for this re-creation of the purple prose of Abelard the subject in abrasive immaturity is sharply distinct from all that precedes and follows it. Never, in his earlier sarcasms at the expense of William of Champeaux and his school, did Abelard permit himself sneers of the kind that are directed against Anselm of Laon, nor do the criticisms of his adversaries expressed in the rest of the *HC* and in his other writings lapse into such a depth of denigration. Singular in style, uncertain in register, and inconsequent in its allusions, this set-piece of polemic is both exceptional in Abelard's autobiography and anomalous in his oeuvre.

Yet it is not without later analogies, one of which it may be useful to indicate. Self-aggrandisement by belittling straw-opponents was a trait, or a foible, of another satirist of scholarship given to casting his achievements in the heroic mould. In his nervous brilliance and neurotic puerility, A. E. Housman bears more than a passing resemblance to Abelard the subject. The differences between them are, that Housman never grew out of the habit, nor did he employ the inverted commata which Abelard the narrator interposes between his account and the subject's sneers. No inverted commata surround William of Champeaux's departure from the stage of the *HC*. Even during his absence, the spell he exercised on Abelard remained bewitching. When William became resident-bishop of Châlons, his pupil declined to dominate the Parisian scene, for which he had struggled so hard and so long. Returning from Brittany, he went to study with William's teacher, Anselm, at Laon. This did not imply an apostolic succession of learning from generation to generation. William remained, for Abelard, the one and only *magister*. That term, in his poetic diction, is nothing less than a title. Extolling the claims of the *magistri*, he stations their chairs directly after the thrones of kings in a hierarchy at whose summit sits God.[35]

That is why it is a slight when Abelard grants Anselm that title in relation to William and his other pupils, but denies it to him in respect of himself. Never *magister*, Anselm is demoted to the state of *senex* in Abelard's report of his brief sojourn at Laon, where he continued to pursue his quest for fame.

---

[35] *Hymnus Paraclitensis* 87, 1, ed. Szövérffy, *Peter Abelard's Hymnarius Paraclitensis* ii.187.

The power and authority that attended it provide the terms of a contrast between Anselm and William. *Guillelmus in episcopatu Catalunensi polle-bat*: the verb is unequivocal; William ruled as bishop of Châlons. Anselm, more ambiguously, 'held at that time the greatest authority on account of his antiquity' (*maximam ex antiquitate auctoritatem tenebat*).[36] *Tenebat*, not *habebat*: a holder rather than a possessor of authority, his grasp of the treasure that Abelard coveted was less secure than William of Champeaux's grip on episcopal power. Why? On account of Anselm's age, which might have been a motive for compassion (the delight of the envious, as Plutarch perceived).[37] *Antiquitas*, lightly ironical, need not be denigratory. It is made so in this burst of venom:

And so I proceeded to this old man who had acquired a reputation more by hoary experience than by ability or memory. If anyone knocked at his door uncertain about a problem, he returned more unsure. He was wondrous in the eyes of those who listened to him, but a nonentity in the view of critical enquirers. He had a marvellous way with words, but their meaning was beneath contempt and without reason. When he lit a fire, he filled his house with smoke, rather than illuminating it with light. His tree seemed remarkable for its flourishing completeness to those who looked at it from afar, but, as one came closer and gazed more carefully, it was found to be barren. And so when I drew near to pluck fruit from it, I discovered that it was the fig-tree which the Lord cursed or that old oak-tree with which Lucan compares Pompey, when he says: 'There stands the shadow of a great name … '.[38]

The word *invidia* never occurs in this passage. Envy, however, is its theme. Malice parades as indignation; spite affects a tone that is both self-righteous and self-regarding.[39] Abelard considers himself the opposite of Anselm: the proud possessor of *ingenium* and *memoria* rather than the tedious tenant of *usus*. The object of envy is depicted as a subject for whom

[36] *HC* 7, ed. Pagani, 122.

[37] *De invidia et odio*, 538C, ed. S. Lanzi, Corpus Plutarchi Moralium 39 (Naples, 2004) 88.

[38] 'Accessi igitur ad hunc senem, cui magis longaevus usus quam ingenium vel memoria nomen comparaverat. Ad quem si quis de aliqua questione pulsandum accederet incertus, redibat incertior. Mirabilis quidem erat in oculis auscultantium, sed nullus in conspectu quaestionantium. Verborum usum habebat mirabilem, sed sensu contemptibilem et ratione vacuum. Cum ignem accenderet, domum suam fumo implebat, non luce illustrabat. Arbor eius tota in foliis aspicientibus a longe conspicua videbatur, sed propinquantibus et diligentius intuentibus infructuosa reperiebatur. Ad hanc itaque cum accessissem, ut fructum inde colligerem, deprendi illam esse ficulneam, cui maledixit Dominus, seu illam veterem quercum, cui Pompeium Lucanus comparat dicens: "Stat magni nominis umbra … " ', *HC* 8, ed. Pagani, 122–4.

[39] For these categories, inherited from classical Latin, see the excellent discussion of Kaster, *Emotion, Restraint and Community*, 84ff.

no one could feel such an emotion. But the colours are too crude. Failing to paint the picture of a senile fool, warts and all, they offer an inverted self-portrait. The likeness, ugly but graphic, is of Abelard's craving for Anselm's *auctoritas*. About his teaching, little is said in many malignant words. The malignity is verbose, not eloquent. Its bombastic style is untypical of the narrator. He stands back while the subject sounds off. No comment of 'presumption' or 'misjudgement' is passed as previously. These qualities are left to speak for themselves. They do so with the stridency and muddle of a prize-essay in invective. The stridency is amplified by variants on the same theme; the muddle, alien to a narrative otherwise limpid and linear, is betrayed by the mixed metaphors. Chief among them is the tree, or the trees, with which Anselm is compared unfavourably. His arboreal reputation had to be cut down to size. Abelard the subject aims two blows at the trunk, both of which miss their mark.

Anselm's teaching of theology was based on the Bible and the Latin Fathers, especially Augustine, which is why it is meant to be telling when Scripture is cited against him. But as a justification of the obvious animus, the fig-tree cursed by Christ on the way from Bethany to Jerusalem (Matthew 21:19; Mark 11:12–14) is inadequate. Exegetes since Augustine had wondered why it was blamed for not producing fruit before Easter. 'What [wrong] had the tree done in being fruitless? What was its fault in barrenness?', asked the saint, echoed by the bewilderment of others that the tree's creator knew less than its cultivator.[40] No one construed literally this malediction by Jesus, who preached love of one's enemies.[41] Blind in his enmity to Anselm, Abelard fails to make his readers see his point. His point, such as it is, might have been better sustained by the fig-tree thought to be cursed because Judas hanged himself on it,[42] and it is possible that the one has been confused with the other. Abelard the subject is more confused than caustic. The Biblical analogy he has chosen, understood figuratively by others with a compassion which he lacks,[43] does not sustain the meaning he wishes to put on it.

Nor does the quotation from Lucan (*Bellum civile* 1.135). As the subject intends this half-verse to be read, the stress should fall on 'shadow'

---

[40] *Sermo* 98, 3 in *Sant'Agostino. Discorsi. II/2 (86–116) sul Nuovo Testamento*, tr. L. Carrozzi (Rome, 1983) 202.

[41] See Speyer, 'Fluch' and E. Schwartz, 'Der verfluchtete Feigebaum' in *Zum Neuen Testament und zum frühen Christentum: Gesammelte Schriften* V (Berlin, 1963) 42–7.

[42] Cf. A. Murray, *Suicide in the Middle Ages* II: *The Curse on Self-Murder* (Oxford, 2000) 334.

[43] Cf. Abelard, *Sermo* 10: 'Ad terrorem hominum et correptionem malorum gestum est in arbore quod gerundum erat in homine … ad paenitentiam invitat' (PL 178, 460D–461A).

(*umbra*). It does not necessarily do so. Equal, if not greater, emphasis can
be attached to the verb that occupies initial position. Anselm's reputation
remains (*stat*), despite the attempt to cast aspersions on it. The solemnity with which Abelard's classical quotations have been studied takes no
account of their misuse.[44] If the half-line from Lucan is intended to elevate
scholarly combativeness to an epic register,[45] the effort backfires and the
effect is bathos. The subject fares no better with oaks than with fig-trees.
Inconsequent allusion to the Bible is coupled with inept quotation from
Roman poetry, revealing nothing much about Anselm, but a great deal
about Abelard's attitude to him at Laon. Striving for cleverness, the subject
achieves no more than clumsiness. Inadvertently he exemplifies the truth
that: 'slander is the tribute that malice pays to shame'.[46]

The shamelessness of the subject, unglossed by the narrator, is further
exposed by what follows. Had Anselm of Laon been so temporary a tenant of *nomen* and *auctoritas*, it would have sufficed to describe how he lost
them; and this is what the narrator proceeds to do, by treating the previous polemic as the digression it is. The style becomes explanatory; and
when envy recurs, it is referred to Abelard's show of contempt for Anselm,
which turned his pupils against the young man.[47] Yet the same predicament in which he had placed himself during his first clash with William
of Champeaux at Paris now leads to a difference. Abelard, at Laon, transformed hostility into admiration by expounding, without formal training
in theology, a difficult book of the Bible. Then nemesis intervened. Forced
to withdraw, yet again, he was pursued not only by the *invidia* of Anselm
but also by that of his would-be successors, Alberic of Reims and Lotulf of
Novara.[48] Their enmity, claims Abelard, enhanced his reputation.

If the symmetry is familiar, the inferences drawn from it are not. There
are, it appears, two ways to acquire authority and power as a *magister*. One
is, by teaching well what you have not studied; the other is, by putting up
your rivals' backs. Not the most plausible line of reasoning but, even if it
is given the benefit of the doubt, the fact remains that Anselm of Laon
was not Abelard's rival, except in Abelard's eyes. Their illness of envy (in
Plutarch's terms)[49] skewed his vision, as the impropriety of his moral diction

[44] Cf. D. De Robertis, 'Il senso della propria storia ritrovato attraverso i classici nella *Historia
calamitatum* di Abelardo', *Maia* 16 (1964) 6–54.
[45] Cf. von Moos, 'Lucan und Abaelard' in *Abaelard und Heloise*, 99–128.
[46] Kaster, *Emotion, Restraint, and Community*, 101.   [47] *HC* 9, ed. Pagani, 124–6.
[48] *HC* 10, ibid., 128.
[49] *De invidia et odio*, 537A, ed. Lanzi, 80. For the tradition of the metaphor, cf. ibid. 100–2, and
Kaster, *Emotions, Restraint, and Community*, 85ff.

indicates. Anselm vetoed his Biblical teaching 'shamelessly' (*impudenter*). That is the same adverb applied to William of Champeaux's return to Paris, where, like Anselm at Laon, he did no more than stand on rights violated by Abelard's trespassing.

Attributing to them his own faults, the subject enlists allies. His pupils rejected as specious (*praetendens*) Anselm's reason for his ban on Abelard's exegesis. The old master did not want errors committed by a freshman (*rudis*) in theology to be ascribed to him. This, the students thought, was 'envious slander' (*livoris calumnia*). No bad description of Abelard's previous polemic, nor an argument he could afford to dismiss so high-handedly, for it was exactly what he said himself when claiming that his theological views had been misrepresented by his own pupils. Choosing to ignore how close his double-edged rhetoric cuts to his own bone, Abelard the subject huffs and puffs. Aware that the hot air is fanned not only by arrogance but also by fragility,[50] Abelard the narrator pleads like a counsel unconvinced of the defendant's innocence.

If Abelard the narrator is unconvinced, that is because Abelard the subject is unconvincing. Brilliant he may be, but he is not intelligent. Rather than learn from his mistakes, he repeats them. *Invidia*, recognised at Melun to be a treacherous weapon, wounds him once more at Laon. The vulnerability of the subject is hardly less evident than his vaingloriousness. His words, harsh and haughty, are wronged and indignant as well. Their inverted moralism was resonant with associations for Abelard's contemporaries. Many of them would have associated it with a familiar type. That type was familiar from the literature of religious guidance.[51] Here is an example, previously unpublished, taken from a treatise read by the regular canons of Abelard's generation:

Arrogant masters who know nothing of charity, if unable to win a most praiseworthy reputation from others' pupils, blacken their characters cruelly. Inflamed by the spark of envy, they do not want to live for others whom they perceive they are unable to dominate. True masters, by contrast, allow others to be praised for their teaching by their own pupils … for every form of *magisterium* is put to the test by the charity it displays … not only do they not envy others' praise, but they even put themselves out to help and advance them.[52]

---

[50] Cf. Taylor, *Deadly Vices*, 48–9.

[51] A brief but useful survey is provided by Bynum, *Jesus as Mother*, 267–9.

[52] ' … arrogantes magistri et caritatis ignari, si plenissimum nomen laudis ex alienis discipulis consequi nequeunt, eorum vitam crudeliter insequuntur. Invidie enim face succensi nolunt aliis vivere, quos se conspiciunt non posse possidere. Veraces vero magistri concedunt, ut ex eorum discipulis alii quandam laudem magisterii habe[a]nt … omne enim magisterium in examine caritatis approbatur … non solum aliis laudem non invident, sed utilitatem eis

This passage and others like it provide a further reason for Abelard's distinction, in the *HC*, between the subject and the narrator. The narrator did not need to point out the resemblance between the subject and the type of *arrogantes magistri* delineated here; the 'cruel' attempt 'to blacken' Anselm of Laon's 'character' spoke for itself, as did the repeated efforts to filch Anselm and William of their pupils' praise. Abelard the subject, on the ample evidence of his own words, then fitted into a moral category that fell short of the ideal of *caritas* which would later become central to the ethical thought of the narrator.[53]

Of ethical thought, at this stage of the *HC*, there is not a glimmer.[54] Abelard portrays himself as a moral midget. More darkness than light is cast by the unprincipled inversions of his rhetoric, which attributes to others the deadly sin of envy under which he labours.[55] The effect is, to highlight his loneliness. The only company kept by this fragile figure is that of the *invidiosi* whom he cannot bear; nor is it clear that the narrator can stand the subject. His hostility to rivals, adversaries, and antagonists is expressed in terms of self-love which are undermined by the narrator's more subdued, though no less telling, criticisms. The structure is dialectical. And in this *sic et non* of affirmation and denial of Abelard's former self, his sufferings acquire comic features. They are not amusing because he possessed a sense of humour when he inflicted them on himself. There is little wit and no joy in the account of Abelard's youth and early manhood. The nearest he then came to such sentiments was, *Schadenfreude* at worsting William of Champeaux on the issue of universals, and even then the gratification did not last. Never light-hearted, always disgruntled, frustrated, slighted, the subject of the *HC* exemplifies the insight that envy is the only one of the seven deadly sins which is 'no fun at all'.[56]

et provectum exorant.' BAV. Ottob. lat. 175, 53*v*. On this manuscript, see J. Leclercq, 'Un témoignage sur l'influence de Grégoire VII dans la réforme canoniale', *Studi Gregoriani* 6 (1959–1960) 173–227.

[53] See M. Perkams, *Liebe als Zentralbegriff der Ethik nach Peter Abelard*, BGPTMA 58 (Münster, 2001) and Chapter 5 below.

[54] For the view that Abelard's career is 'split into two halves: an earlier period (up to 1117), when his interests were almost entirely in logic, and a later period, when his main interest came increasingly to lie in questions connected with Christian doctrine', see J. Marenbon, 'Life, Milieu, and Intellectual Contexts' in *The Cambridge Companion to Abelard*, ed. J. Brower and K. Guilfoy (Cambridge, 2004) 20ff.

[55] Cf. C. Casagrande and S. Vecchio, *I sette vizi capitali: Storia dei peccati nel Medioevo* (Turin, 2000) 36ff.

[56] J. Epstein, *Envy: The Seven Deadly Sins* (Oxford, 2003) 1.

Our strongest enmities, Paul Valéry remarked, are directed against those who are what we would like to be.[57] That, on the evidence of Abelard's autobiography, is perhaps not quite right, for, if he coveted the *auctoritas* of Anselm of Laon, at whom he sneered, he acquired the position vacated by William of Champeaux without changing his tune of grudging respect towards this master previously dominant in the Parisian schools. Then, at the moment of success, the subject became – or, rather, remained – the worst foe of himself. Glory, popularity, and money were his undoing.[58] Fame, so secure that readers cannot fail to know about it,[59] wrought havoc on Abelard when he obtained it at last. He was ruined by prosperity, he declares in the words of Proverbs 1:32, accepting as applicable to himself that Biblical definition of stupidity.

Stupidity is a category which Abelard the subject had not hesitated to apply to others, generally on intellectual grounds. His stupidity, by contrast, was moral. Why and how, the narrator explains with clarity. When the subject is described as thinking himself the only philosopher in the world, it is not just the evident conceit that is at issue. The issue is also, Abelard's lack of ethical intelligence. It is revealed in his susceptibility to the first and the last of the seven deadly sins.[60] Pride (*superbia*) and licentiousness (*luxuria*) represent, to the narrator, foolish lapses from the ideal that required philosophers and theologians to be continent. Purity of thought entails chastity of life; appearances must correspond to reality. This was the ethical objective at which the subject ought to have aimed. He fell short of it because he did not understand, when he reached the highest goal of his youth, that fame alone was insufficient.

Fame was insufficient, for Abelard's standards of moral solipsism led only to what he came to regard as immoral folly. The sneerer at Anselm of Laon had been incapable of formulating such a thought; he was too verbose in his vulnerability. The loudness of the subject is silenced temporarily by the narrator who, enlarging on his curt comments of presumptuousness and misjudgement, surveys the main calamities of this troubled life. The castration that followed at Paris in *c*.1117 and the condemnation at Soissons of 1121 were providential. Delivering him from pride and licentiousness, they taught him the virtue of 'being humbled'.[61] *Humiliatum*, not *humilem*: the least likely quality of the subject is neither natural to nor acquired

---

[57] Quoted by Epstein, ibid., 65.   [58] *HC* II, ed. Pagani, 128–30.
[59] 'ex fama te quoque latere non potuit', *HC* II, ibid., 130.
[60] Cf. Casagrande and Vecchio, *I sette vizi capitali*, 3ff., 149ff.
[61] 'divina pietas humiliatum sibi vendicaret' *HC* II, ed. Pagani, 132, cf. 'illius libri … combustione me humiliando', ibid., 130–2.

by him, but imposed on him by God, according to the narrator. This act of 'kindness' (*pietas*, not *crudelitas*) is seen as a sign of grace. No sign of grace enlightened the gloom of Abelard the subject. He, who had never been humbled without a bellow of protest against envy, quietly accepts his castration and his condemnation as salutary in the role of narrator. Bent on understanding where and when he had erred, he then invites the reader to participate in the subject's process of learning, not from hearsay, but by following the chronological order of events.[62] This is how Abelard understands therapeutic writing about the self; this is the point at which the narrator, ignoring the defensive rhetoric of the subject, begins to make more than passing remarks on what lay behind his defects.

Seeking the causes, not the symptoms, Abelard diagnoses them in an account of his *éducation sentimentale*. It is significant that the feeling with which he deals first is not the one he came to prize most highly. *Caritas*, for him and others, meant primarily love of God and, by extension, love of one's neighbour.[63] At this point in his development the subject feels *caritas* for no one. Nor is it clear that love was the sentiment he experienced with Heloise. *Amor*, in Abelard's diction, is a neutral and insipid term which takes on colour and acquires taste with an accompanying adjective or an explanatory noun in the genitive. Neither of these aids to understanding is provided in his report of his affair with Heloise. 'Affair' may indeed be the nearest approximation to the Latin *amor*, for it is evident that Abelard had difficulty in pinning a name to what was less an emotion than a calculation. The difficulty should not be ascribed to lack of skill. If he was not entirely sure of how he should specify his feeling for her, one of the reasons was, he had already deprecated it as 'licentiousness' (*luxuria*).

Luxuria, when it first occurs in the *HC*, has an archaic air. The air is not that of twelfth-century Paris with its secular clergy, where the cosiness of concubinage remained more than a memory, but that of a harsher world of asceticism and rigour. *Luxuria* is more suited to the vocabulary of an earlier moralist, such as Peter Damian. Carnality, that saint argued, was to be countered with 'thoughts of the grave'.[64] Decomposing flesh, devouring worms, the stench of putrefaction: none of these macabre fantasies appears

---

[62] 'Cuius nunc rei utramque historiam verius ex ipsa re quam ex auditu conoscere te volo, ordine quidem quo processerunt', ibid., 132.

[63] See H. Pétré, *Caritas: Étude sur le vocabulaire latin de la charité chrétienne* (Louvain, 1948) and Perkams, *Liebe als Zentralbegriff*, 26ff. See further Chapter 6.

[64] *Ep.* 132, in *Die Briefe des Petrus Damiani*, ed. K. Reindel, MGH *Epistolae* III, 2 (Munich, 1989) 442, 5–22.

in the *HC*, because Abelard's affair with Heloise hardly amounted to *luxuria*. Sex, yes; licentiousness, no: the distinction is pertinent and pointed. It points in the direction of the anti-Augustinian thesis of the naturalness of desire advanced in *Scito te ipsum*.[65] Natural, but not crudely carnal, the relationship between the lovers was both sensual and scholarly. What attracted Abelard to Heloise was, above all, her accomplishments in learning.[66] Erudition and eros are placed in parallel. Fondling books and caressing breasts, love-talk instead of tutorials, kisses rather than lessons[67] – the charm verges on preciosity and lapses into narcissism.

Such were his fame and figure, declares Abelard, that he might have had any woman.[68] It is not only envy that speaks the language of self-love. Why then did Narcissus-Abelard, with the world of women at his feet, deign to stoop to Heloise? She was good-looking – the point, often obscured by mistranslation, deserves emphasis[69] – and she was 'supreme in scholarship'.[70] Beauty not neglected, brains win out. They win out, because they satisfy a higher criterion. Through favourable contrast with the ignorance of others, Heloise's erudition made her famous. Fame remains the ultimate, the dominant, and – in this instance alone – the reciprocal standard of Abelard's judgement. *In toto regno nominatissima*, the learned lady offered him a feminine reflection of his own image. This is self-satire. And it intensifies, as the narrator reveals the full extent of the subject's odiousness. There is nothing romantic about the way Abelard describes what is still celebrated as one of the great romances of the Middle Ages. His diction is calculating. He reckoned it 'very easy' (*facillime*) to 'couple' (*copulare*) Heloise in love with him[71] – the verb is not only explicitly sexual;[72] it also connotes manipulation – because she was 'more accommodating' (*commodiorem*). Why the comparative? More accommodating than whom? Than other women, less susceptible to the learning displayed in the letters with which Abelard preyed on Heloise's

---

[65] See Chapter 7 below.   [66] *HC* 12, ed. Pagani, 132–4.

[67] 'Apertis itaque libris, plura de amore quam de lectione verba se ingerebant; plura erant oscula quam sententiae; saepius ad sinus quam ad libros reducebantur manus', *HC* 14, ibid., 138.

[68] *HC* 12, ibid., 134.

[69] 'cum per faciem non esset infima' (*HC* 12, ibid., 134) does not mean 'se d'aspetto non era certo l'ultima' (ibid., 135) because the double negative, in Abelard's usage, is positive. Similar errors are to be found in English, German, French, and Spanish versions.

[70] 'per abundantiam litterarum erat suprema', *HC* 12, ibid., 134.

[71] 'Hanc igitur ... commodiorem censui in amorem mihi copulare et me id facillime credidi posse', *HC* 12, ibid., 134.

[72] See J. Adams, *The Latin Sexual Vocabulary* (London, 1982) 179.

taste for scholarship. This made his task 'easier' (*facilius*).[73] The odious
adverb is repeated.

The repetition emphasises that spontaneity was as far from Abelard's
sentiments for Heloise as was concern for her as a person in her own right.
Amor, here, means not an affair of the heart but the solipsism of a seducer.
He compounds his errors of taste and failures of feeling in his behaviour
towards her uncle. Fulbert was ingenuous. He did not suspect Abelard's
designs on his niece and, motivated by a desire to further her education,
urged him: 'to concentrate his efforts on teaching her both day and night
and, if I found her laggardly, *vehementer constringerem*'.[74] 'Discipline
severely' was what Fulbert meant (if he said this): 'embrace tightly' was the
sense which the subject chose to twist from the ambiguous verb. And as if
the innuendo were not all too obvious from the phrase 'day and night', this
ponderous pun is rubbed in.[75]

The writing is intended to draw attention to itself. That attention is not
favourable. The narrator inverts the commata around the subject's tale,
told with insufferable heavy-handedness. Everything has to be spelt out,
including how 'extremely' – *vehementer*, again – Abelard was 'astounded'
at Fulbert's surrender of Heloise's 'tender lamb' to his 'starving wolf'. These
coarse clichés of self-felicitation jar, and are meant to be heard to jar, with
the sobriety of the self-criticism voiced two chapters previously. The discord is deliberate, and enables the reader to understand what the narrator
meant when he described the subject as stupid. The moral and emotional
stupidity of Abelard at the time of his affair with Heloise is conveyed by
the garrulous style. But after the subject's verbosity has lowered the tone,
the narrator raises it with an observation that is brief and poignant. If
Fulbert was not suspicious, he explains, that was on account of 'his love for
his niece and my past reputation for continence'.[76]

The key word is 'past' (*preterita*). Once the supreme ideal, *fama* has
dwindled into a base illusion. The betrayal is double: of Fulbert's trust and
of Abelard's self. All that remains of both is, shadow without substance;
and when the subject explains that he wished to marry Heloise secretly,
in order to avoid 'loss of reputation',[77] that expression amounts to nothing more than keeping up appearances. To them Abelard clings with all

---

[73] 'tanto autem facilius hanc mihi consensuram credidi', *HC* 12, ed. Pagani, 134.
[74] 'tam in die quam in nocte ei docendae operam darem et eam, si negligentem sentirem, *vehementer constringerem*', *HC* 13, ibid., 136.
[75] 'Qui cum eam mihi … vehementer constringendam daret', ibid.
[76] 'amor … neptis et continentiae meae fama preterita', *HC* 13, ibid., 136.
[77] 'dummodo id secreto fieret, ne *famae detrimentum* incurrerem.' *HC* 16, ibid., 142.

the obduracy of his desire to remain the centre of attention. Did we not witness the popularity of the love-songs he composed when he ought to have been teaching?[78] No, we did not: what we notice is, while his fans sing to his tune, his students lament his distraction from scholarship. Both, for different reasons, still look to him. Obsessed by *fama*, Abelard has acquired a mixed reputation, but no ethical intelligence.

This moral midget affects to look down on those who are taller than he, such as Heloise's uncle. Before the subject shows us the extent of his arrogance towards Fulbert, the discovery of the affair and the consequences for the lovers are related.[79] The terms used are the most emotive yet to figure in the *HC*. All of them belong to the vocabulary of penance. None of them is employed in its strict sense. If Fulbert felt pain (*dolor*), so did the couple when it was separated. But Abelard and Heloise reunited in the symmetry of their sentiments. He, confounded and mortified (*erubescentia confusus*), experienced remorse (*contritio*) for her sufferings, together with shame. She was aggrieved by his grief (*quantos maeroris … aestus!*). Then a pattern studied in the first three chapters of this book emerged. Symmetry became inversion. Penitential emotions made Abelard and Heloise impenitent in their ardour. Shame gave way to shamelessness, inhibitions yielded to acts. Which acts, is indicated by an allusion to the fable of Venus and Mars. Only when they were caught *in flagranti* did the lovers interrupt this pirouette of *fictio*.

That concept was much discussed when Abelard wrote the *HC*. He alone treated *fictio* lightly. The academic category of *Sic et non* and the criterion of ethical literalism in *Scito te ipsum* is a figure of fun when applied here to his own experience. Bernard of Clairvaux would not have been amused. A handful of years earlier, in *De gradibus humilitatis et superbiae*, he had analysed feigning with the censoriousness he reserved for religious inauthenticity and spiritual insincerity. If Bernard's solemnity on the subject of *fictio* contrasts with Abelard's irony, the reason is not that the narrator of the *HC* was disposed to underrate the importance of penance. At this point he signals an issue which the subject treated flippantly, before he passed with equal superficiality over others that might have had a claim to serious attention.

Little attention is paid to familial relationships in the *HC*. When the couple realised that Heloise was pregnant, Abelard eloped with her to Brittany. There he left her with his sister until their son Astralabe was born. The son is named; the sister is not. Anonymous or marginal, this

---

[78] 'sicut et ipse nosti', *HC* 14, ibid., 138.   [79] *HC* 15, ibid., 140.

unenviable duo reappears in the *HC* but once.[80] Forthright about inverted
sentiments of penance, Abelard breaks his silence on the subject of natural
feelings (had he any) only in a cryptic diminutive (*parvulus noster*). In the
drama that unfolds, Astralabe has a bit-part. An obstacle in his father's way,
he is bundled off to his unnamed aunt. The attention which the subject
denies to his own offspring and relatives is trained on himself. He is auto-
referential even when he purports to be sympathising with the misfortunes
of Fulbert, who was nearly driven insane by a combination of grief and
shame which 'no one could understand but from experience'.[81] Urged to
bear witness to the popularity of Abelard's love-songs, we are debarred
from comprehending the torment of Heloise's uncle. So is the subject.
He claims to have sympathised with (*compatiens*) Fulbert, and to have
reproached himself for a betrayal equivalent to high treason. But Abelard's
compassion expressed itself as condescension.

Appealing to Fulbert's *savoir-faire* as a man of the world – which this
canon of Nôtre-Dame should not have had – the subject rehearsed his
banalities about the force of love and the ruinous effect of women on 'male
greatness' (*summos … viros*), such as his own. It is fame that extenuates for
Abelard's behaviour, and the threat of its loss that explains why he makes
the offer, 'beyond Fulbert's hopes', to marry Heloise secretly. Marriage as
a barrier to a clerical career in medieval Paris is not the only consideration
at this point. Equally significant is the ineptitude of the subject's attempt
to strike an ethical pose. Married and sensual, Abelard wishes to seem single and continent. He does so not out of concern for Fulbert or Heloise,
but because he is the dupe of his own illusions. If the threat of 'loss of
fame' entails keeping up appearances, *fama*, here, is equivalent to an empty
boast. The devaluation of this key term in the moral vocabulary of the *HC*
is now complete; and readers understand, with the lucidity of the narrator's hindsight, why Abelard regarded his castration as just punishment. It
was not unjust when Fulbert accepted his offer to marry Heloise 'in order
to betray me more easily'. For, among the kisses and oaths of their hypocritical accord, treachery embraced treachery.

As the narrative reaches this nadir, Heloise moves to centre-stage. Abelard's
dramatic imagination casts his characters as foils. Heloise plays the part of
altruistic intelligence; the subject takes the role of self-centred obtuseness.
Did he love her? The answer depends on what is meant by *amor*. Here that

[80] *HC* 20, ibid., 158.   [81] 'nemo nisi experiendo cognosceret' *HC*, 16 ibid., 142.

neutral noun is lent vivid colour and concrete meaning by the prominence which the narrator gives to her reported speech. The subject, previously reticent about her feelings except as viewed from his own standpoint, now falls silent; and in the longest ethopoeia of the *HC* resounds the eloquence of its leading lady.[82] Heloise's eloquence, learned and perceptive, is set against the subject's dim wordiness.

There are no ornamental quotations, no misleading allusions among her wealth of examples. Every one of her many references is to the point. Heloise's point is not just an argument against matrimony; she also develops further the narrator's reflections on continence.[83] It, as interpreted by the mother of Abelard's child, is little less than a natural virtue. Characteristic of both pagan and Jewish philosophers, who in this respect may be compared to monks, sexual abstinence is more than a question of discipline. Not confined to Christianity, at earlier periods and in different cultures, chaste living distinguished from the mass of the people an élite of the wise. Their *singularitas*, visible in the harmony they achieved between theory and practice, was ethical.

Ethical rather than theological, Heloise's thesis on continence is addressed to Abelard's 'standing as a philosopher' (*philosophi ... dignitatem*). She appeals to his 'love of uprightness' (*amor honestatis*), but does not refer to his *amor* for her. Nor does she mean what a theologian might have meant by grace when she distinguishes it sharply from the 'the constraint of the marital bond' (*vis ... vinculi nuptialis constringeret*). That is why it is mistaken to represent her as an advocate of 'free love' against marriage. Heloise urges on Abelard the virtue of continence in order to remind him of his proper role as philosopher. For her part, she claims only to be his *amica*. *Amica* does not mean 'girlfriend' (in the sense of 'mistress'), as opposed to 'wife'. The term refers to a bond of affection, gratuitous and reciprocal, devoid of legal constraints and social sanctions. *Gratia* is one of its defining qualities, which includes a spontaneity alien to the calculating seducer.

Abelard did not answer Heloise's case. The arch-dialectician lacked counter-arguments. He merely asserted his will, and she yielded out of fear of offending him. Consent, the moral and canonical basis of marriage,[84]

---

[82] *HC* 17–19, ibid., 144–56.   [83] *HC*, 19 ibid., 150.

[84] See H. Ziementz, *Ehe nach der Lehre der Frühscholastik: Eine moralgeschichtliche Untersuchung zur Anthropologie und Theologie der Ehe in der Schule Anselms von Laon und Wilhelms von Champeaux, bei Hugo von St. Viktor, Walter von Mortagne und Petrus Lombardus*, Moraltheologische Studien. Historische Abteilung 1 (Düsseldorf, 1973) 111ff.; J. Noonan, 'Power to Choose' *Viator* 4 (1973) 419–34; J. Gaudemet, 'La définition romano-canonique du marriage' in *Speculum iuris et ecclesiarum* (Vienna, 1967) 107–14; J. Brundage, 'Concubinage

was not what she gave to his insistence. Nor did he learn from what might be called her cultural relativism. Conceding that a measure of goodness can be possessed by pagan philosophers, whom he placed on the same level as monks, in the second book of his *Theologia christiana*,[85] Abelard may perhaps have inspired Heloise's thought.[86] But if he did not learn from her in this respect, he did in another. For the second time in the *HC*, its narrator condemns the subject as stupid.[87] Experience had taught him what, a decade and a half earlier, he did not wish to understand. Wilfully ignorant of the criterion of consent as he then was, Abelard marks sharply the difference between his former self and the morally intelligent Heloise.

Intelligence made her prophetic. Foreseeing grief in the future equal to the passion of the past, Heloise was confirmed in her accuracy by 'the entire world'.[88] Complicity on the part of an anonymous *amicus* is not sought. The facts, no longer slanted by insinuation or bent by collusion, are evident to all. And before dealing with the notorious facts of his castration, which represented one of the two most traumatic experiences of his life, Abelard pays homage to the foresight of the woman who considered herself the cause of his woes. It is in the light of this tribute that the feelings of guilt and self-recrimination later expressed in Heloise's letters must be considered. Abelard has been reproached for his 'apparent lack of sympathy, [his] failure to engage with her plight'.[89] To him, this was not the issue. The issue here, amplified in his other writings on the subject, was that Heloise had no responsibility for his calamity and its consequences.

They were his fault alone. This frankness in acknowledging fault is different from the narrator's previous criticisms of the subject. The shortcomings of Abelard's former self are not judged in terms of an ancient ideal that demanded chastity from philosophers. The criterion here is strictly personal. His conduct is condemned in the terms that, to him, had mattered most. 'The entire world' attests to Heloise's innocence; *fama* is on her side. Alone in the ignominy of a castration which he deemed he had brought

and Marriage in Medieval Canon Law', *Journal of Medieval History* 1 (1975) 1–18; and I. Rosier-Catach, *La parole efficace: Signe, rituel, sacré* (Paris, 2004) 324ff.
[85] See Marenbon, *Philosophy*, 306 and I. Bejczy, 'The Problem of Natural Virtue' in Bejczy and Newhauser (eds.), *Virtue and Ethics*, 139 with relevant texts and bibliography.
[86] See, further, J. Marenbon, 'Abélard: les exemples des philosophes et les philosophes comme exemples' in *Exempla docent: Les exemples des philosophes de l'Antiquité à la Renaissance*, Actes du colloque international 23–25 octobre 2003 Université de Neuchâtel, ed. T. Richlin (Paris, 2006) 119–34.
[87] 'cum meam deflectere non posset stultitiam', *HC* 17, ed. Pagani, 156.
[88] 'Nec in hoc, *sicut universus agnovit mundus*, prophetiae defuit spiritus', *HC* 19, ibid., 158.
[89] Marenbon, *Philosophy*, 72.

on himself, Abelard experiences the opposite of his craving to have all eyes trained on him. The desire to look away from himself and his guilt, at this moment, might have overcome another author. Retrospection was not consoling. Nor did the circumstances in which he wrote the *HC* offer comfort to Abelard. In the wilds of barbarous Brittany, amid the squalor of Saint-Gildas, where murderers who were monks only in name resisted his reforms and threatened his life, a lesser man might have composed a lamentation on what seemed to him the beginning of calamities without end. That is what a copyist considered Abelard had done when he disfigured this work with the title by which it is now known; and familiarity has bred, if not contempt, a tendency to take too much for granted.

Everyone knows about his castration, but everyone does not appear to have reflected on the problems, ethical and literary, with which the writer who had suffered it was confronted when he had to find a place for this appalling theme in his autobiography. No one before Abelard had described his own unmanning in the learned or vernacular languages of medieval Europe. The only analogy to his own case that he detected was that of Origen, and it hardly helped him to frame his experience, for he goes on to emphasise the differences between them.[90] The situation, unparalleled and unprecedented, tempted to silence or self-pity. Abelard resisted that temptation and faced the facts with resolution.

His castration, described as 'most cruel and shameful', is also accepted as an act of revenge, undertaken in a punitive spirit.[91] Punishment had not been a category which the subject had cared to acknowledge. He saw only *invidia*, which was his way of saying that, when things went wrong, he was never to blame. Now the narrator of the *HC*, with a circumlocution that might have become pompous in less skilled hands, detects a precise symmetry between his crime and his castration.[92] The punishment was just in terms of God, of Fulbert, and even of his enemies whose malice revelled in 'such manifest equity'.[93] There, in the obviousness to everyone, lay the pain. Less physical than social, it derived from the same source that bore witness to Heloise's innocence. As the world looked on 'with the utmost amazement',[94] which he had felt at her uncle's ingenuity, Abelard suffered the agony of shame.

---

[90] See Chapter 5.
[91] 'crudelissima et pudentissima ultione punierunt' *HC* 20, ed. Pagani, 158.
[92] 'eis ... corporis mei partibus amputatis, quibus id quod plangebant commiseram', ibid.
[93] 'Occurrebat animo ... quam iusto Dei iudicio in illa corporis mei portione plecterer, in qua deliqueram, quam iusta proditione is, quem antea prodideram, vicem mihi retulisset; quanta laude mei aemuli tam manifestam aequitatem efferrent', *HC* 21, ibid., 160–2.
[94] 'quam summa admiratione mundus excepit', *HC* 21, ibid., 158 and cf. 21 *ad int.* ibid., 160.

Shame, the 'emotion of self-protection',[95] left him with nowhere to turn. Disgraced before others, he felt revulsion at himself. The pity of his pupils, the gloating of his enemies, the concern of his friends – all of this was worse than the injury of the wound. Mortification rather than castration caused a torment which is described in penitential language.[96] Embarrassment (*erubescentia*) and shame (*pudor*), in this context, acquire a different flavour from the spice of the illicit savoured by Abelard and Heloise when Fulbert discovered their affair. That was a private matter. The emotions it evoked were fickle and ephemeral. This public scandal, by contrast, attracted universal attention, intolerable because it was the exact contrary of what he had always sought. Fingers pointing, tongues tattling, everyone everywhere singling him out as a 'monstrous prodigy':[97] for this slave of fame, accustomed to seeing himself as others saw him, there was no alternative perspective. Too blinkered to look inside himself, he was now compelled, by his moral myopia, to interiorise *infamia*.

Its effect is summed up, in a further play on penitential language, as *contritio*.[98] Felt both by Abelard and by his friends and relatives, the emotion had nothing to do with active contrition for sin. Abasement, passive and involuntary, was thrust upon him and his sympathisers. The term serves to highlight his lack of vocation when he entered the life of perpetual Lent at Saint-Denis. Abelard needed protection not from the remorse for his faults which he ought to have felt but from the sense of being lowered which was their consequence. Humiliated rather than penitent, more confused than contrite, he sought refuge from his shame by acting as if he believed that the habit made the monk. *Fictio*, in one of its graver forms, was committed by Abelard when he took vows. Their religious sincerity was meant to be expressed in a consent which he did not give wholeheartedly.[99]

Few flouted the criterion of consent more blatantly than its later exponent in *Scito te ipsum*. First Abelard insisted on marrying Heloise against

---

[95] G. Taylor, *Pride, Shame, and Guilt* (Oxford, 1985) 81.

[96] 'plus erubescentiam quam plagam sentirem et pudore magis quam dolore affligerer', *HC* 21, ed. Pagani, 160.

[97] 'quanta dilatatione haec singularis infamia universum mundum esset occupatura … qua fronte in publicum prodirem *omnium digitis* demonstrandus, *omnium linguis* corrodendus, *omnibus monstruosum spectaculum* futurus', *HC* 21, ibid., 162. On legal aspects of the problem, see the interesting study by S. Murphy, 'The Letter of the Law: Abelard, Moses, and the Problem with Being a Eunuch', *Journal of Medieval History* 30 (2004) 161–87 and cf. Y. Ferroul, 'Bienheureuse castration: Sexualité et vie intellectuelle à l'époque d'Abélard', *Bien dire et bien apprendre* 4 (1986) 1–28.

[98] 'In tam misera me contritione positus confusio, fateor, pudoris potius quam devotio conversionis ad monasticorum latibula claustrorum compulit', *HC* 21, ed. Pagani, 162–4.

[99] Constable, *Reformation*, 18.

her wish. Then he entered monasticism without conviction. And he also omitted to obtain the agreement of his wife which canon law required. His successive actions *c.*1115–*c.*1118 make it clear that the idea of *consensus* had never entered his head. What motivated Abelard's conduct was, self-will. The self-will of the subject, in its disregard of others' interests, is summed up by the paradox, or the oxymoron, with which the narrator describes his next offence. Abelard forced Heloise to take the veil 'at my command, voluntarily' (*ad imperium nostrum sponte velata*).[100] What this means is, she conformed her will to his. Her 'spontaneity' defined in terms of acquiescence in his dominance, the implicitly self-critical phrase combines two elements: the one original, the other borrowed. *Sponte* derives from the famous speech of Lucan's Cornelia (*Bellum civile* VIII.98) which Heloise goes on to quote;[101] *ad imperium* is Abelard's own. His own, therefore, is the admission that, yet again, her consent was coerced.

Coercion is an act of moral violence alien to the nature of monasticism. Monasticism, however, admitted the idea of self-punishment. Even the exercise of free will, in this context, could be regarded as punitive. Those who took vows were thought to commit themselves to serve out a life-sentence of penance for their sins. When her acquaintances, moved by compassion for her youth, tried to deter Heloise from such an 'unbearable punishment' (*tamquam intolerabili poena*),[102] the expression was in keeping with ordinary usage. Far from ordinary was her own reference to the same term. For how could she accept punishment when, on Abelard's account, she was innocent of blame? What Heloise did not say is significant. She refrained from contradicting his judgement. But to accept his assertion of her guiltlessness would have amounted, in her view, to a disavowal of her husband. Were they not united – one flesh and, above all, one will? It was his will, not hers, that had determined her every action, from their affair to their marriage; and it followed from his imperiousness that, on the issue of her taking the veil, 'at my command, voluntarily,' his remained the last word. Abelard's last word left Heloise with few of her own; and it is indicative of her speechless state that what follows, in the *HC*, is a quotation within a quotation.

No matter whether she really recited the lines from Lucan attributed to her,[103] nor is it of much moment that ethopoeia could be flexible in Latin. What counts here is, to note a telling change in the style. Heloise's

---

[100] *HC* 21, ed. Pagani, 164.
[101] The best study is by von Moos, 'Cornelia und Heloise' in *Abaelard und Heloise*, 129–62.
[102] *HC* 21, ed. Pagani, 164.
[103] Cf. von Moos, *Abaelard und Heloise*, 152 and n. 78.

reported quotation is introduced with *ait*, not *dixit* or *locuta est*. The shift from the perfect tense of the narrative to the historic present sends a signal that use is being made of the inverted commata in which Abelard was expert. More expert than he in citation, Heloise employs Cornelia's speech to compare him with Pompey the Great in defeat. The figure to whom Abelard had likened Anselm of Laon is restored to his proper role of pathos. That pathos is enhanced by parallels between Heloise's quotations and her previous utterances. When, for example, she cites Cornelia's lament on the greatness of her husband – 'Oh, greatest of husbands, you do not deserve to be wed to me!' (*O maxime coniunx! / O thalamis indigne meis!* (*Bellum civile* VIII.94–5)) – these verses can be construed as a poetic paraphrase of her speech against matrimony. A 'disgrace', a 'humiliation', and a 'curse' for Abelard's standing, his marriage with her, Heloise had argued, would oblige the world to punish her severely: *quantas a ea* [= *Heloissa*] *mundus poenas exigeret*.[104]

This is the thought that can be linked with her citation of Cornelia's willing acceptance of punishment: *nunc accipe poenas, / sed quas sponte luam* (*Bellum civile* VIII.97–8). More is meant than the punitive character of monasticism. What Heloise struggles to express is, a sense of transferred guilt. Neither directly nor indirectly responsible for Abelard's castration, she assumes the blame for it, because repeated subordination of her will to his leads her to identify with his plight. Taking the veil is the effect, not the cause, of Heloise's self-recrimination, which produces her distinctive paradox of guilt in innocence. Without a will of her own, she claims to act 'voluntarily' (*sponte*). Abelard has already explained the meaning of that adverb. It does, and can, not imply spontaneity, because that has been taken from Heloise by her thrall to him. So it is that she again resorts to ventriloquism. Cornelia is not her model but her mouthpiece. Quotation provides the measure of Heloise's inarticulateness.

In these circumstances, which strained the limits of language, understatement was required; and the narrator's verbal minimalism enhances his dramatic effect. Heloise 'hastens' (*properat*) to the altar and, taking from it a veil blessed by the bishop, 'without ado' (*confestim*) makes her monastic profession 'before everyone' (*coram omnibus*).[105] Prompt in her obedience, this Christian Iphigeneia offers herself up as a sacrifice to her husband's shame. Unlike Jephtha's daughter in Abelard's *planctus* on the not unrelated subject of her immolation in fulfilment of her father's rash vow,[106] Heloise

---

[104] *HC* 17, ed. Pagani, 144.   [105] *HC* 22, ibid., 164–6.
[106] Ed. and trans. P. Zumthor, *Abélard: Lamentations* (Paris, 1992) 47–61.

says nothing; nor does the narrator. 'Before everyone' – that omnipresent, omniscient audience whose favour Abelard had courted and whose attendance on his downfall he had deplored – the facts speak for themselves.

There is no place here for a *planctus*. Nor has the scene much to do with the defeat of Pompey the Great and the sorrow of his wife. Heloise bears no real resemblance to Cornelia at this point and medieval modes of reading the *Bellum civile*, which selected passages that became proverbial,[107] are irrelevant to Abelard's eloquent reticence. He cannot enlist a friend's sympathy, because he feels none for himself. Everyone witnesses Heloise's tragedy, and no one doubts its cause. Its cause is his self-will; its effect is an equation. By the inflexible rules of Abelard's solipsism, his calamity became Heloise's. She is his victim; she therefore suffers 'voluntary punishment'. In that paradox, the conscience of the narrator has passed a verdict without appeal on the unconscionable subject.

---

[107] Cf. E. Sanford, 'Quotations from Lucan in Medieval Latin Authors', *American Journal of Philology* 55 (1934) 1–19 and von Moos, *Abaelard und Heloise*, 137ff.

CHAPTER 5

Cain and conscience

Cain, for the High Middle Ages, was not only the murderer of Abel. He was also a killer of the conscience. This anti-type of the penitent, obdurate in mortal sin, never failed to attract ignominy. St Augustine's founder of the earthly city was a *figura* of the Jews who crucified Christ for St Ambrose.[1] Destined to wander, *vagus et profugus* (Genesis 4:12, 14), in a no man's land of alienation, the cursed outcast became the equivalent of a moral leper. Who would liken himself to Cain? Abelard, is the answer – at least twice in the *HC*. The one analogy is explicit and self-explanatory;[2] the other, implicit in his account of the council of Soissons and its sequel, marks the point at which the subject endures a trauma of speechless alienation from God, from others, and from himself. There is no term in Latin to define this condition of moral muteness. Incapable of definition, it had to be evoked with the connotations of Cain. Abelard does so with a skill that was unmatched and remains unappreciated. His achievement is both conceptual and literary. As the subject of the *HC*, who had become the slave of fame, casts off the self-made chains that bound him, the narrator shows how he acquired a different moral identity.

'Conscience' is not used at this turning-point of the narrative; and those who have studied Abelard's ideas on the subject rarely take it into account.[3] They confine themselves to what he states. Latent meaning is hardly

---

[1] Augustine, *De civitate Dei* XIV.15ff. *S. Aurelii Augustini De civitate Dei XI–XXII*, ed. Dombert and Kalb, CCSL 48, 436ff; Ambrose, *De Cain et Abel* I.2.5, ed. K. Schenkl, CSEL 32, 1 (Vienna, 1896) 341, 16ff. For context, see the valuable article by S. Schrenk, 'Kain und Abel' in *RLAC* XIX, 943–7 and cf. B. Töpfer, *Urzustand und Sündenfall in der mittelalterlichen Gesellschafts – und Staatstheorie*, Monographien zur Geschichte des Mittelalters 45 (Stuttgart, 1999) 59ff.; and R. Markus, *Saeculum: History and Society in the Theology of St. Augustine* (Cambridge, 1970) 45ff. Not directly related to this theme, but stimulating in their implications for it, are K. Hoheisel, 'Die Auslegung alttestamentlicher Opferzeugnisse im Neuen Testament und in der frühen Kirche', *Frühmittelalterliche Studien* 18 (1984) 421–36 and A. Angenendt, 'Sühne durch Blut' *Frühmittelalterliche Studien* 18, 437–67.
[2] *HC* 53, ed. Pagani, 226.
[3] The exception is Perkams, *Liebe als Zentralbegriff*, 264–6 with brief but pertinent remarks.

recognised as an issue in his thought. Yet if philosophy is restricted to an explicit set of propositions or a specific series of doctrines, these a-historical limits exclude not only the medieval tour de force which is Peter Abelard's autobiography but also the modern masterpiece of therapeutic investigation, Ludwig Wittgenstein's *Philosophische Untersuchungen*.[4] Both of them were concerned with what, in ethics, can be seen but not said. Inexpressibility is a theme which Abelard develops, in the *HC*, when relating the events of Soissons and their sequel. There emerges, perhaps for the first time in his extant works, a view of the conscience which cannot simply be defined in such terms as: 'most generally ... our power to recognise obvious truths',[5] or 'the application of reasoned reflection to known precepts' by an 'authority', comprehensive and subjective, which 'judges one's own personality'.[6]

Different though they are, these definitions are complementary. Both appear to rest on the assumption that, when the word 'conscience' is absent, the concept too is lacking. Each of them attributes priority to intellectual cognition. For good reasons. Was it not a premise of ancient thought, influential during the Middle Ages, that definite knowledge was required before a choice could be made or a decision taken?[7] The application of this premise to Abelard's morality of intended actions is valid, as far as it goes. But does it go far enough? It explains nothing about the emergence of that morality on the part of one who, to judge by his autobiography up to 1121, had not thought about ethics. How did Abelard become a prominent figure in a field where, by his own admission, he had been a midget? Through experience, which forced him to reflect in categories with which he had been unfamiliar. Logic was insufficient to overcome the trauma of Soissons. At that council and afterwards, the dialectician was faced with an existential dilemma in which knowledge could not be definite, truth was uncertain, and reason was hardly capable of assessing itself or others. This was the state of moral malaise which Abelard treated by developing his earliest ideas on the conscience.

∽

Their development in the *HC* is gradual but dramatic. That analogy, drawn in the previous chapter, is again meant literally. Abelard depicts a drama of the inner life which unfolds at a calculated pace. The absence of moral

---

[4] See D. Pears, *Paradox and Platitude in Wittgenstein's Philosophy* (Oxford, 2006) and cf. J. Gibson and W. Huemer (eds.), *The Literary Wittgenstein* (London, 2005).
[5] Marenbon, *Philosophy*, 274 and cf. Marenbon in *Peter Abelard, Collationes* 8, n. 11: 'a sort of intellectual honesty'.
[6] Perkams, *Liebe als Zentralbegriff*, 121 and 125.   [7] Dihle, *Theory of the Will*, 67ff.

actors matters, as does the point at which they are admitted to the scene. Although conscience began to make a late entry at the time of his castration, it was far from occupying the limelight. Acknowledging his guilt and accepting his punishment as just, the subject of the *HC* was incapable of facing infamy. He fled from it into Saint-Denis. And in that act of *fictio*, attenuated only by diminished responsibility on grounds of humiliation, he did not reflect that he had been humiliated earlier by himself. When Abelard married Heloise in secret, the unthinking minion of *fama* allowed the ideal of his youth to degenerate from the criterion by which he asserted his intellectual authority against that of his elders into a source and a cause of deception. If Fulbert's henchmen made him a eunuch, Abelard had unmanned his ethical identity before their blows struck.

Now he had only the potential one of a monk, which others attempted to reconcile with his former role as a teacher. Abelard did not become a 'philosopher of God' on his own initiative. The initiative is attributed to 'clerics' who entreated him and his abbot that he should continue to lecture. Like the students who supported him at Laon against Anselm, they offered not only evidence of his didactic popularity but also proof of his enduring fame. Casting a 'net baited with philosophical flavour',[8] and becoming an apostolic fisher of minds and of souls, he modified the part he had played, without radically changing his character. Gratified as ever by the flattering attentions of his admirers, Abelard was still susceptible to *fama*.

Even more susceptible to *infamia*, he acquired a zest for attributing it to others. Strikingly full of himself, even in reversal, the subject of the *HC* is even more remarkable for his lack of self-consciousness. In terms that recalled the behaviour which had led to his just punishment, this humiliated monk set about humiliating his abbot. Adam of Saint-Denis led a 'filthy life', worse than that of his subordinates. So had Abelard; and this no doubt made him alert to the *infamia* with which he reproached his superior 'frequently and emphatically' (*frequenter atque vehementer*) both in private and in public.[9] The rapidity of Abelard's transformation from an unethical seducer to an inverted moralist appears to have prevented him from recognising the symmetry between Adam's case and his own. But another symmetry with his past did not fail to make itself obvious. Yet again he became 'intolerable and odious beyond measure' (*supra modum onerosum atque odiosum*).

[8] *HC* 22, ed. Pagani, 166.   [9] *HC* 23, ibid., 168–70.

Supra modum acknowledges that a limit has been trespassed. The expression is the narrator's, not the subject's. He, at this stage of his development, recognised no limits, because he saw everything in relation to himself. That relationship, too close to his immediate past for comfort, might have given Abelard grounds to reflect on the just measure of criticism. He did not. Ostracism followed. When he was effectively relegated to an outpost (*cella*) of Saint-Denis, he faced a problem different from the ones with which he had been familiar. It was nothing new when Abelard's teaching there provoked envy (*invidia*). Novel, in the *HC*, is the hatred (*odium*) he inspired in his rivals, who alleged that he taught what he had not studied in violation of his duties as a monk. Now the charge against Abelard was not only intellectual and personal but also institutional. The ecclesiastical establishment was urged to intervene. And what he did was, nothing.

Nothing was done by Abelard to counter the charges made against him to the authorities because he viewed this problem at a different level. At the level of argument and of learning, he thought it sufficient to discredit his opponents by accurate citation of the Bible and the Fathers.[10] Worsting others in scholarship, Abelard believed he had won. Capable of registering *odium*, he did not understand how he provoked and deepened it in Abbot Adam and his rivals. He continued to parrot the language of self-love. Can this conduct be interpreted as a *faux pas*? If the question is debatable,[11] it is clear that, responsive only to reason and to the applause of pupils, allies, and partisans, Abelard placed his confidence in the support of those who, rejecting empty verbosity, wanted 'what can be understood rather than said'.[12] These, in his eyes, were the terms of the debate between himself and his enemies; and as he defines them, the themes of inexpressibility and of rational understanding are introduced. They are relevant to the crisis of 1121.

We cannot verify Abelard's account of proceedings at the council of Soissons. The sources are too scant. Enough is known, however, to establish an affinity between his trial for heresy before a synodal court and the one that, in the previous century, had secured the condemnation of Berengar of Tours.[13] The *damnatio memoriae* of Berengar suggested the need for a

[10] *HC* 27, ibid., 180.
[11] No, B. Jussen, 'Nicht einmal zwischen den Zeilen'; perhaps yes, on other criteria, G. Algazi, 'Gelehrte Zerstreutheit und gelernte Vergeßlichkeit' both in *Der Fehltritt* ed. von Moos, 105ff., 235ff. See further below.
[12] 'plus quae intelligi quam quae dici possent efflagitabant', *HC* 24, ed. Pagani, 172.
[13] J. Miethke, 'Theologenprozesse in der ersten Phase ihrer institutionellen Ausbildung: die Verfahren gegen Peter Abelard und Gilbert von Poitiers', *Viator* 6 (1995) 91ff.

strategy of rehabilitation,[14] which was another of Abelard's motives for writing the *HC*. An obvious tactic was, to impugn the prosecutors and the judge. This he does, but less bluntly than his notoriety as a polemicist might lead one to expect. Absent are the sneers and the sarcasm directed at the dullness of Anselm of Laon or the ambition of William of Champeaux in the earlier part of the work. Irony takes their place. What Abelard describes, with a dramatist's flair for revealing gestures and telling expressions, is a cross between a tragedy, a comedy, and a farce.

The villains of the piece are already familiar from his encounter with them at Laon: Alberic of Reims and Lotulf of Novara, envious of his celebrity and eager to do him down. Their ally in high places is Raoul le Verd, archbishop of Reims, who combines the roles of power-broker and windbag. Between the accused and his adversaries stands Geoffrey of Lèvres, bishop of Chartres, who plays the unenviable part of prisoner's friend. And above this mixed cast of characters (or below it) teeters the comic figure of Cuno of Preneste, cardinal and papal legate, who never opens his mouth except to put his foot in it.

Naturally, Abelard does not say so. He implies as much. His implications are subversive of the hierarchical status that constituted Cuno of Preneste's only claim to authority. A different claim to *auctoritas*, based on scholarship, is advanced by antithesis in Abelard's description of Cuno as 'less learned than would have been required' (*minus quam necesse esset litteratus*).[15] The impersonal verb, characteristic of the pomposity of prelates which he goes on to mock, is couched in the hypothetical subjunctive. A question is begged: 'would have been required' *for what?* To judge competently, is the answer hinted by the euphemism. Euphemism is not assertion. Much hinges on tone. And in this tone of understated irony, the scene is set for a clash.

Before the clash is enacted between the authority of the ecclesiastical establishment, represented by Cuno of Preneste and Raoul of Reims, and the authority of scholarship, in the persons of Abelard and Thierry of Chartres, a travesty of a trial takes place. Unexamined, the *Theologia 'Summi boni'* by the accused is condemned to be thrown into the flames with his own hands. This is the point where righteous indignation might have given vent to polemic. With a dramatic sense of suspense, Abelard holds back. Only after the work was burnt did one of his enemies – unnamed, as if anonymous – speak out.

---

[14] See G. Macy, 'Berengar's Legacy as Heresiarch' in *Auctoritas und Ratio: Studien zu Berengar von Tours*, ed. P. Ganz, Wolfenbüttler Mittelalterliche Studien 2 (Wiesbaden, 1990) 47–67.
[15] *HC* 30, ed. Pagani, 184.

Or rather he did not speak out. He 'murmured' (*submurmuravit*). The verb connotes a furtive insinuation, not an open charge. Furtive because the evidence for it had just been destroyed, the insinuation that Abelard believed only God the Father to be omnipotent was made 'in order to avoid giving the impression that they [his enemies] had said nothing'. Abelard himself says little in the way of direct comment. But he implies a great deal with *sub-*. The prefix is repeated. When the legate 'got wind of' (*subintellexit*) this insinuation, he exclaimed that even 'a little child' (*puerulus*) would not have made so elementary an error. That the error was Cuno of Preneste's – who had not understood that Abelard attributed power to God in particular, without denying it to the other two members of the Trinity – was pointed out by Thierry of Chartres who 'subjoined' his corrective quotation from the Athanasian Creed 'with a scoff' (*irridens subintulit*).

The function of this triad of *sub*-s is to reduce authorial intervention to a minimum. Abelard's verbal minimalism here serves to maximize his comic effect. Repetition of the prefix hints, with untranslatable economy, at an interpretation that he refrains from spelling out. Beneath the level of reasoned argument and demonstrable proof, proceedings at Soissons were first conducted in an underhand manner by the prosecution, then with inferior competence by the judge. *Sub-* delineates a sequence – from insinuation to error and correction – which sets the unnamed enemy, the papal legate, and Abelard's defender on the same stylistic level, in order to emphasise their differences. And rather than interpose a plaidoyer for himself, this master of understatement allows Thierry of Chartres to steal the show, the farcical nature of which is exposed by his scoff or laugh.

No one laughs today at the *HC* in the spirit of complicity which its author aimed to inspire in his readers. That complicity depends on recognition of Abelard's irony. Not to state but to imply that his adversary was malevolent and the legate ignorant demanded restraint. And since restraint is not commonly attributed to Abelard, it may be worth noting that it is enhanced by a further quality never ascribed to his autobiography. It is not the least of his achievements that, when recounting his traumatic experiences at Soissons, he was capable of presenting them as a tragi-comedy whose farcical aspects are funny. Ignored by detractors whose sense of humour is not equal to Abelard's, they have done nothing to hinder the misplaced solemnity with which the *HC* has often been read.

Solemnity, feigned to mask deviousness, and pomposity, employed to lend an air of respectability to bluster and bluff, are Abelard's next targets. Both are embodied in Raoul of Reims. The archbishop upbraided Thierry of Chartres 'as if he had committed *lèse-majesté*' or worse. Worse, because the Latin *in maiestatem loqui* is ambiguous, referring both to treason and to blasphemy. To that double-edged rebuke Thierry replied with the unequivocal authority of the Bible. Capping his quotation from the Athanasian Creed, he went one better in boldness with a Scriptural allusion (Daniel 13:48ff.) to Susanna's trial on false charges. And as the scholar undermined the prelate's authority by appeal to another that could not be challenged, Raoul 'changed the terms of the debate, as was proper' (*verbis prout oportebat commutatis*).[16]

'As was proper': here the irony directed at Cuno of Preneste becomes satire of Raoul of Reims. The parallel reinforces the piquancy. *Oportebat*, the second impersonal verb aligned with *necesse esset*, is indicative, not subjunctive, because Abelard wishes to emphasise, in the unqualified language of propriety, the improper nature of the tactic. Why was it 'proper' for Raoul of Reims to change the terms of the debate? Because, on those set by Thierry of Chartres, he could not win. Pretending to defer to the legate's opinion, the archbishop effectively took matters in hand – not by answering Thierry but by launching into an argument *ad hominem*. Anyone who did not hold the belief that all three members of the Trinity were omnipotent must be deviant and should not be heard. That meant Abelard. And as if to complete the trap, Raoul of Reims proposed that the accused should expound his faith 'to be approved or reproved and corrected'. Yet even then this pompous prelate did not get to the point. He hedged it about with formulas of courtesy (*si placet*), of commendation (*bonum est*), and of decorum (*prout oportet*). It is that last expression which Abelard satirises with his own *prout oportebat*. The echo magnifies Raoul's empty rhetoric of Pharisaïsm.

The pharisaical archbishop betrays his designs with his own words, some of which resound like Abelard's. He, ordered Raoul of Reims, was to expound his faith publicly (*coram omnibus*). But the accused had already done so. Every day, before the council sat, Abelard had explained his position *in publico omnibus*.[17] Synonymy highlighted difference. Raoul applied the expression to a show-trial: Abelard employed it of the people and the clergy who had received his teaching with acclaim. 'He speaks boldly' (*palam loquitur*), his public had said. The lucidity of the defendant contrasts with the verbosity (deprecated by Abelard's pupils) of the prosecutor-cum-judge. And the Biblical flavour of the language serves to

---

[16] *HC* 31, ibid., 186.   [17] *HC* 26, ibid., 176.

spice the antithesis. *Palam loquitur* alludes to John 7:26. There the Jews go on to ask: 'Do the rulers indeed know that this is the very Christ?' Christ-like previous to the council that condemned his book, Abelard portrays himself as crucified by the travesty of a trial at Soissons. Travesty is disfigured into grotesque by his enemies' refusal to let him express himself and by their insistence that he recite the Athanasian Creed, 'of which any child (*puer*) would have been capable'. The echo is again ominous. Assigned the role of a *puer*, whom Cuno of Preneste had deemed unworthy to commit Abelard's 'error', one of the most advanced theologians of the age was reduced to the level of a beginner. Compelled to read aloud the text, held before him as if he did not know it off by heart, he submitted to a humiliating ritual of enforced penance.

The humiliation endured by Peter Abelard recalled an ancient form of *poenitentia publica* not yet defunct in the twelfth century. Recollection was painful, because what he suffered at Soissons amounted to a caricature of the model. The voluntary nature of public penance had been fundamental since late antiquity. Of their own will, sinners expressed grief in self-abasement before the faithful, motivated by a sense of personal responsibility towards God. Abelard, in 1121, had no choice; responsibility was taken from him. Atonement appeared indistinguishable from punishment. In these cruel circumstances, even the character of his emotions was distorted. The 'sobs, sighs, and tears' with which he read aloud the Athanasian Creed were, or seemed to be, identical to the sorrow displayed by penitents on such occasions. In a symmetry of inversions, Abelard was compelled to play a role he rejected without consciousness of guilt or consolation of forgiveness.

Made to seem what he was not, he went on to reflect on the moral difference between appearance and reality. At stake was his ethical identity. Reconstructing it in the sequel to Soissons, Abelard was aided by the thought of Saints Ambrose and Gregory the Great on the relevant subject of penance. Both of them attached cardinal importance to spiritual sincerity. Both of them were suspicious of emotional ostentation, dismissing the stage-effects of *poenitentia publica* as beside the point.[18] The point was not the theatrical effect wrought on men by self-punishment but grief for offences committed against God. That contrast between outward show and inner authenticity shaped Abelard's reflection on his experience, and contributed to the antithetical terms in which he went on to formulate his doctrine of contrition. The essence of *contritio*, as Abelard interpreted

---

[18] See Chapter 2 above.

it,[19] was the personal responsibility denied him in 1121. That responsibility was to be expressed directly, without intermediary, by the sinner to God. Neither of these ideas was novel. Distinctive of Abelard's approach was the exclusion he took them to entail. Excluded was human justice, capable only of assessing actions; the focus being set instead on the divine tribunal, which knows the *arcana cordis*. As Abelard interprets the canonists' maxim, ecclesiastical courts are unequal to retributive justice, which he reserves to God.[20] If this antithesis owes much to his condemnation by human misjudgement, it is also informed by the opposition between the external and internal spheres of the moral life that is characteristic of the *Moralia in Iob*.[21] These factors combined to lend Abelard's thought on the subject of penance an anti-institutional cast.

It is not true, as is sometimes asserted, that he devalued confession in favour of contrition. The priority of *contritio*, not its predominance, is his (far from original and wholly orthodox) argument. Yet it is noteworthy that Abelard's overriding concern with the personal responsibility of the sinner to God obscured a distinction drawn by other theologians and canonists. They claimed that, if the Church was incapable of judging the secrets of the heart in an ecclesiastical court, it could do so in the forum of penance, as *Ecclesia Dei*. After Soissons, Abelard was understandably inclined to regard these two tribunals as one and the same; and his scepticism towards both precluded sympathy for the doctrine, consolidating during and shortly after his lifetime, which likened the confessor's knowledge of sin to that of God.[22] Divine infallibility, for Abelard, was separate from and superior to the aberrant opinions of men. When he cited the case, standard in the penitential handbooks over centuries,[23] of a mother condemned, although guiltless of intending to smother her baby, one of his aims was to demonstrate that the exemplary punishment of inadvertent offenders had nothing to do with moral justice.[24] The cast of mind behind this example and others, in *Scito te ipsum*, of the incompatibility between legal formalism and the claims of the conscience has its origins in Abelard's trauma of 1121. And that is why it was consistent both with his faith in the efficacy of contrition and with his misgivings about the administration of

---

[19] A formal analysis of this concept is provided by Anciaux, *Théologie* 64ff., 176ff., 286ff.
[20] *Ethics*, ed. Luscombe, 40, 7ff.; *Scito te ipsum* 1.25, ed. Ilgner, 26, 683ff. and see Kuttner, 'Ecclesia de occultis non iudicat'.
[21] See Dagens, *Saint Grégoire*, 168ff.   [22] See Chapter 3 above and Chapter 6 below.
[23] See Chapter 2 above.
[24] *Ethics*, ed. Luscombe, 38, 13ff. and *Scito te ipsum*, ed. Ilgner, 24, 3ff.; 25, 658ff. See further Chapter 7 below.

penance that he denied it independent status as a sacrament, subsuming it under *caritas*[25] – a virtue notably lacking at the council that had humiliated him.

∽

These tensions in Abelard's moral and doctrinal thought first emerge in the *HC*. The Christ-like expounder of his own theology before the beginning of the trial became the crucified reciter of another's creed at its end. 'As if' (*quasi*) 'guilty and convicted', he was handed over to the monastery of Saint-Médard 'as though' (*tamquam*) 'it were a prison'.[26] The hypothetical heretic deserved a notional jail. And in this dialectic between appearance and reality, an anti-type of the penitent begins to make his presence felt. Latent behind the scene at Soissons, he enters the limelight of ethical scrutiny at Saint-Médard. The abbot and monks of that community, to which he was consigned after the council, offered Abelard a warm welcome.[27] He was unable to respond. The singularity on which he previously insisted had become isolation. In his moral solitude, he felt the emotion predominant after he had been unmanned, shame. Shame yielded to anger when he addressed God. Neither the vengeful deity of the Old Testament nor the merciful saviour of the New was invoked. Abelard called on the 'judge of equity' to witness his inequitable treatment, and proceeded to rail against Him with 'mental bile and bitterness' (*quanto ... animi felle, quanta mentis amaritudine*).

An anti-type is evoked by this word. *Amaritudo*, as he knew from the exegetical tradition of Job 10:1,[28] is the Biblical metaphor *par excellence* for remorse in penance. Not directed against himself and his sins, as penitential doctrine required, but against God, the bitterness felt by Abelard made what ought to have been the subject of remorse into what was the object of recrimination. The recrimination of the blasphemer, couched in terms familiar from Augustine's interpretation of Psalm 144:22 and from the Benedictine Rule, often quoted in twelfth-century literature of spiritual guidance,[29] voiced despair. And despair gave way to horror at

---

[25] Cf. R. Weingart, *The Logic of Divine Love: A Critical Analysis of the Soteriology of Peter Abelard* (Oxford, 1970), 196ff. and 200ff. and Weingart, 'Peter Abelard's Contribution to Medieval Sacramentology', *RTAM* 34 (1967) 159ff.
[26] *HC* 31, ed. Pagani, 188.   [27] *HC* 32, ibid., 188.   [28] See Chapter 2.
[29] 'Deus, quid tibi feci? Quare mihi abstulisti, et illis dedisti? Iniquis das, et tuis tollis. Accusas Deum quasi iniustum, et te laudas quasi iustum. Conuertere; accusa te, lauda illum. Tunc eris rectus, cum in omnibus bonis quae facit, *Deus tibi placet; in omnibus malis quae pateris, Deus tibi non displicet. Hoc est inuocare Deum in ueritate*', *S. Aurelii Augustini Enarrationes in Psalmos CI–CL*, ed. Dekkers and Fraipont, CCSL 40 2104, 28ff. For the influence of this

his heinousness. The outcast portrays himself as abominable in his own eyes, taking the measure of his alienation from God, from others, and from himself with the connotations of Cain.

To Cain Abelard was led, in reading that affected his self- interpretation, by St Ambrose, who linked that polyvalent figure with the doctrine of penance. The crucial text was Genesis 4:9. There Cain, like Adam at Genesis 3:9, replies to God with the evasiveness of his father. It was less the murderer's insolence in answering the divine enquiry about Abel's whereabouts that disturbed Ambrose than Cain's failure to accuse himself.[30] Self-accusation, because voluntary, was the most effective means of admitting guilt.[31] Acknowledgment of sin served to purge it.[32] Punishment inflicted on oneself invited God's mercy. These ideas of penitential self-transformation were lost on Cain. Incapable of regaining his innocence and of being redeemed, he acquired a black image whose shades became ever more sombre as the twelfth century elaborated on the doctrine of atonement. Cain's despair was emphasised.[33] And despair, violating the duty of trust in God's forgiveness, was deemed blasphemy against the Holy Spirit. The despairing blasphemer, the cursed outcast, the moral leper: such were the associations of this figure with which Peter Abelard was familiar when, describing his state after the council of Soissons, he likened himself to Cain.

Cain was not only abominable but also pitiable, because so alone. It is that state of ethical abandonment, prior to *contritio*, which Abelard conjures up. He does so with a term whose force was to be qualified later in *Scito te ipsum*. 'Out of his mind' (*insanus*) – and therefore innocent of sin, imputable only to those capable of reasoning, according to the criteria formulated in his tract on ethics[34] – he felt the emotions attendant on the sacrament of penance. Yet the pain (*dolor*) and embarrassment (*erubescentia*)

---

text, cf. Hildebert of Lavardin, *De paenitentia* (*Sermo tertius in Quadragesima*), PL 171, 455A. On the category of inverse *amaritudo* in the religious literature of the twelfth century, cf. the canonical treatise in BAV. Ottob. lat. 175, 63v: 'zelus amaritudinis, quae separat hominem a Deo et ducit in infernum'. This reference is to the seventy-second chapter of the Benedictine Rule.

[30] *De Cain et Abel* II.7.24, ed. Schenkl, 399, 13ff.
[31] *De Cain et Abel* II.9.27, ibid. 401, 10ff.
[32] *De Cain et Abel* II.9.32–3, 38, ibid. 405, 27ff; 409, 12ff.
[33] See G. Dahan, 'L'exégèse de l'histoire de Caïn et Abel du XIIe au XIVe siècle en Occident', *RTAM* 49 (1982) 65ff. and 70ff. Encyclopedias of medieval art making room for Cahors and Cairo, but none for Cain, A. Ulrich, *Kain und Abel in der Kunst: Untersuchungen zur Ikonographie und Auslegungsgeschichte* (Bamberg, 1981) is welcome. Cf. L. Hödl and J. Engemann in *Lexikon des Mittelalters* V (Munich, 1997) 838–45 and J. Illies (ed.), *Brüdermord: Zum Mythos von Kain und Abel* (Munich, 1975).
[34] *Ethics*, ed. Luscombe 56, 18–22; *Scito te ipsum* 1.38, ed. Ilgner, 37, 967–70.

that Abelard suffered did not liberate him with the cathartic purge of sin recommended by St Ambrose. On the contrary: shame, which 'looks to what I am',[35] saw nothing but a victim. Victimised, as he then considered himself, by loss of fame, Abelard struggled to preserve the tenuous self-regard typical of that condition.[36] His struggle is conveyed in a deliberate misuse of analogy. Just before the charged term *erubescentia* and immediately after *insanus*, he compares himself to St Antony, repeating what he describes as the 'complaint': 'Good Jesus, where were you?', from that bestseller of monastic literature which was the saint's Life.[37] No medieval reader would have failed to recall that Antony did not complain. Bewilderment, not bitterness, on being delivered from his torments lay behind the question he addressed to Christ. The humble incomprehension of the saint has nothing in common with Abelard's desperate sense of abandonment. Wandering in a labyrinth of mistaken identity, he discovered no way out by analogy nor any alternative to reason.

How to reason about a self defined by false analogies and by shocking antitheses? Abelard, in 1121, knew what he was not – neither guilty nor penitent nor sane – but he could place no trust in others' perceptions. Others perceived him as a condemned prisoner. Rejecting that role and finding no other, he appealed to a concept without a name. That is what Abelard implies by the semi-paradox that he could feel but not express his condition; and that is why he evoked this state of moral muteness with the connotations of Cain. The mode of evocation here is consonant with his subject, which is what could not be said. The eloquence of his latent meaning, at this turning-point of the *HC*, is highlighted by contrast with a later passage in the same work. There, as abbot of Saint-Gildas under attack by his monks, Abelard identifies explicitly with Cain, the persecuted outcast, before seeking cold consolation in the memory of the attempt to poison St Benedict.[38] No consolation was to hand at Saint-Médard, nor was identification with another possible for one estranged from himself. The indeterminacy of the anti-type acquires its meaning in a pattern of affirmation and negation which is Abelard's *sic et non* of crisis. Trapped in a prison more of his own making than of others' and deprived of a future, his only means of escape had to be a return to his past.

---

[35] B. Williams, *Shame and Necessity*, Sather Classical Lectures 57 (Berkeley, 1993) 93.
[36] Cf. Nussbaum, *Upheavals of Thought*, 196ff. and A. Morrison, *Shame: The Underside of Narcissism* (Hillsdale, 1989) 66ff.
[37] Evagrius of Antioch (translator of Athanasius), *Vita B. Antonii abbatis*, PL 73, 132D.
[38] *HC* 53, ed. Pagani, 226.

Abelard's past was rich in calamities, the most spectacular of which was his castration at Paris. Comparing that event with the condemnation of Soissons, he drew a distinction that was to be formative of his ethical thought:

I compared all that I was now enduring with my physical sufferings then, and considered myself the most wretched of men. I deemed that betrayal small in comparison with this injustice and lamented the fame I had forfeited much more than my bodily loss, since I had incurred that through a fault, while I had been made to undergo such manifest violence by the upright purpose and love for our faith which were my motives in writing [the *Theologia 'Summi boni'*].[39]

Self-criticism balanced with self-defence, Abelard emphasises the difference between personal injury and moral injustice. If the 'betrayal' perpetrated by Fulbert's henchmen had been caused by a fault to which he admits, his castration paled into insignificance before the brutality of his condemnation. *Fama* remains a criterion and Abelard laments its loss, while attempting to compensate for this external standard of judgment by an internal one. It is his 'upright purpose' (*sincera intentio*) that acquits him from responsibility for wrongdoing and makes his condemnation – not his castration – into an act of 'manifest violence'. The incompatibility between human and divine justice that is a prominent theme of *Scito te ipsum* is already present here in the *HC*. The language is penitential. *Sincera intentio* recalls both Ambrose's and Gregory's stress on spiritual authenticity and the lip-service paid to the concept of motivation in the *libri poenitentiales* whose prime concern, however, was the regulation of conduct.[40] If the word 'conscience' is not used, the idea is inherent in the contrast which he draws between a moral agent's perception of inner truths and the way he is viewed from the outside. The relationship between *fama*, to which Abelard had been enslaved, and *conscientia*, in ignorance of which he had misled his previous life, is conceived as antithetical.[41] It is that antithesis which is missing from such definitions of the Abelardian conscience as 'the power

---

[39] 'Conferebam cum his quae in corpore passus olim fueram quanta nunc sustinerem, et omnium hominum me aestimabam miserrimum. Parvam illam ducebam proditionem in comparatione huius iniuriae, et longe amplius famae quam corporis detrimentum plangebam, cum ad illam ex aliqua culpa devenerim, ad hanc me tam patentem violentiam *sincera intentio amorque fidei nostrae* induxissent, quae me ad scribendum compulerant.' *HC* 32, ibid., 188.
[40] See Chapter 2 above and L. Mauro, 'Tra *publica damna* e *communis utilitas*: L'aspetto sociale della morale di Abelardo e i "libri paenitentiales" ', *Medioevo* 13 (1987) 103–22.
[41] Cf. Abelard, *Sermo* 29: 'Dominus, cui conscientia magis quam lingua loquitur, non solum ab infamia verum etiam a morte ipsam [= insaniam] liberare non differens ... ', PL 178, 562D.

to recognize obvious truths' or 'the application of reasoned reflection to known precepts'.

The truths and precepts for which he groped in 1121 were neither obvious nor known to him. More than intellectual cognition was at stake. Moral and emotional insight was needed to refute the error imputed to him by others on whose opinion he had depended. The concept sought and found here is, integrity (*sinceritas*). The integrity of Abelard's motivation, religious as well as scholarly, is asserted in this passage, contrary to the adverse verdict on himself and his book; and the symmetry is reinforced by his use of penitential terms to reject the penance forced on him. Contrition, pertinent to his behaviour at Paris, was inapplicable at Soissons. Refusal to accept punishment in the second case is rendered more persuasive by acknowledgement of its validity in the first. No longer at odds with himself like Cain, Abelard begins to refashion his moral identity with categories from which would be developed, in *Scito te ipsum*, his ethic of intended actions.

Unintended actions also play a revealing role in the *HC*. They reveal the extent, and the limits, of Abelard's sense of humour. It does not always stretch to himself, although the narrator is sometimes capable of being ironical at the expense of the subject. Comedy, in the *HC*, is more sustained at the cost of others, such as those who attacked Abelard at Soissons. Their farce of a trial became slapstick.[42] Victims of the *fama* they had turned against him, they acquired a bad name for their cruelty. Unwilling to admit their collective fault, each of them tried to pin the blame on the others. But none of them repented, save the foolish figure of the papal legate. And Cuno of Preneste did so, as usual, for the wrong reasons. *Poenitentia ductus* – the expression used by St Matthew (27:3) of Judas' remorse, before suicide, at his betrayal of Christ – he had the prisoner released after a few days' detention, not on moral or religious grounds but because he realised that he had made himself unpopular. Shame, not guilt, motivated Cuno's 'repentance' at the very moment when Abelard struggled with the same emotion against the appearance of *poenitentia*. The ethical symmetry, so characteristic of the *HC*, is too elegant to be wholly credible. However, none but a pedant will insist. Our sources are scant and, even if they could be verified on this point, who would wish to spoil the joke?

---

[42] *HC* 32, ed. Pagani, 188–90.

Abelard invites us to enter into his spirit of irony without qualification. But when it is qualified, in respect of himself, we are less likely to give him the benefit of the doubt. Soon after his release from Saint-Médard and return to Saint-Denis he chanced to remark to some monks of that foundation, which prided itself on its links with Dionysius the Areopagite, that he had been bishop of Corinth, not Athens, according to the Venerable Bede. Abelard made this remark 'jokingly, as it were' (*quasi iocando*).[43] The humour was lost on its audience. Local patriotism was affronted; defensive piety came to its aid. Deprecating Bede, the monks cited the research undertaken into the question by Hilduin, the ninth-century abbot of Saint-Denis. Then tension escalated into crisis.

How did this *faux pas* become a *débâcle*? Abelard, in 1121/22, had no means of answering that question, nor does he appear to have acquired any later. He might have asserted, correctly, that he had not committed a sin, in the sense defined in *Scito te ipsum* of consenting to perform an action recognised as wrong.[44] But that was hardly the point. Sure-footed in guiding an imaginary debate between a Jew, a Christian, and a philosopher in his *Collationes*, he faltered and fumbled in the rougher reality of human intercourse. Perhaps, after the trauma of Soissons, Abelard was unsettled and inclined to over-react. Yet never, in the course of the two decades that followed his abrupt departure from Saint-Denis, did he reflect on inadvertent errors of this kind. It is true that Medieval Latin terminology hardly helped him. It was associative and imprecise.[45] An oxymoron such as *error in veritate* might have done the job, since the assertion was both true in its own terms and aberrant in its effect. Yet it was not Abelard's own assertion and, if his intentions were jocular, the adverb *quasi* acknowledged that there was room for doubt. It might have been dispelled by making the monks see the joke. He did not do so, because his sense of humour in this instance did not run to himself. So it was that he committed an offence to the claims not only of local piety but also of tact. The ancient name for this quality, known to but neglected by Abelard, is *urbanitas*.

With no tact and much impetuousness, Don Quixote remounted his high horse. Ample experience ought to have taught him that he would be dismounted. But Abelard had not learnt to bridle his head-strongness, and he charged at a windmill even more illusory than those of the past. Proclaiming the universal authority of Bede, he refrained from accusing

---

[43] *HC* 33, ibid., 190.   [44] See Chapter 6 below.
[45] See P. von Moos, 'Fehltritt, Fauxpas und Transgressionen in Mittelalter' in von Moos (ed.), *Der Fehltritt*, 1–96.

his opponents of being provincial, leaving them to draw the inference. And he trampled further on their sensibilities by declaring that he did not care whether the Areopagite was the patron-saint of Saint-Denis.[46] All of this is narrated without a hint of irony or a word of criticism at his former self. Narrator and subject speak in one voice. Its tones are tragic. It was 'wickedness' (*nequitia*) when the monks turned against him; and, in his despair, he sensed a cosmic conspiracy.[47]

The rhetoric is moral, but the optic is partisan. How partisan, is betrayed by the motives ascribed to others. Abelard knew that he had alienated Adam of Saint-Denis. To repeat that the abbot feared criticism of his morals was not strictly relevant.[48] More relevant were the political strings to be pulled by this head of a foundation linked with the crown, to which Adam threatened to appeal. Faced with that threat, Abelard resorted to the sole expedient he knew – and fled. Wandering from Saint-Denis to Provins and the Paraclete, he reverted to peripatetic type. Constant only in his errancy, he did not detect a likeness between himself and Boethius' fortune (*Philosophiae consolatio* 1, metr. 4, 28ff.). Humourless in his laments over a misfortune brought upon himself by his impolitic conduct, Abelard chooses to insist.

The insistence, meant to be compensatory for the failure, serves only to highlight it. The monks, who are said to have revelled in the 'highest glory' (*maxima gloria*) when he entered the abbey, are alleged to have feared 'dishonour' (*dedecus*) if he left.[49] This allegation is amplified, but not explained. How could 'the greatest scandal' (*maximum … opprobrium*) be incurred by Abelard's departure, when it had already taken place before he rode his high horse out of the gates? Did Adam not claim that he had slighted the 'crowning glory of the kingdom' (*regni sui gloriam et coronam*)?[50] Was it probable or plausible that the abbot and others considered this monk such an ornament to the foundation he was taken to undermine? Stripped of these self-flattering frills, a simpler explanation suggests itself: that Adam's threat of excommunication amounted to no more or less than an attempt to reduce to obedience an awkward member of that community – of almost any community – hardly noted for being obedient.

Obedience, as Abelard came to understand that monastic virtue, was owed primarily to God, not to men. Human relations, in the subtler sense of playing down a *faux pas* and preventing what might have remained

---

[46] *HC* 34, ed. Pagani, 192.
[47] 'penitus desperatus, quasi adversum me universus coniurasset mundus', *HC* 35, ibid., 194.
[48] 'quanto ceteris turpius vivebat, magis me verebatur', *HC* 34, ibid., 192.
[49] *HC* 36, ibid., 194.   [50] *HC* 34, ibid., 192.

a minor incident exploding into a major episode, were not, and never became, his strong point. Yet he had ties with those who excelled at ecclesiastical and lay politics. Stephen of Garlande, royal chancellor and seneschal, sponsored him at various stages of his career,[51] but there is no sign that Abelard learnt much from him in the ways of the world. Capable, on occasion, of enlisting the sympathy of a lay magnate like Theobald, count of Blois, who interceded on his behalf with Abbot Adam, or of involving Burchard, bishop of Meaux, in his case,[52] he remained ultimately reliant on the good offices of Stephen. A gad-fly of one patron, who appears to have used him to sting his enemies, such as William of Champeaux, Abelard was emphatically not a master of the art of the possible. When, later in the *HC*, he states that Heloise achieved more to endow the Paraclete in one year than he would have managed in a century,[53] there is reason to take him at his word.

This might have meant solitude, had Abelard not been compelled to earn his keep. Hence the pupils who thronged to him in that oratory of learned anachoretism which they built near Troyes.[54] At the Paraclete,[55] in a community made to his measure, subordinate to the intellectual authority he craved, Abelard practised his own version of the ideal known as *vita communis*.[56] His model, lengthily cited on this subject, was Jerome. A scholarly saint, at loggerheads with the world, he combined erudition and antagonism in a measure which Abelard tailored to his own. What he could not yet cut down to size was, calumny. Calumny asserted that he was mistaken to dedicate his oratory to the Holy Spirit. This attack was made on one who continued to feel like Cain. Although he saw himself as 'a fugitive, in despair' (*profugus ac iam desperatus*),[57] in terms reminiscent of Genesis 4:12ff., Abelard did not suffer from the self-alienation endured in the sequel to Soissons. A change had occurred in his circumstances and in his outlook. He found 'a small measure of respite by the consoling grace of God' (*divinae gratia consolationis aliquantulum respirassem*). In the wasteland of the *HC*, where human enmities blight the landscape, this phrase

---

[51] See R.-H. Bautier, 'Paris au temps d'Abélard' in *Abélard en son temps*, ed. J. Jolivet, Actes du 9e centenaire de la naissance de Pierre Abélard (14–19 mai 1979) (Paris, 1981) 54–67, 77.

[52] *HC* 35–6, ed. Pagani, 194.   [53] *HC* 47, ibid., 216.

[54] See E. Kantorowicz, 'Die Wiederkehr gelehrter Anachorese im Mittelalter' in *Selected Studies* (New York, 1965) 339–51 and P. von Moos, 'Les solitudes de Pétrarque: Liberté intellectuelle et activisme urbain dans la crise du XIVe' in *Entre histoire et littérature*, 611–47.

[55] *HC* 37ff., ed. Pagani, 196ff.

[56] See von Moos, 'Le "bien commun" et "la loi de la conscience" ' in *Entre histoire et littérature*, 475ff.

[57] *HC* 39, ed. Pagani, 202.

about divine grace comes as a bolt out of the blue. Wholly unexpected, it is justified by a long defence of Abelard's choice of name. With the Paraclete is identified not only his refuge, but a moving force of his faith. It is grace that gives him a novel approach to the old problem of persecution.

Persecuted, as he interpreted their actions, by those 'new apostles',[58] who may be Bernard of Clairvaux and Norbert of Xanten,[59] Abelard is no longer content to refer to the familiar motif of envy. He enlists God as his witness (*Deus ipse mihi testis est*) and appeals not to the sympathy of a friend nor to the opinion of the world but to divine knowledge (*Deus scit*).[60] *Fama*, likened to an empty echo,[61] may make him tremble at the thought of an ecclesiastical meeting convened to damn him as heretical but, even as he admits to his anxiety at the malevolence of men, he declares his belief in the understanding of God. Here the image of the conscience adumbrated in the sequel to Soissons assumes clearer contours. Again its fundamental feature is, opposition between the errancy of human judgement and divine infallibility.

On one issue, however, Abelard allows for implicit doubt about God's understanding. Seeking respite from the 'persecutions' that led him to imagine fleeing from the Christian fold,[62] he accepted election as abbot of Saint-Gildas in Brittany. *Deus sciat* – 'may He know'[63] – he writes, in the optative subjunctive of a verb previously used in the indicative, why he fell into that precipice while avoiding the menace of a sword. The limitations revealed in Abelard's account of the *débâcle* at Saint-Denis are transcended when he describes sufferings not of his own making. Recording his Breton hell-hole, another writer might have been tempted to style himself a martyr. Little ingenuity was required to cast the suffering abbot of Saint-Gildas as a champion of Christ and his monks as Satan's agents.

If Abelard resisted the temptation, that was because he had abandoned his self-heroising and self-commiserating styles. Others' interest in or acquaintance with his plight at Saint-Gildas is assumed, but not in order to gratify or to console his vanity. The dangers faced there, he declares with new insight, threatened both body and soul.[64] His soul, previously unmentioned in the *HC*, was imperilled if he failed to do his duty by reforming the abuses, while his body was endangered should he make the attempt. Torn between these conflicting sentiments, menaced by a local 'tyrant',

---

[58] *HC* 40, ibid., 206.
[59] Bibliography on this question is summarised by Pagani, ibid., n. 209.
[60] *HC* 42, ibid., 208.   [61] *HC* 41, ibid., 206.   [62] *HC* 42, ibid., 208.   [63] *HC* 43, ibid., 210.
[64] 'tam animae meae quam corporis pericula pensarem, neminem iam latere arbitror.' *HC* 44, ibid., 210.

and prey to a deeper form of despair, Abelard drew a conclusion which was not quite accurate. None of his earlier afflictions (*molestias*), he claimed, was comparable to what he endured at Saint-Gildas.[65] The inaccuracy lies in his omission of Paris. There, after his castration, he had admitted that he was to blame. Now he does so again.

The fault to which Abelard admits, or of which he accuses himself, is different from his earlier concessions to earthly justice and human revenge. At Saint-Gildas the *mea culpa* is directed to the Holy Spirit. After deserting that 'consoler', when he left the Paraclete, he was tormented by his inability to have mass celebrated there. Then providence intervened in the person of Heloise, 'now my sister in Christ rather than my wife' (*nostra illa iam in Christi soror potius quam uxor*).[66] Expelled from Argenteuil, together with her nuns, she offered Abelard 'a God-given opportunity to provide for my oratory' (*oblatam mihi a Domino intellexi occasionem, qua nostro consulerem oratorio*).[67] Not the most gallant expression of concern for ladies in distress, it is, however, the prelude to a contrast between his failure at Saint-Gildas and her success at the Paraclete.[68] After being accused of neglecting Heloise, Abelard assumed the role of spiritual guide to her community.

The restrictions imposed by his role are no less notable than its achievements. The hymns, the sermons, and the Rule are expressions, and proofs, of his concern for the Paraclete. For Heloise, by contrast, his sympathy has been found wanting. This criticism perhaps ignores what was expected of a spiritual guide. He was required, by St Paul's injunction cited in the first chapter, to respect the inviolability of his charges' consciences. When Heloise wrote her confessional letters to Abelard, whose role she sought to amplify but not to question, he could reply by advising and exhorting her, but he had no right to challenge her testimony. The propriety with which he adhered to his description of Heloise as 'my sister in Christ rather than my wife' was pastoral; and his correctness was reinforced by defensiveness.

Malicious tongues had wagged about him and her. Faced with the same problem that had always vexed him, Abelard found a new solution. The narrator's tone is no longer that of the victim, nor is irony deployed to dramatic effect. Already able to relativise his calamities, Abelard goes on to face the problem of their relationship to fame. He, who had collapsed at its reversal or withdrawal, recognises that even a clear conscience offers

---

[65] 'Desperabam penitus cum recordarer quae fugerem et considerarem quae incurrerem, et priores molestias quasi iam nullas reputans crebro apud me ingemiscens dicebam: "Merito haec patior … " ' *HC* 45, ibid., 212.
[66] *HC* 46, ibid., 214.   [67] Ibid.   [68] *HC* 47, ibid., 216.

no security. 'The usual wickedness of his detractors' had attributed erotic motives to his visits to Heloise at the Paraclete. The 'sincere charity' with which he had attempted to provide for her spiritual needs and those of her nuns had not served to protect him from slander.[69] *Sincera caritas* is virtually the same expression used to affirm his innocence in 1121.[70] Adequate to assert the claims of the conscience then, it is unable to ward off *invidia* now.

'Envy' (*invidia*) is not 'hatred' (*odium*). Nor are 'detractors' (*derogantes*) identical to 'enemies' (*inimici*). Both represent more nuanced references to fame (or *infamia*), the demands of which Abelard is now prepared to admit – but not to accept – even when they are unjust. This, the second, turning-point of the *HC*, is unlike the tragic peripeteia of Soissons. Gone is Abelard's tactic of repudiation. Suppressed is his dialectic of crisis. And in the stability of a self confident of its moral identity but uncertain about how it is perceived, he develops a remarkable argument. After citing St Jerome and the Bible, he turns to the example of the most famous – the only? – castrated philosopher before him.[71] Origen, acting without judgement (*minus provide*), had committed a significant crime (*non modicum crimen*) in unmanning himself. Abelard, by contrast, states that he had benefited from divine mercy, because the deed had been done by others. They were guilty of a fault (*culpa*). He had merely suffered a punishment – the word *poena* is used twice in the same sentence – which was short and sharp, for he had hardly felt it in his sleep. His castration could even be seen as a liberation.

This most radical of Abelard's relativisations hinges on the criterion of personal responsibility. Not only intentions but also actions count. Actions count, however, as manifestations of conscious choice, which is why it is significant that he chooses to admit to pain. That pain, once again, is not primarily physical. Abelard continues to be tormented 'more from loss of fame than from diminution of the body' (*plus ex detrimento famae quam ex corporis crucior diminutione*). An echo of his analysis of the sequel to Soissons, this phrase points to a crucial difference between his ethical state now and then. Conspicuous by their absence are the emotions that had driven him into the cloister at Paris and into isolation at Saint-Médard.

---

[69] 'In quo nec invidiae mihi murmur defuit, et quod me facere *sincera caritas* compellebat, solita derogantium pravitas impudentissime accusabat, dicens me adhuc quadam carnalis concupiscentiae oblectatione teneri, qua pristinae dilectae sustinere absentiam vix aut numquam paterer.' *HC* 48, ibid., 218.

[70] Rightly noted by Perkams, *Liebe als Zentralbegriff*, 265.

[71] *HC* 48–9, ed. Pagani, 218–20.

They do not need to be mentioned, because they have become irrelevant. Still at odds with envy (*invidia*), Abelard no longer feels either shame (*pudor*) or embarrassment (*erubescentia*).

If the victim has vanished, the target remains. And, significantly, Abelard is able to acknowledge his vulnerability. Quoting St Augustine on the need to balance the claims of fame and conscience,[72] he explains his own disequilibrium in terms of proper pride. Thwarted by others' misjudgements, the moral agent does not simply appeal to the tribunal of the conscience, as he had done after Soissons. He both accepts his role as the object of envy and goes on to compare himself with Cain.[73] The comparison, this time, is explicit and unabashed. Still an outcast, Abelard no longer feels the horror or the indeterminacy evoked by the connotations of Cain at Saint-Médard. His circumstances are menacing, but his identity is secure. Attempts to assassinate him, ambushes, injury, living as if a sword were suspended above his neck:[74] if these perils frighten him, they do not undermine Abelard's sense of himself. It is reinforced by a higher purpose which his reader has come to share. Neither the complicit friend nor the collusive witness of the early part of the *HC*, this figure, about whom the narrator has long been silent, changes with him in the interval. A partner in the same enterprise, he is the spiritual companion whom Abelard now needs in the 'godly way of life'. The therapy which makes a monk of Cain also transforms the reader, his *alter ego*, into 'a most beloved brother in Christ'.[75]

❧

Does this amount to a 'counter-morality'?[76] Better, perhaps, a morality developed in a dialectic of antitheses. The antithesis between fame and conscience is depicted in the *HC* as a battle until it concludes, if not in an Augustinian peace, at least in an Abelardian truce. Before that truce is established, he traces, through his calamities, the uneven course of his moral development. Abelard's categories evolve as his character alters; and this evolution is most striking in the metamorphoses of *fama*. The highest goal of his youth, it becomes his bane when internalised as *infamia*,

---

[72] *HC* 49, ibid., 220.   [73] *HC* 53, ibid., 226.   [74] *HC* 52–4, ibid., 224–8.

[75] 'dilectissime frater in Christo et ex divina conversatione familiarissime comes', *HC* 55, ibid., 230. The literalism which leads Pagani, following G. Orlandi, ad loc. to print *diutina* (transmitted by only one manuscript against the consensus of the tradition) implies the biographical fallacy.

[76] The expression is applied to the *HC* and the *planctus* by W. Olten, 'Fortune or Failure: The Problem of Grace, Free Will, and Providence in Peter Abelard', *Augustiniana* 52 (2002) 371.

until it establishes an alliance, as proper pride, with *conscientia*. One of the achievements of the *HC* is its acknowledgement of the precariousness of that alliance. Abelard's acceptance of vulnerability is the goal, inconceivable at the beginning of the work, reached at its conclusion. There he refashions Augustine's heritage to attain a form of self-knowledge which is his own. And that is why the natural and necessary complement to *Scito te ipsum*, his tract on ethics entitled with the Delphic principle which he derived from experience, is the *HC*.

Its drama of interiority reaches a nadir after Soissons. Deprived of fame and not yet in possession of conscience, Abelard evokes the indeterminacy of his ethical state with an anti-type of penance. Penitential emotions provide him with the cognitive capacity to reshape his identity. Shame (*pudor*) and embarrassment (*erubescentia*) are key terms. Their meanings change. Shame, as experienced at Paris in its public and social forms, is not identical to the self-alienation of Saint-Médard. Nor does bitterness (*amaritudo*) signify remorse at that terrible moment. It means recrimination. Using such terms in the opposite of their orthodox sense, Abelard demonstrates how he overcame immoral feelings to achieve a measure of reconciliation with himself, with others, and with God. Decisive, at the Paraclete, is his recognition of divine grace. It enables Abelard to refine his analysis. He does so most effectively in the comparison of his unmanning with that of Origen, where the omission of shame, embarrassment, and bitterness serves to amplify his doctrine of personal responsibility. Now the author of his emotions, not their slave, he is able to control them and to choose what – or what not – to feel. The moral intelligence of his feelings, mastered by the adult Abelard at the end of the *HC*, measures the distance that separates him from the ethical adolescent of its opening.

At the opening and throughout the narrative up to 1121, a dominant characteristic of the subject is, self-will. Imperious, impetuous, and on occasion stupid, Abelard may never have learnt tact in human relations, but there can be no doubt about the sincerity of his submission to an axiom of monasticism drawn from the Lord's Prayer. 'Thy will be done', with which his autobiography concludes,[77] remained the leitmotif of his conduct following his last and worst calamity at the hands of Bernard of Clairvaux. On that, we have the verdict of the most judicious abbot of the twelfth century. Peter the Venerable, describing Abelard's behaviour at Cluny after his second condemnation in 1141, praised him as a model member of the

---

[77] *HC* 56, ed. Pagani, 232.

community.[78] Humility, a virtue never ascribed to the notoriously arrogant writer of the *HC*, was practised by him in the sense perceptively defined as 'not a peculiar habit of self-effacement, rather like having an inaudible voice, [but of] a selfless respect for reality.'[79] That reality, lived at Cluny but anticipated a decade earlier in his autobiographical therapy, was religious.

It is religion, or rather God, that provides a point of comparison and contrast between Abelard's autobiography and one of the few by a Western philosopher after Rousseau to achieve similar stature. If aspects of Bertrand Russell's life (particularly his affairs of the heart) can be construed as a history of calamities, it is also noteworthy that the agnostic author of *Why I am not a Christian* recorded moments of 'mystic illumination', in which he became 'a completely different person'.[80] Religious language, otherwise absent from Russell's narrative, figures at its turning-points, none of which is more finely drawn than a passage dealing with his 'vain search for God.'[81] But among the many qualities of this thinker, humility was not salient; nor did he face the problems of moral identity posed by converting the *fictio* of a monastic profession into the reality of a monastic vocation. Abelard faced them with a courage all the more convincing for being acknowledged to fall short of sainthood and, in doing so, he laid ghosts perhaps more real, because less cerebral, than the spectres that haunted the disconsolate Russell.

---

[78] *Ep.* 115, *The Letters of Peter the Venerable* I, ed. G. Constable (Harvard, 1967) 306–37. This letter is translated, with commentary, in Godman, *The Silent Masters*, 5ff.

[79] I. Murdoch, *The Sovereignty of Good* (London, 2001) 93 and cf. 101.

[80] B. Russell, *Autobiography* (London, 2000) 149.

[81] 'What Spinoza calls "the intellectual love of God" has seemed to me the best thing to live by, but I have not had even the somewhat abstract God that Spinoza allowed himself to whom to attach my intellectual love. I have loved a ghost, and in loving a ghost my inmost self has itself become spectral … human affection is to me at bottom an attempt to escape from the vain search for God', ibid., 261.

CHAPTER 6

Feminine paradoxes

Abelard's autobiography takes its place in a tradition of therapeutic writing about the self, yet nothing in Latin literature is quite like it. As original and idiosyncratic as its author, the *HC* has no immediate model nor any direct descendants. It stands alone in the singularity with which it depicts Abelard's moral metamorphoses. At the end of the work he ceases to play Proteus, finding a stable identity as an adherent to monastic values. This has consequences for the other characters in his ethical drama. If the reader is drawn onto the scene, not much room is made for the leading lady. Heloise no longer occupies centre-stage. Styling himself her spiritual guide, Abelard highlights the religious character of their relationship. Its other aspects are consigned to the past. But where did that leave her in the present? If he had refashioned his role, what was hers?

An answer to these questions is formulated, brilliantly, in the words of greeting (*salutatio*) with which Heloise's first letter to Abelard plays on the philosopher's taste for paradox:

To her lord Abelard or rather her father, to her husband or rather her brother, his handmaiden or rather his daughter, his wife or rather his sister Heloise.[1]

Perhaps reminiscent of a triad attested in Roman poetry,[2] this *salutatio* is certainly provoked by Abelard's description of Heloise as 'now our sister in Christ rather than our wife' in the *HC*.[3] Against his emphatic *potius* is set her understated *immo*. In this *sic et non* of synonyms, the dialectic turns on Heloise's identity. Not Abelard's spiritual sister rather than his

---

[1] 'Domino suo immo patri, coniugi suo immo fratri, ancilla sua imma filia, ipsius uxor immo soror, Abelardo Heloisa.' *Ep.* ii, ed. Pagani, 234.
[2] Cf. Juvenal iii.93ff. On the stock roles of *uxor/matrona*, *ancilla*, and *meretrix* (which Heloise introduces later) in Roman *fabula palliata*, see E. Courtney, *A Commentary on the Satires of Juvenal*, (London, 1980) 169ff. Pagani, 234 cites Ovid, *Heroides* iii.52.
[3] 'nostra illa iam in Christo soror potius quam uxor', *HC* 46, ed. Pagani, 214.

wife but both at once and more, she declines the predominantly religious part he assigns her, affirming the compatibility of her multiple roles. The *forte* of her insistence tempered by a tone of deference (*dominus, pater*), the melody is enlivened by an *allegro* of virtuosity.

The virtuosity of Heloise, in this *salutatio* which marks her entry into European literature, is neither Roman nor Romantic. The rhetoric of passion and pathos employed by Ovid's abandoned heroines provided her with little comfort and less understanding. The tragedies of Briseis, Dido, and the rest consisted not only in plights loosely parallel to Heloise's but also in their inability to overcome them. To achieve that, she had to look elsewhere. She looked not only to classical literature, about her command of which we have perhaps heard too much, but also to legal and theological tradition, about her interest in which we have undoubtedly heard too little. There Heloise advances with confidence, for she knows that, on the battleground of debate about marriage and monasticism, she is a march ahead of Abelard.

Jurists and theologians agreed that, after the entry of husband and wife into the religious life, their marriage was not dissolved.[4] It was transformed into a spiritual union.[5] Spirituality is the aspect singled out by Abelard; union the dimension emphasised by Heloise. More balanced than his one-sidedness, the implied argument of her *salutatio* rests on a firmer basis. The basis of marriage, it has been seen, was the doctrine of consent.[6] That doctrine, derived from Roman law, was also applied to the monastic profession.[7] The likeness drawn between the voluntary agreement that ought to have been a precondition for both was close and common – although the author of *Scito te ipsum*, in which consent looms large, was inclined

---

[4] See J. Hourlier, *Histoire du droit et des institutions de l'Eglise en Occident*, X: *L'âge classique* (1140–1378). *Les religieux* (Paris, 1974) 159ff. and J. Leclercq, 'Amour et marriage vus par des clercs et des religieux, spécialment au xiie siècle' in *Love and Marriage in the Twelfth Century*, ed. W. van Hoecke and A. Welkenhuysen (Leiden, 1981) 106ff. Cf. C. Brooke, 'Aspects of Marriage Law in the Twelfth and Thirteenth Centuries' in *Proceedings of the Fifth International Congress of Medieval Canon Law*, ed. S. Kuttner and K. Pennington, Monumenta Iuris Canonici C, 6 (Vatican City, 1986) 341–3.

[5] Cf. Egbert of Schönau, *Sermo 5* (*contra Catharos*): 'Fit quidem nunnunquam, ut tales [vir et mulier] migrant pariter ad monasticam vitam et separatas ab invicem mansiones eligant … sed talem separationem Deus operatur, non homo, et quidem tales non omnino ab invicem discedunt, neque rumpitur inter eos vinculum coniugale, quia indivisa in eis manet *unitas mentium*. Nam quanto liberius divinae dilectioni vacant, tanto purius atque firmius se invicem diligere possunt', PL 195, 27D. (The idea of marriage as a union of minds, applied by Augustine to Mary and Joseph, was widely discussed in the twelfth century. See M. Müller, *Die Lehre des heiligen Augustinus von der Paradiesehe und ihre Auswirkung in der Sexualethik des 12. und 13. Jahrhunderts bis Thomas von Aquin* (Regensburg, 1954)).

[6] See Chapter 4.   [7] Ibid.

to ignore them until they were recalled by his wife and spiritual sister in the pointed terms of her *salutatio*. They are pointed because Heloise had assumed neither of these states freely. She had been forced into marriage and monasticism by Abelard.

His first thought, on donating to her the Paraclete, had been to provide for that abandoned oratory.[8] Abelard's second thought, hardly more flattering to Heloise and her nuns, was to minister to their needs, in order to win their esteem (*quo me amplius revererentur*).[9] His motivation, both charitable and self-referential, was not primarily ethical. Obligation and duty, moral or otherwise, took second place to Abelard's drive to compensate for failure at Saint-Gildas by success at the Paraclete. Having renounced self-will in respect of God, he does not appear to have abandoned it with regard to Heloise and her nuns. She, however, had learnt the lesson of his dominance. Having known consent only as acquiescence in Abelard's wish that she assume the double role of wife and spiritual sister, Heloise chooses to adhere to both her parts. Such is the meaning of her *salutatio*, which combines deference with defiance. Then this reluctant bride and involuntary nun goes on to assert her rights. They are grounded, in her first letter, on a concept of moral responsibility summed up by the recurrent term 'debt' (*debitum*) which Abelard never uses, with regard to her or anyone else, in the *HC*. Obligation of this kind was a moral category alien to him when he received her first letter. In 1116, when he married Heloise; in 1117, when he compelled her to take the veil; and in the early 1130s, when he composed the *HC*, he thought of himself, his identity, and his reputation. Abelard did not think of what, as a corollary of decisions taken arbitrarily by himself, he owed to her.

This is not just a further instance of 'her teaching him', which we are urged to applaud as 'feminism', but a problem of intellectual history that needs to be addressed in less anachronistic terms. The terms in which Abelard addressed it were different from those of Heloise. His reply to her first letter is not couched in the same categories nor phrased in the same language. *Debitum*, frequently employed by her, is conspicuous by its absence – even if Abelard's writings for the Paraclete may be interpreted as a qualified acknowledgement of the appeal made by the concept of debt. The effect of his reserve was to make Heloise wary of the word. *Debitum* occurs only

[8] *HC* 46, ed. Pagani, 214.   [9] *HC* 52, ibid., 224.

once in her second letter; and there its reference is transformed into the hypothetical duty of performing funeral rites for him.[10]

For Abelard, when he came to reflect on moral obligation, the cardinal principle was *caritas* – which meant, above all, love of God.[11] It is love of God that motivates love of one's neighbour, he argues in the *Theologia 'scholarium'*[12] and elsewhere; and this is the sense he gives to his *caritas* on behalf of the Paraclete in the passage cited from the *HC* above. Spiritual, spontaneous, and selfless, *caritas* evokes none of the contractual associations of *debitum*. The language common to jurists and theologians, on which Heloise draws, did not come naturally to Abelard nor, on the rare occasions when he uses it, is it to the same purpose. Her key term, in her first letter, belongs to a different order of discourse from his. *Debitum* is distinct from *caritas* in being less metaphysical, more concrete, and – given the context in which Heloise employs it – paradoxical. For, both on her account and on that of her husband in the *HC*, this determined defender of their marital bond had been its vehement opponent.

Where then lies the coherence of Heloise? In her theory of the will – assumed and asserted, rather than argued – in its freedom of choice, as evoked by *consensus*, and in its obligations, as emphasised by *debitum*. Presenting her case, Heloise both reckoned with and played on Abelard's susceptibilities. He took a dim view of *consensus* in matrimony, equating it with servitude;[13] and she refrained from pressing the point with an array of authorities. Her tact is noteworthy. She, who (as reported in the *HC*) could not take the veil without citing a line from Lucan and who strews her arguments against matrimony with a florilegium of *auctoritates*, confines herself, in her first letter, to quoting verbatim only the Bible and St Augustine, Cicero and Seneca – none of whom is adduced to support her assertions about *consensus* or *debitum*. On both subjects, she acquired a newfound, if partial, readiness to speak out in her own voice after becoming a nun. Yet those who maintain that they are listening to Heloise are curiously deaf to what she has to say.

She is eloquent in her silences, to which it is as necessary to attend as it is to read between her lines. Ovidian pathos is an explicit but minor feature of Heloise's writing. More remarkable is its restraint. She abstains

---

[10] *Ep.* IV.3, ibid., 272.   [11] See M. Perkams, *Liebe als Zentralbegriff* 33ff., 45ff., 300ff.

[12] *Theologia 'scholarium'* I, 6, *Petri Abaelardi Opera Theologica* III, ed. E. Buytaert OFM and C. Mews, CCCM 13 (Turnhout, 1987) 320, 67ff., and see Perkams, *Liebe als Zentralbegriff*, 115.

[13] Cf. his solution to her fourteenth problem: 'Quippe quae maior servitus est dicenda quam ut proprii corporis vir aut uxor potestatem non habeat, nec ab usu carnis abstinere, ut vel orationi vacent, nisi ex consensu, queant?', *Problemata Heloissae*, PL 178, 701D.

from spelling out much with which she assumes Abelard to be familiar, such as the doctrine that, in the order of grace, the *debitum* of husband and wife was equivalent and reciprocal.[14] Amplified by him in his 'feminist' writings,[15] a version of this theology of spiritual parity is implicit in Heloise's insistence on the binding character for them both of their 'marital debt' (*debitum coniugale*).[16] And if she never uses that term in its sexual or, at least, procreative sense, the reason is not only its irrelevance to the castrated Abelard. In keeping with jurists and theologians who, before Gratian, argued that reciprocity of will, not *coitus*, was constitutive of marriage,[17] his wife teaches her husband a lesson which he might have learnt from Anselm of Laon, the master at whom he preferred to sneer.[18]

'I suffer not a woman to teach' (*docere autem mulieri non permitto*), admonishes the Apostle at I Timothy 2:12. Heloise circumvents St Paul's prohibition by adopting the stance of the suppliant. 'I entreat' (*obsecro*), she writes with characteristic ambivalence,[19] for Abelard's 'handmaiden' has the didactic assurance of a mistress.[20] It is qualified, however, by caution at seeming to overturn the hierarchical order; and order becomes Heloise's theme. Abelard fails to understand the hierarchy of his obligations. At its lower rung – that of the fictive 'friend' and 'companion' who is none other that the reader of the *HC* – he may have done his duty but, higher up the scale where the nuns of the Paraclete, superlative in their filial friendship (*non tam amicas quam amicissimas, non tam socias quam filias*),[21] are situated, he has not repaid a debt undertaken voluntarily.

[14] R. Metz, 'Recherches sur la condition de la femme selon Gratien', *Studia Gratiana* 12 (1957) [= *Collectanea S. Kuttner* II] 377–96.

[15] Splendidly studied by M. McLaughlin, 'Peter Abelard and the Dignity of Women: Twelfth-Century "Feminism" in Theory and Practice' in *Pierre Abélard – Pierre le Vénérable: Les courants philosophiques, littéraires, et artistiques en Occident au milieu du XIIe siècle*, ed. J. Jolivet and R. Louis (Paris, 1975), 287–94.

[16] *Ep.* II.8, ed. Pagani, 242.

[17] See P. Vaccari, 'La tradizione canonica del *debitum* coniugale e la posizione di Graziano', *Studia Gratiana* 1 (1953) 535–47.

[18] 'quedam etiam sic necessarie coherent, ut sine his coniugium non sit, ut consensus; quedam sic ut, licet absint, coniugium tamen manere possit, ut coitus ... *matrimonium non facit coitus, sed voluntas*, hoc significavit quod coniugium potest esse sine coitu, non sine consensu.' *Anselms von Laon systematische Sentenzen*, ed. Bliemetzrieder, 140. The italicised phrase is a quotation from ps.-Chrysostom, *Opus imperfectum in Matthaeum* 32.9, known to Anselm of Laon from Pope Nicolas I's famous letter of doctrinal definition to the Bulgarians of 13 November, 866, conveniently printed in H. Denzinger, *Enchiridion symbolorum definitionum et declarationum de rebus fidei et morum. Kompendium der Glaubensbekenntnisse und kirchlichen Lehrentscheidungen lateinisch-deutsch*, ed. P. Hünermann, 37th edn (Freiburg im Breisgau, 1991) 866, n. 643. For Abelard and Anselm of Laon, see Chapter 4.

[19] *Ep.* II.5, ed. Pagani, 238.   [20] See Chapter 7.   [21] *Ep.* II.5, ibid., 238.

The consent of choice and the obligations of responsibility that follow from it are linked in a phrase intended to jog Abelard's memory: 'you have bound yourself to us with a greater debt' (*maiori te debito nobis astrinxisti*).[22]

That verb recalls the account of his seduction of Heloise in the *HC*.[23] There he puns ponderously on the vocabulary of binding and embracing. Understandably less amused than Abelard at his verbal ingenuity, she recalls and reverses the sense of *constringerem* in his autobiography with the synonym *astrinxisti* in her first letter. For the irresponsibility of the seducer is substituted the obligation of the founder. Founder of the Paraclete, now a community of nuns, Abelard is linked to them by a substantial debt of his own making (*quanto ... debito te erga [nos] obligaveris*).[24] If the verb is singular, the *debitum* is double: 'weigh up the measure of the debt by which you are bound to me, so that what you owe collectively to women devoted to you be repaid by you to your one and only more devotedly' (*quanto autem erga me te obligaveris pensa, ut quod devotis communiter debes feminis unicae tuae devotius solvas*).[25] The repetition of *obligaveris* – twice in successive paragraphs, with *obligatum* in the next – underlines the correlation between choice and duty. Just as the initiative was Abelard's, so is the liability, both communal and individual. Binding him with these moral chains, Heloise adds a sacramental shackle: 'you know that you owe me a debt that is all the greater for your being recognised to be further fettered by the bond of the marital sacrament' (*cui [= mihi] quidem tanto maiori debito noveris obligatum, quanto te amplius nuptialis foedere sacramenti constat esse astrictum*).[26]

This from the reluctant bride who, Abelard relates, had wished to spare him marriage, 'so that no force of constraint should bind me' (*ut me non vis aliqua vinculi constringeret*).[27] That 'constraint' (*vinculum*) has been transformed into a 'bond' (*foedus*) – the term applied by Anselm of Laon and others to the compact hallowed by a sacrament that signified the union between Christ and the Church[28] – and Heloise has become Abelard's ball and chain. He cannot deny her case, which is known to be

---

[22] Ibid.   [23] *HC* 12, ed. Pagani, 134 and see Chapter 4.
[24] *Ep.* 11.6, ibid., 238, where Pagani argues for the necessary correction to the manuscript tradition, but fails to print it. The reading *eas* of T, adopted by J. Monfrin, *Abélard: Historia calamitatum* (Paris, 1967) 112, is not preferable.
[25] *Ep.* 11.7, ed. Pagani, 246.   [26] *Ep.* 11.8, ibid., 242.   [27] *HC* 18, ibid., 158.
[28] S. Heaney, *The Development of the Sacramentality of Marriage from Anselm of Laon to Thomas Aquinas*, Catholic University of America Studies in Sacred Theology 134 (Washington, 1963) 11ff.

true (*noveris*) and, should he wish to cavil, she increases the pressure in her impersonal verb, the generality of which is no less calculated than his own *necesse est* and *oportet* in the *HC*.[29] Here as elsewhere Heloise imitates distinctive traits of Abelard's style, in order to assert the opposite of what he and others thought. *Constat* represents the sacramentality of a marriage contracted without voluntary consent as an established fact, rather than the *quaestio vexata* in the theology and jurisprudence of the twelfth century that it was.[30]

On this subject, Abelard was not disposed to tolerate sleights of hand. Although he recognised matrimony as a sacrament, it was grudgingly, as a poor second-best to chastity;[31] and many are the aspersions cast by him on what he considered an inferior state.[32] Sceptical or indifferent towards human contracts and conventions, even those sanctioned by the Church, Abelard was less practical, less applied, and less aligned with orthodox opinion of the *nuptiale sacramentum* than Heloise. She bought it at the price of abandoning her former critique of marriage's woes. After quoting explicitly and extensively St Jerome's anti-matrimonial polemic,[33] she now adduces Anselm of Laon and his likes without naming names. Tacit citation lending her claims the support of borrowed voices, there is no need to raise her own.

Among the voices which Heloise echoes and alters to her own ends, none is more significant than Abelard's. Constructing a case opposed to his, she takes pains to base it on the same or similar criteria. The most prominent of them, when he narrates his youth in the *HC*, is fame (*fama*), as distinct from conscience (*conscientia*).[34] Appealing to that second criterion in her remarks on Abelard's *debitum*, Heloise links it to the first. 'The entire world', 'as everyone sees', 'were all to be silent, the facts speak out for themselves' (*mundus universus; ut omnibus patet; si omnes taceant, res ipsa clamat*): such allusions to *fama*, recurrent in the *HC*,[35] serve to marshal

[29] See Chapter 5.
[30] A good survey, with rich bibliography, is provided by Colish, *Peter Lombard*, II, 628ff.
[31] See R. Weingart, 'Peter Abelard's Contribution', 172–3.
[32] Eg: *Sermo* 31 (PL 178, 570A), *Problema Heloissae* 14 (ibid. 697B), *Problema Heloissae* 40 (ibid. 722A–B), *Problema Heloissae* 42, (ibid. 725Dff.), *Sermo* 33, (ibid. 582D).
[33] Cf. *HC* 18, ed. Pagani, 146ff. with P. Delhaye, 'Le dossier anti-matrimonial de l'*Adversus Iovinianum* et son influence sur quelques écrits latins du XIIe siècle', *Mediaeval Studies* 13 (1951) 65–86.
[34] For the distinction, see Chapters 4–5.
[35] eg. 'sicut universus agnovit mundus', *HC* 19, ed. Pagani, 158; 'summa admiratione mundus excepit' 20, ibid., 158; 'singularis infamia universum mundum … occupatura … omnium digitis demonstrandus, omnium linguis corrodendus, omnibus monstrandum spectaculum

what she represents as unanimous backing for her position. Against his, it is superfluous to argue, for the truth of Heloise's assertions is evident to almost all.

To all, that is, except Abelard. He is isolated into a minority of one by her rhetoric of public opinion, which echoes his own. The pressure brought to bear on him by the impersonal verb *constat* in Heloise's phrase about the sacramentality of marriage is heightened and hardened when she completes her sentence: 'you are all the more bound to me by the measureless love with which I have always embraced you, as everyone sees' (*et eo te magis mihi obnoxium, quo te semper, ut omnibus patet, immoderato amore complexa sum*).[36] And why does measureless love entail a special obligation? For reasons plain to everyone (*ut omnibus patet*), apart from Abelard. Against him, everyone appears to take Heloise at her word: 'her thoughts … are evidently and objectively true.'[37] The 'objectivity' here is not reasoned but rhetorical; the appeal to unspecified witnesses serving to manoeuvre Abelard into a corner. Playing deftly on his susceptibility to *fama*, Heloise aims to shame him into acknowledgement of his ill-defined debts.

They are ill-defined because Heloise begs a series of questions which she leaves unanswered. How can debts be incurred by a love depicted as gratuitous and selfless? Is this not a contradiction in terms? No, no – for those terms have changed. After giving without thought of return, Heloise now stakes out her claims, which are founded on reciprocity of obligation. Obligation, not feeling, is the core of her case, she goes on to explain, because Abelard's past conduct was motivated rather by lust than by love (*libidinis ardor potius quam amor*).[38] This is less an explanation than a reproach. And the reproach is meant to sting, for Heloise stresses that this opinion is not just hers but widespread, common, and public (*non tam mea est quam omnium coniectura, non tam specialis quam communis, non tam privata quam publica*). The effect of such gossip is *vilitas* – a demeaning loss of self-worth which, first attributed to herself, is then projected on to Abelard. Her affirmation of his heartlessness is intended, dialectically, to provoke a denial.

∽

If none of this is taken into account in Abelard's first reply to Heloise,[39] the reason is neither lack of concern nor evasiveness. His homily on the virtues of women's prayer is not simply addressed to her and the nuns of

---

futurus' 21, ibid., 162; 'in publico omnibus' 26, ibid., 176; 'omnibus patebat' 30, ibid., 184; 'quasi adversum me universus coniurasset mundus' 35, ibid., 194. See further below.
[36] *Ep.* II.8, ibid., 242.   [37] Dronke, *Women Writers*, 116.   [38] *Ep.* II.14, ed. Pagani, 250.
[39] *Ep.* III, ibid., 254–66.

the Paraclete but also to a wider readership. Predominantly clerical and monastic, its members were aware of the proprieties of spiritual guidance. They had also been alerted, in the *HC*, to the tongues of gossip that had wagged about the couple's relationship. Both of them are conscious that the eyes of the world are upon them. Hence Abelard lends emphasis to Heloise's reproach that he had not written to her since she had taken vows,[40] and she claims that the *HC* had come to her attention 'by chance' (*forte*).[41] That may be the only inauthentic word in their correspondence. There is nothing fortuitous about the epistolary exchange of Abelard and Heloise. Documentary proof of their separation, designed to counter the calumny from which they had suffered, their works also aim to show how, as abbot and as abbess, they had changed. The tone is set by Heloise's allusion to Seneca's *Epistolae morales*.[42] It not only supports her request for frequent communications but also demonstrates that she understands the philosophical and paraenetic genre in which he situates the *HC*. Ethical guidance and spiritual comfort are sought from her confessor. Confession, however, does not mean submission. Humble as woman, wife, and ecclesiastical inferior, Heloise emerges, from her correspondence with Abelard, as at least his equal in moral thought.

It is as a thinker about ethics that she asserts and achieves independence. Heloise does not follow Abelard's line, even when they write about the same subjects. Nor does she defend the dignity of women – that task is left to him – but affirms, with a determination at variance with her professions of modesty, her theological competence in writings that take the most flexible form available to a Latin author of the twelfth century. Semi-public in function,[43] the *epistola* was regularly used as a medium of discussion and debate.[44] The term was metonymic; and did not just mean 'letter'. A continuation and extension of the project of ethical enquiry begun in the *HC*, Heloise's correspondence with Abelard is animated by a seriousness of purpose which enables her both to waive the ban on written confession[45] and to honour in the breach the Rule's prohibition of epistolography to monks and nuns.[46] But if she, as abbess, and he, as abbot, were

[40] *Ep.* III.1, ibid., 254.   [41] *Ep.* II.1, ibid., 234.   [42] *Ep.* II.4, ibid., 236–8.

[43] See R. Köhn, 'Dimensionen und Funktionen des Öffentlichen und Privaten in der mittelalterlichen Korrespondenz' in *Das Öffentliche und Private in der Vormoderne*, ed. G. Melville and P. von Moos, Norm und Struktur 10 (Cologne, 1998) 309–57.

[44] L. Ott, *Untersuchungen zur theologischen Briefliteratur der Frühscholastik*, BGPTMA 34 (Münster, 1937).

[45] On the prohibition of written confession, see Chapter 3.

[46] G. Constable, 'Monastic Letter Writing in the Middle Ages', *Filologia mediolatina* 11 (2004) 1–24.

empowered to dispense themselves from such restrictions, they were not free to compose those literary exercises in self-portrayal suggested by the misnomer 'personal'.[47] It suggests an anachronism beneath the dignity and below the decorum of medieval *epistolae*.

Decorum, intellectual or religious, has not troubled those bent on find-ing, in Heloise's 'personal letters', the secrets of her heart. They used to believe that they had discovered them on the subject of 'pure' or disinter-ested love,[48] until it was pointed out how commonplace this notion was in the twelfth century.[49] But 'pure' love is not the only version of that senti-ment, nor is it the first one to which Heloise refers. She speaks of her 'meas-ureless' or 'immoderate' love for Abelard. He may have winced on reading this expression. *Immoderatus amor* for humans is a concept that grated on his monastic mentality, which repudiated 'carnal affections' of this kind;[50] and, in the marital relationship stressed by her, he considered it tolerable only as a palliative to worse.[51] Irreprehensible, by contrast, was the meas-ureless *caritas* praised by Saints Augustine and Jerome, even if extended to those who did not deserve it and would not be saved.[52] Nonetheless, as a product of irrational will, it falls short of Abelard's ideal of reasoned love for God. *Amor* and *caritas*, it has been seen, are not synonyms in his dic-tion. Depending on their referent, human or divine, they can amount to antonyms. For excesses of amatory idealisation, applied to men or women rather than to God, Abelard displays a marked aversion.

Heloise does not argue against that position. On the contrary: she brands her own as insane. 'Measureless love' produced 'such madness' (*tanta insa-nia*) that she renounced her desire for him and, with it, her secular and affective identity (*tam habitum ... quam animum*).[53] This resourceful dia-lectician finds another, however, as a virtuosa of ethical paradox. Open blame of herself entails none too oblique criticism of Abelard. If Heloise had lost that reason which he considers indispensable to love, it was his fault, since he ordered her to act on her *immoderatus amor* against her own

[47] J. Muckle, 'The Personal Letters between Abelard and Heloise: Introduction, Authenticity, Text', *Mediaeval Studies* 15 (1953) 47–94.

[48] A summary of the older research is offered by M. Feo, 'L'amore perfetto' in *Petrarca e Agostino*, ed. R. Cardini and D. Coppini (Rome, 2004) 111–20. His view that Heloise tells 'lies' ('bugie') represents a travesty of the text.

[49] Cf. Marenbon, *Philosophy*, 298–303.   [50] *Sermo* 33, PL 178, 583A and 586B.

[51] *Problema Heloissae* 42, ibid., 726B.

[52] *In Romans* 13: 10, *Petri Abaelardi Opera Theologica* I: *Commentaria in Epistolam Pauli ad Romanos. Apologia contra Bernardum*, ed. E. Buytaert, OFM, CCCM 11 (Turnhout, 1969) 293, 239–45. See Perkams, *Liebe als Zentralbegriff*, 134–6.

[53] *Ep.* 11.9, ed. Pagani, 242, 244.

interest. Her irrationality added to the grounds for his guilt; she is said, implausibly, to idolise him.[54] Now, it is true that Heloise's paeans of praise rise to hymnic heights. But then they descend to the level and seemingly limitless plateau of Abelard's moral debts. Her sole cause of pain and grace of consolation, *solus* as her source of grief and happiness, he is also *solus* in the magnitude of all he owes her because, rather than offend him, she was prepared to lose herself. Another QED in the long list of questions that Heloise persists in begging. Why self-sacrifice does not speak for itself, rather than calling in debt after debt, Abelard is not invited to enquire. Nor do those who, oblivious to the intimidation of her moralising rhetoric, attribute to Heloise a secular religion of love which puts him in the position of God.[55]

This is to confuse an identification with an analogy. The analogy derives from Abelard's role as confessor, whose position as God's intermediary was being redefined, during Heloise's lifetime, in terms outlined in the third chapter. They add ambiguity to what is taken to be her famous declaration of selfless love, at which it is worth looking again:

God knows that I never sought anything in you but yourself, desiring you purely and not your things. I did not aspire to the bond of marriage or a dowry, nor indeed did I aim to satisfy my pleasures and desires but yours, as you know. And if the name of wife seems more hallowed and respectable, the word 'girlfriend' has always been sweeter to my taste or, if you will forebear, those of concubine and whore, so that, by humbling myself more fully for your sake, I may acquire an ampler measure of your grace, and thus detract less from the glory of your excellence.[56]

Between Abelard's mode of knowing and God's, Heloise draws an analogy. 'God knows' (*Deus scit*) in the first sentence is parallel to 'as you know' (*sicut ipse nosti*) in the second. And what is Abelard supposed to know? Not so much her actions as her intentions, on which she rings the changes

---

[54] Ibid.
[55] Cf. Gilson, *Heloïse et Abélard*, 115: 'littéralement la détresse de l'adoratrice délaissée par son dieu'; R. Mohr, 'Der Gedenkenaustausch zwischen Heloisa und Abälard über eine Modifizierung der Regula Benedicti für Frauen', *Regulae Benedicti Studia* 5 (1976) 308, citing L. Grane, *Peter Abelard. Philosophie und Christentum im Mittelalter* (Göttingen, 1969) 74; 'idolatrous devotion' according to Newman, 'Authority, Authenticity, and the Repression of Heloise', 139.
[56] 'Nihil umquam, Deus scit, in te nisi te requisivi, te pure non tua concupiscens. Non matrimonii foedera, non dotes aliquas expectavi, non denique meas voluptates aut voluntates sed tuas, sicut ipse nosti, adimplere studui. Et si uxoris nomen sanctius ac validius videtur, dulcius mihi semper exstitit amicae vocabulum aut, si non indigneris, concubinae vel scorti ut, quo me videlicet pro te amplius humiliarem, ampliorem apud te consequerer gratiam et sic etiam excellentiae tuae gloriam minus laederem', *Ep.* II.10, ed. Pagani, 244.

in no less than three verbs ('sought', 'aspired', 'aimed': *requisivi, expectavi, studui*). The same assertion is repeated and reinforced later:

> You alone, on the basis of your experience, can judge my constant intention toward you; I entrust everything to your scrutiny, I yield on every point to your testimony.[57]

Invoked both as a witness and as a judge, in Biblical language reminiscent of Kings 2:3, Abelard is portrayed as capable of penetrating the secrets of Heloise's heart.

All of which is exactly what he denied, in *Scito te ipsum*, that anyone was able to do for (or to) another.[58] 'The Church does not judge the secrets of the heart': as Abelard interpreted this maxim of the canonists, intentions are knowable only to God. He alone, therefore, is equal to retributive justice: courts or individuals, imperfect and erring, can assess no more than actions. Heloise asserts the opposite. God-like in his knowledge of her motivation, Abelard is both put in the position of her confessor and reassigned his role as her object of 'measureless love'. But the language is not just amatory, nor is the thought idolatrous. Both are in line with the orthodox opinions of Cardinal Robert Pullen and the ruling of Pope Eugenius III,[59] neither of whom imagined a woman addressing in these double-edged terms an ex-lover and present husband who was also her spiritual guide. The ambiguity was without precedent, the agility unparalleled; and Abelard did not attempt to match either. He continued to insist on the limits of his and others' knowledge.

Limits afford protection. It was needed by one who believed himself to be the victim of a cosmic conspiracy. There is defensiveness, as well as propriety, in Abelard's semi-public stance while corresponding with Heloise, which points to a difference between them evident in their attitudes to *fama* and *invidia*. She recalls her past eminence as his beloved with nostalgia. He is more fraught. What concerns Abelard is less their former relationship than the attitude of others, whom he assumes to be hostile. *Invidia*, for him, is a negative category without nuance. Enmity, malice, and rivalry versus subordination and obedience: these are the extremes between which Abelard's view of human relations veered. He never conceives of empathy on the part of his adversaries. Heloise was

---

[57] 'Quem autem animum in te semper habuerim solus, qui expertus es, iudicare potes: tuo examini cuncta committo, tuo per omnia cedo testimonio', *Ep.* II.13, ibid., 250.
[58] *Ethics*, ed. Luscombe, 40, 7ff.; *Scito te ipsum* I.25, ed. Ilgner, 26, 683ff. The self-judgements of the individual conscience are well discussed by Perkams, *Liebe als Zentralbegriff*, 118–25.
[59] See Chapter 3.

more generous and less inclined to be on guard. Even as she reminisces about the pinnacle of fame from which she was toppled, she thinks without animus about the women who had envied her. When they witnessed her *débâcle* in love and in life, these rivals felt compassion for her.[60] Or so Heloise imagines, as Abelard does not.

This difference in their moral imaginations is a factor in the formulation of her next paradox: 'I, who have done most harm, am most innocent, as you know' (*quae plurimum nocens, plurimum, ut nosti, sum innocens*).[61] A less refined thinker might have found a variant on the words of Pontius Pilate (Matthew 27:24): 'I am innocent of the blood of this just man' (*innocens sum a sanguine huius iusti*), which are readily adaptable to fit both the facts of Heloise's case and Abelard's imitation of Christ. But self-exculpation is not her aim. It is self-accusation attenuated by blamelessness of motivation. Again she appeals to his knowledge (*ut nosti*) as one warrant of her nuanced truth. The other is impersonal: that 'equity' (*aequitas*) which weighs 'not what is done but in what spirit it is done' (*nec quae fiunt, sed quo animo fiunt*) and which is often compared with the phrasing of Abelard's commentary on Romans and *Scito te ipsum*.[62] Yet again it is not the verbal similarity between his and Heloise's ideas on intentionality – far from uncommon in the second quarter of the twelfth century – that is noteworthy, but the conceptual difference between their notions of equity.

Against the equity of God, Abelard rails in the sequel to Soissons, portraying himself as a raving madman (*insanus, furibundus*).[63] Out of his mind, he returned to it in a distinction between his castration as just punishment for an acknowledged fault and his condemnation as 'manifest violence' against the upright motives (*sincera intentio amorque fidei nostrae*) for which he had written the *Theologia 'Summi boni'*.[64] Opposition between the intentions of the moral agent and the malevolence with which they are perceived is Abelard's premise for the second part of this distinction. Here *fama* and *conscientia*, the chief ethical categories of the *HC*, declare war. More at peace with herself and others, even in the affective isolation of the Paraclete, Heloise regards the inner and outer spheres of the moral life as operating in harmony or, at least, not in obvious conflict. Others

---

[60] 'Quam tunc mihi invidentem, nunc tantis privata deliciis *compati* calamitas mea non compellat?', *Ep.* 11.13, ed. Pagani, 248.
[61] Ibid.   [62] Rightly criticised by Marenbon, *Philosophy*, 91–2.
[63] *HC* 32, ed. Pagani, 188 and Chapter 5.   [64] Ibid.

might be right to consider her harmful because, at one level, that is how she considers herself.

A degree of equity is conceded to human judgement by Heloise. None at all is granted by Abelard, who assimilates that concept to divine *caritas*. In this world it is not merely customary but correct to level exemplary punishments on inadvertent offenders or, following procedural rules, to find guilty the falsely incriminated.[65] These are less instances of judicial propriety than examples of human incapability to fathom motivation. Products of Abelard's pessimism about moral justice on earth, they count among the negative reasons for his concentration on God's *caritas*, to which his ethical thought is turned. Not yet estranged from the erring perceptions and fallible verdicts of men, Heloise, who imagines and seeks compassion, makes the mistake of turning to him.

Abelard may not be her Samson, but she is his anti-type of Dalila. In the words of that treacherous temptress (Judges 16:15), Heloise declares her loyalty: 'my heart was not with me but with you' (*non enim mecum animus sed tecum erat*).[66] With the self-interest of Dalila is contrasted the altruism of Heloise, ambivalent as ever between reverence and reproach, present and past. In the past, when she was 'on everyone's lips' (*in ore omnium*),[67] Abelard composed love-poetry for her: in the present, she needs a prose consolation from him if she is to attend to divine service. The symmetry adds wit to her partial admission of his view of her as 'our ... sister in Christ'. But the tone is *basso* compared with the *forte* of her insistence on his obligations or her love. And about one of the strongest possible links between those two themes, Heloise is strikingly silent.

She never mentions maternal love or refers to Astralabe in her letters to Abelard. Their son does not appear in her works until after his father's death, when she wrote, requesting a job for him, to Peter the Venerable (who replied with the timeless truth: 'It's so difficult to find a job nowadays').[68] From Heloise's first letter, which justifies its declaratory rather than demonstrative character in repeated appeals to common knowledge,[69] one of the most salient facts about her relationship with Abelard is omitted. Discretion was not the motive; her pregnancy and the birth of their son are narrated in the *HC*.[70] Why then this reticence about

[65] *Ethics*, ed. Luscombe, 38, 5ff.; *Scito te ipsum* 1.24, ed. Ilgner, 25, 658ff.
[66] *Ep.* ii.15, ed. Pagani, 252.   [67] *Ep.* ii.16, ibid.
[68] *Epp.* 167 and 168 in *The Letters of Peter the Venerable* I, ed. Constable, 400–2.
[69] Eg: 'Quanto autem debito te erga <nos> obligaveris, *non argumentis non testimoniis indiget* ut quasi dubium comprobetur et si omnes taceant, res ipsa clamat', *Ep.* ii.6, ed. Pagani, 238.
[70] *HC* 15, ed. Pagani, 140, 142; *HC* 20, ibid., 158.

Astralabe, the one product of their marriage who, more obviously than any other, continued to be the responsibility of them both? Did parenthood not establish an obligation at least as reciprocal, moral, and binding as the rest listed by Heloise? Her letter to Peter the Venerable and Abelard's *Carmen ad Astralabium* suggest that they acknowledged that obligation later. But if later, why not then? These questions cannot be answered, for, as he argued, the *arcana cordis* are inscrutable.

The silences of Heloise, on this and other issues, are no less notable than her overt eloquence. When she speaks in borrowed voices, they are neither predominantly nor significantly Ovidian. Reflecting on marriage and the role of the confessor, this learned lady finds variants on themes played by contemporary virtuosi of theology. But if these variants are in tune with the music of orthodoxy, they are unmistakably her own. Heloise's own, not her husband's, is her vivid and discriminating style. Perhaps seen at its subtlest in her combination of amatory language with ecclesiological analogy, the refinement of her writing is also evident in its divergences from Abelard's. Often quoting Cicero (*De inventione* 1.41.76) on sameness as the mother of excess, he elevates the citation into a hermeneutic principle in the prologue to his *Sic et non*.[71] His stylistic practice does not always conform to his theory. A tiresome feature of Abelard's Latinity is his fondness for pronominal adjectives in correlative constructions, such as *tanto ... quanto*.[72] Repeated *ad nauseam* in the *HC*, they are toned down by Heloise, who practises more effectively than her ex-master the variation he preaches.[73]

Alert to his mannerisms, she is not above mimicking them with wit. When, for example, Heloise writes 'should everyone be silent, the facts speak out for themselves' (*si omnes taceant, res ipsa clamat*), her echo of Abelard's 'were I to be silent, the facts speak out for themselves' (*si ego taceam, res ipsa clamat*) transforms the egotism of his pseudo-objectivity into an appeal to public opinion against him.[74] Understated imitations of

[71] *Sic et non*, ed. Boyer and McKeon, 89 with Bezner, *Vela veritatis*, 562ff.
[72] Noted, but not analysed, by J. Benton and F. Prosperetti Ercoli, 'The Style of the *Historia Calamitatum*: A Preliminary Test of the Authenticity of the Correspondence Attributed to Abelard and Heloise', *Viator* 6 (1975) 63.
[73] *HC* 3, ed. Pagani, 112; 5, ibid., 118; 10, ibid., 128; 11, ibid., 130; 12, ibid., 134; 15, ibid., 140; 23, ibid., 166; 24, ibid., 174; 30, ibid., 184; 38, ibid., 200; 42, ibid., 208; 47, ibid., 216; 48, ibid., 218; 49, ibid., 220; 51, ibid., 224; 52, ibid., 226; 54, ibid., 228; 55, ibid., 230. *Ep.* ii.1, ibid., 234; 3, ibid., 236; 4, ibid., 236; 8, ibid., 242.
[74] *Ep.* ii.6, ibid., 238; *HC* 6, ibid., 120.

Abelard's stylistic ticks or tacit corrections of his excesses like these cannot be assessed by databases or by yet another computation of *cursus*,[75] because no count of words or rhythm is adequate to fathom the dialectical qualities of Heloise's thought. And her thinking transcends dialectic with his to achieve originality in paradoxes of the conscience not only unattested in Abelard's works but also incompatible with his mentality. Prominent in Heloise's first letter, they are prevalent in the second.

She begins her second letter to him with a touch of tartness.[76] Heloise chides Abelard for having placed her name before his in the greeting with which his reply to her first letter opens. A *salutatio* should not only follow epistolary conventions but also observe the order of nature; it is correct and fitting that superiors precede inferiors. The universal perspective linked to the bird's-eye view, Heloise teaches Abelard a lesson in ambiguous humility, combining self-effacement with self-assertion. That paradox, fundamental to both these letters, is more than a figure of rhetoric or a brand of argument. Its function is existential. Preserving the form while subverting the content of inferiority, Heloise holds in equilibrium the tensions between her multiple roles as wife, abbess, and author. Abelard was incapable of so delicate a balancing-act. Either humble or proud, he never rose to the feat of being both at once. Nor does his inner life appear to have been subject to the same pressures. After Soissons, his calamities occurred from the outside. They did not arise from within. Alien to, or at least unexpressed by, Abelard were the strains, at times erupting into self-division, that are formative of Heloise's paradoxical style and thought.

Neither her thought nor her style, in her second letter, is modelled on his. This is the case even when concepts and criteria used by them both are, or appear to be, similar. Foreseeing his death, Heloise observes with regret and reproach, Abelard has not provided consolation but caused desolation.[77] Its effect is again parallel to that of a trauma described in the *HC*.[78] Should he pass away, Heloise imagines herself as deranged (*insana*) in anger against God. But if that was Abelard's state after Soissons, it was provoked by shame, not by grief for another. And since he is not yet dead, nor is she railing against God. Banished to the realm of speculation, Heloise's blasphemy at this point is hypothetical, unlike his in the sequel to the council of 1121. The real analogy between their situations is offered by Abelard's criterion of *sincera intentio*, misunderstood by the malice of his enemies,

[75] Cf. J. Ziolkowski, 'Lost and Not Yet Found: Heloise, Abelard and the *Epistolae duorum amantium*', *The Journal of Medieval Latin* 14 (2004) 171–202.
[76] *Ep.* IV.1, ed. Pagani, 268.   [77] *Ep.* IV.3, ibid., 270–2.   [78] *HC* 32, ibid., 188.

which is then employed to counter his admonitions to her.[79] Yet Heloise's concern for her husband at Saint-Gildas does not make her incapable of prayer at the Paraclete; it simply renders her unable to pray *sincere*. The reference is both to a cardinal term in his analysis of the conscience and to a standard which they shared with their contemporaries.[80] In prayer, when God saw the heart, word and deed were expected to be in harmony.[81] Although prevented from achieving that harmony by the prospect of grief, Heloise is neither out of her mind like Abelard in 1121 nor inclined to view her plight with the solemnity displayed by him on the subject of himself.

Next to nothing has been written about Heloise's sense of humour. But it is there, in her conceits of 'unfortunate fortune' (*infortunata fortuna*) emptying its quiver on her so completely that others had no fear of its assault and of her body being left without any place for a wound.[82] Anxious only that it might destroy her too quickly, the personified malevolence conjured up by Heloise is a figure less of pathos than of bathos. Her hyperbole is not that of a *planctus*,[83] but a mimicry of Abelard's rhetoric of victimisation.[84] For his tragic history of calamities, she substitutes a black comedy with elements of grotesque. There is little self-pity in Heloise, and much indignation. That indignation is represented as moral. What happened to her and, especially, to him was a perversion of all the laws of equity (*omnia in nobis aequitatis iura pariter sunt perversa*).[85] This diction was meant to shock. *Aequitas*, in the legal and theological discourse of the twelfth century, was reserved to divine justice.[86] Accusing it of perversion, Heloise now commits a blasphemy which is by no means mitigated by the arguments with which she seeks to justify it. Punished not when they fornicated but when married and living in chaste separation, the couple, as she sees it, was further divided by a punishment inflicted on Abelard alone. It is that division, contested in her first letter but confirmed in his reply to it, which Heloise again challenges with her concept of union in guilt: 'you

---

[79] 'Confectus maerore animus quietus non est, nec Deo *sincere* potest vacari mens perturbationibus occupata', *Ep.* IV.3, ed. Pagani, 272. Cf. Abelard's *Expositio dominice orationis*, ed. De Santis, 212, 122ff.

[80] See Constable, 'The Concern for Sincerity and Understanding in Liturgical Prayer'.

[81] See Augustine on Psalm 139:5 in *S. Aurelii Augustini Enarrationes in Psalmos CI–CL*, ed. Dekkers and Fraipont, CCSL 40, 2015. For a useful survey, see E. von Severus, 'Gebet', *RLAC* VIII, 1134–1258.

[82] *Ep.* IV.4, ed. Pagani, 272.

[83] P. Dronke, 'Heloise and Marianne: Some Reconsiderations', *Romanische Forschungen* 72 (1960) 232.

[84] *HC* 21, ed. Pagani, 160ff. and 32, ibid., 188ff.   [85] *Ep.* IV.5 ibid., 274.

[86] See I. Bejczy, 'Law and Ethics: Twelfth-Century Jurists on the Virtue of Justice', *Viator* 36 (2005) 197–216.

were alone in punishment, but two were to blame' (*solus in poena fuisti, duo in culpa*).[87]

Empathy is one premise of this declaration, selflessness is another. Neither was a quality at which Abelard excelled. If he reflected on Heloise's idea, it was by elaborating, in *Scito te ipsum*, the distinction between moral justice and exemplary punishment which she draws by antithesis. But antithesis serves a different purpose in his ethical tract, opposing the infallibility of God's tribunal to the erring opinions of men. They are incapable of true *aequitas* because, unlike Him, they do not 'see in the dark' (cf. Ezekiel 8:12). Heloise, by contrast, considers both divine and human justice mistaken in respect of Abelard's punishment,[88] on the disarming grounds that she was complicit in his crime. That is why she formulates her sense of guilt for suffering deserved by them both but endured only by him as a self-accusation. The moral perspectives of the couple are diametrically opposed. If Abelard detects in his castration the equitable hand of providence,[89] Heloise regards it as outrageous as the slings and arrows of fortune. He is serene and detached: she indignant and distraught.

How distraught, is indicated by the twists and turns of her argument, which veers from self-accusation to self-defence, ending with self-condemnation. Heloise begins with a parade of misogynistic clichés, reminiscent of her invective against marriage.[90] But then, at the end of her Biblical examples of women's nefarious effect on men, she thanks God that, unlike those *femmes fatales*, she had not consented to 'guilt' (*culpa*). Absence of consent, in her view, demonstrates an 'innocence [which] purifies my soul'. The term *consensus* is the same as that used in *Scito te ipsum* and the argument would be similar to Abelard's, did Heloise not add a qualification. The sexual sins she committed before the 'crime' of his castration prevent her from asserting her complete guiltlessness. If she suffers now, it is rightly so, for her erotic pleasures in the past stand to her *poena* in a relationship, temporal and ethical, of cause and effect: *praecedentium in me peccatorum sequentia merito facta sunt poena.*[91]

This sequence of sinfulness had little meaning for Abelard. In terms of his ethical theory, Heloise was conflating two categories that should be kept separate. Although she was sinful, because aware of consenting to wrong, in her 'pleasures of carnal vice' (*carnalium illecebrarum voluptates*), they do not establish her co-responsibility for his castration. Presumably

[87] *Ep.* IV.5, ed. Pagani, 276.
[88] '[Quanto enim amplius te pro me humiliando satisfeceras…] tanto te minus apud Deum quam apud illos proditores obnoxium poenae reddideras', ibid.
[89] *HC* 32, ed. Pagani, 188; 49 ibid., 220.   [90] *Ep.* IV.5–6, ibid., 276–8.   [91] *Ep.* IV.7, ibid., 280.

ignorant of what Fulbert was plotting and certainly not in agreement with it, Heloise had nothing to do with this 'crime', because culpability at one remove cannot be imputed to a moral agent. It is *consensus*, informed and unmediated, that determines guilt, Abelard argues in *Scito te ipsum*. For him, the first of Heloise's propositions is coherent, but not the second. It represents a confusion of cause and effect, as she herself admits: 'I have been made the cause of the evil committed by its effect' (*quam* [= *me*] *tamen in causam commissae malitiae ex effectu convertit*).

Moving in its emotivity but mistaken in its analysis, Heloise's conscience voices its pessimism in the words of Leo the Great: 'a perverse conclusion is to be attributed to bad beginnings' (*malis initiis perversus imputandus est exitus*).[92] Note the adjective *perversus*. It typifies the dialectical character of her style and thought. What she counters here is the optimism with which Abelard concludes the account of his calamities: 'all perverse happenings are put to an excellent end [by God]' (*quaecumque perverse fiunt optimo fine ipse terminat* [*Deus*]).[93] *Perverse* – *perversus*: the word is the same, but the ideas are antithetical. The antithesis is a product of two mentalities which, although related to one another, are hardly compatible. Style, most elusive of criteria, should not be analysed mechanically. To ignore the claims of context is to distort the significance of verbal resemblances. Imitation does not demonstrate common authorship, for the philosopher's pupil had become his critical peer. The independence of Heloise from Abelard is notable even – or especially – when she refers to his writings; and if the conceptual differences between them are most marked when their stylistic similarities appear closest, this is due to their dialectic of the conscience.

---

[92] *Ep.* IV.7, ibid., 280. This source (*Ep.* XII.1) is identified by Pagani, ibid.
[93] *HC* 56, ed. Pagani, 232

CHAPTER 7

Sincere hypocrisy

Rational and reflective yet hardly capable of accounting for the will to choose evil,[1] Abelard's conscience resembles an impartial arbiter. Heloise's is more like an implacable prosecutor, bent on incriminating herself. Not content with self-accusation, she goes on to address the issues, both personal and theoretical, raised by penance.[2] And it is in dealing with these issues, in her second letter, that Heloise develops some of her subtlest paradoxes, among them sincere hypocrisy. She declares that she wishes to do penance for Abelard's sufferings. What does that mean? If the lifelong contrition which she imagines inflicting on herself is identical to a classic definition of monasticism quoted by Abelard,[3] there end her resemblances to him and to virtually every other writer on the doctrine of penance.[4] They taught that *contritio* should be directed to God. Not so Heloise. Impenitent towards Him, whom she accuses of 'extreme cruelty', she criticises divine justice and denies hope in divine mercy.

Too little attention has been paid to this statement, which none of her contemporaries would have taken lightly; too much to her erotic fantasies during mass, which at least some of them were inclined to regard more indulgently.[5] No indulgence was possible for the sin of blasphemy against the Holy Spirit which Heloise commits in defiance and despair.[6] That sin, mortal and irremissible, is compounded by her wish to perform what she describes as mental expiation for Abelard's physical injury, in order 'to satisfy at least you, if not God' (*tibi saltem modo, si non Deo, satisfaciam*). Transposing the

---

[1] Cf. Perkams, *Liebe als Zentralbegriff*, 118ff., 313ff.   [2] *Ep.* IV.8, ed. Pagani, 280.
[3] Cf. his solution to *Problema Heloissae* 14: 'Quid enim vita monastica, nisi quaedam districtioris poenitentiae forma?', PL 178, 700A.
[4] For Abelard's ideas on contrition see *Ethics*, ed. Luscombe 88, 6ff.; 96, 19ff.; *Scito te ipsum* 1.59, 64, ed. Ilgner, 58, 1517ff.; 64, 1676ff. and Chapter 5. For context, see Anciaux, *Théologie*.
[5] See below.
[6] Cf. Abelard, *Problema Heloissae* 13, PL 178, 694B. See Landgraf, *Dogmengeschichte* IV, 1, 15ff. and cf. Merkel, 'Gotteslästerung'; Speyer, 'Fluch'; and Murray, *Suicide* II, 377ff.

138

religious concept of atonement (*satisfactio*) onto a secular plane, Heloise elaborates on the ambiguity of Abelard's role as spiritual guide discussed in her first letter. Elaboration, here, lapses into error. If, as confessor, he received her avowals *in loco Dei*, it did not follow that he could be 'recompensed' for his sufferings by a remorse expressed in blasphemy, nor that he might accept 'contrition' for sins of which he deemed her innocent.

Substituting him for the divine tribunal to which atonement was due, Heloise's misuse of the language of penance produces a symmetry of discord. Not only at variance with Abelard in her insistence on her guilt, she is also at odds with God. This double dilemma of alienation compels her to recognise that she is not in full possession of her faculties. In an expression that sets her tone and serves to account for her vagaries, Heloise describes her state as the 'infirmity … of a most anguished mind' (*miserrimi … animi … infirmitas*). A parallel, implicit and imperfect, is thereby drawn between her at the Paraclete and Abelard at Saint-Médard.[7] Incapable of remorse towards God, what she feels is recrimination. The difference is, that he dismisses his condition then as the raving of a madman, while she, distraught but not demented, remains within the limits of motivated irrationality.[8]

Loss of control, in the Aristotelian sense of ἀκρασία (*incontinentia*, in Latin),[9] is induced in Heloise by a combination of selfless grief and misplaced guilt. Abelard made little allowance for that state, which represented a shade of ethical grey barely perceptible to his black-and-white mentality. What he understood was, the starker contrast between derangement, which he had experienced after Soissons, and sanity, to which such moral psychology as he could muster is confined within a logical framework that recognises, but scarcely explains, irrationality.[10] Assuming as self-evident the desire for good, identified with obedience to God's commands, Abelard acknowledges only that it may be sapped by what he calls 'bad will' (*mala voluntas*) and 'weakness of the flesh' (*infirmitas carnis*).[11]

---

[7] See Chapter 5.   [8] Cf. D. Pears, *Motivated Irrationality* (Oxford, 1984).

[9] The term is used here not only in its technical sense, as a paradox of rational choice, but as an aspect of moral psychology which, construed in terms of the Aristotelian analogy to acting (see below), sheds light on Heloise's dilemma. For a valuable collection of essays on this subject, see *Das Problem der Willensschwäche in der mittelalterlichen Philosophie. The Problem of Weakness of Will in Medieval Philosophy*, ed. J. Hoffmann *et al.*, Recherches de théologie et philosophie médiévales Bibliotheca 8 (Leuven, 2006).

[10] See C. Grellard, '*Fides sive credulitas*: Le problème de l'assentiment chez Abélard, entre logique et psychologie', *AHDLMA* 70 (2003) 7–25.

[11] *Ethics* ed. Luscombe, 16, 22–4; *Scito te ipsum* 1.10, ed. Ilgner, 261–3.

Were this a diagnosis of Heloise's moral malaise, it would be wide of the mark. Her will is not evil but uncontrolled in its altruistic empathy for his sufferings; nor, at this moment, is it her flesh which is weak, but her spirit which is in conflict with God. Her crisis, unlike Abelard's of 1121, is not occasioned by external circumstances; it arises from within. And there he had difficulty in accounting for the phenomenon which he defined as 'being compelled to wish what one wishes not to wish' (*velle coguntur quod nequaquam vellent velle*).[12] The difficulty arose from Abelard's particular, not to say peculiar, theory of the will.[13] If its relationship to his ideas on *consensus*, the decisive moment of assent to wrong or sinful action, is problematic, one of his premises is clear: even reluctant and compelled actions can be regarded as products of intellectual cognition, because thought is assumed to precede them.[14] That is why Abelard claims that: 'we always have control over our will and consent' (*voluntatem vero semper et consensum in nostro habemus arbitrio*).[15]

This claim is not borne out by one of the principal examples which he uses to illustrate it: that of the slave pursued by his cruel master, discussed in Book I of Augustine's *De libero arbitrio* and refashioned in Abelard's ethical tract.[16] Believing that he is about to be murdered or tortured, the slave kills his master. The homicide, according to Augustine, demonstrates evil will. Alert to both the moral and the legal dimensions of the problem, the saint condemns the slave on the grounds that he has failed to act on the principle that to live a life bought at the cost of another is 'better called death'. The elegance of this paradox of moral suicide does not conceal its fragility. Inferring motivation from action, Augustine takes no account of context. The heat of the moment, the urgency of the pursuit, the combination of alarm and threat suggest not only the evil will on which the saint insists but also panic striking out in what was taken to be self-defence. About that, Augustine says nothing. Instead he attributes to the slave an intellectual cognition far from plausible in the circumstances which is meant to establish his moral responsibility. But the slender evidence provided does not exclude a version of that motivated irrationality which

---

[12] Ibid. and see below.
[13] See Saarinen, *Weakness of the Will*, 51–60; Marenbon, *Philosophy*, 262ff.; Perkams, *Liebe als Zentralbegriff*, 107ff.
[14] A different view is argued by J. Müller, 'Das Problem der Willensschwäche bei Petrus Abaelardus', in *Das Problem der Willensschwäche*, ed. Hoffmann *et al.*, 123–45.
[15] *Ethics*, ed. Luscombe, 26, 2–3; *Scito te ipsum* 1.16, ed. Ilgner, 423–4.
[16] 1.4.25–1.4.30 in *S. Aurelii Augustini Opera* II, 2, ed. W. Green, CCSL 29 (Turnhout, 1970) 216, 32ff. – 217, 69 and *Ethics*, ed. Luscombe, 6, 24ff.; *Scito te ipsum* 1.4, ed. Ilgner 4, 90ff.

Augustine describes brilliantly in the eighth book of the *Confessions*. Eloquent there about his own loss of control, he makes no allowance for it here in the case of the slave.

Augustine's reticence on this point is all the more striking because he both provides and suppresses facts which complicate the case. A conflict between equals would have been sufficient to ground his verdict, but he has selected a hierarchical relationship, which places the slave at a double disadvantage. No law may license the murder of the master, as Augustine states, but none prevents him from killing or torturing his slave, as the saint does not. Context has more bearing on the issue of motivation than he cares to acknowledge: the harsh facts of ancient life may have contributed to acratic action on the part of the slave. Arguably neither bad nor good but uncontrolled, his will is open to more than one interpretation. There is room for a judgement of involuntary homicide. Yet Augustine finds this ambiguous agent guilty of both murder and moral suicide, condemning him without right of appeal to time, place, and circumstances.

That circumstances, place, and time are relevant to the assessment of crime, Abelard does not deny. The trouble is, that he, like his contemporaries, hardly distinguishes crime from sin.[17] Sin, properly speaking, can be judged only by God, who knows those *arcana cordis* which Abelard calls intentions. Men guess at motivation on the basis of acts. This antithesis is not neutral; the sympathies expressed in *Scito te ipsum* are plainly for the divine and against the human tribunal, such as the one which condemned its author at Soissons. But recognition of men's imperfection need not have led Abelard to conclude that their legal thought on such issues was irrelevant; which is what he seems to do when, recasting Augustine's example of the slave, he ignores everything that had been written by canonists since the saint about the right of self-defence in emergency.[18]

This is revealing because Abelard, more than Augustine, saw the need for contextual explanation of the case. He adds to the skeletal account of *De libero arbitrio* circumstantial details. The slave's flight was long (*diu*) and, only after repeated attempts to escape, did he finally (*tandem*) capitulate to necessity and kill his master. *Coactus et nolens*: involuntary but intentional, as Abelard understands it, contrary to Augustine, the agent is motivated by a variant on that coerced consent with which he described, in the *HC*, Heloise's taking the veil: 'at my command, voluntarily' (*ad imperium nostrum sponte*). She conformed her will to his.[19] And will, rather than

---

[17] Kuttner, *Kanonistische Schuldlehre*.   [18] Ibid., 334ff.   [19] See Chapter 4.

intention, remains the issue in the case of the slave,[20] for, despite Abelard's urge to view this problem in a perspective different from Augustine's, he continues to employ the same optic. Having described the circumstances as an emergency and the situation as desperate, he concludes that the slave's killing of his master was 'rashness' (*temeritas*).[21] But what is rashness other than an error or misjudgement of the will? *Temeritas* imposes a value-judgement which reinforces the Augustinian voluntarism that Abelard wants to undermine. The effect is, to render the meaning of assent unclear. If *consensus* entails an act of cognition based on definite knowledge, it does not fit the facts of the case refashioned by Abelard. The slave does not *know*; he *apprehends*; and his apprehension is forced (*coactus*) upon him by the circumstances.

The circumstances added by Abelard to *De libero arbitrio* tend to a plea of diminished responsibility for acratic action. He rules it out, sentencing the slave to damnation and death of the soul. Augustine's severity is not tempered, and Abelard remains under the spell of that bewitching saint even when he wishes to differ from him, because he fails to develop the implications of the context whose relevance he admits. An aversion from legal thought is detectable in *Scito te ipsum*, although there are signs that its author was acquainted with canonists' often sophisticated ideas on guilt. Not by chance does Abelard re-write one of the standard examples recurrent in the penitential literature – that of a mother who had inadvertently smothered her child.[22] As in the case of the slave, he adds a wealth of details not to be found in any of his sources. Piling on the pathos – the mother is poor; the 'little boy' (*infantulus*) is suckling; she covers him with rags, moved by pity for his sufferings; and smothers him only because she is overcome, in her weakness, by the force of nature[23] – Abelard ensures that our sympathies are on her side when he argues that punishments are inflicted on works of sin rather than sin itself.

Yet he does not let this distinction alone, adding that 'sometimes punishment is reasonably (*rationabiliter*) inflicted on a person in whom no fault preceded' (*nulla culpa praecessit*).[24] The language, patently legal, evokes the canonists' criterion of *culpa praecedens*. If the adverb 'reasonably' is not ironical, it implies deference to their authority, although Abelard has gone out of his way to make the mother's punishment seem unreasonable, because heavy. *Consensus* is irrelevant to her action, for she was asleep when

---

[20] Cf. W. Mann, 'Ethics' in *Cambridge Companion to Abelard*, 283.
[21] *Ethics*, ed. Luscombe, 8, 17; *Scito te ipsum* 1.5, ed. Ilgner, 5, 121.
[22] See Chapter 2 above.   [23] *Ethics*, ed. Luscombe, 38, 13–18; *Scito te ipsum* 1.24, ed. Ilgner, 25, 658ff.
[24] Ibid., 40, 5; ibid., 1.25; 26, 680 (*ubi culpa non precessit*).

it was performed; but context again has more bearing than he allows. As Abelard has refashioned this example, it raises the issue of lack of foresight which canonists argued could represent a form of guilt.[25] That guilt, however, was assessed in terms less summary than those of *Scito te ipsum*. Both legal and penitential literature referred to mitigating circumstances, such as the long-term effects of a life of deprivation producing culpable but pitiable ignorance.[26] That may be the idea inherent in the pathos with which Abelard elaborates on this standard example of infanticide, but he does not draw its gentler conclusions.

If antipathy to legalism is understandable on the part of the scapegoat of Soissons, allowance must also be made for the fact that *Scito te ipsum* is incomplete. Its unfinished state is mirrored in its author's alternations between divine and human perspectives on justice. Although Abelard passes moral verdicts as if from God's tribunal, the evidence on which they are based is open to the objection of circularity. How, for example, does he know that the slave's intention was wicked? From his action – on the grounds, no different from Augustine's, that motivation must be induced from deeds.[27] Their ethical neutrality is asserted, but the assertion is contradicted, in the case of the slave, by the negative verdict of 'rashness'. If this term points to a 'mental attitude related to the act of consent, but distinct from it' or to a 'second-order will',[28] the status of this entity unspecified by Abelard is not easy to imagine without reference to Augustine's theory that willing is, and must be, present in all action.[29]

Scito te ipsum is a work by an author striving to modify an Augustinian language of ethics who has not yet found another that is consistent in its own terms. The signs are multiple. Abelard preserves the saint's account of the 'stages of sinning' as suggestion, pleasure, and assent,[30] despite the inapplicability of this triad to the case of the slave. For him, suggestion

---

[25] Cf. Kuttner, *Kanonistische Schuldlehre*, 117 and 314.

[26] P. Payer, 'The Humanism of the Penitentials and the Continuity of the Penitential Tradition', *Mediaeval Studies* 46 (1984) 340–51.

[27] Cf. I. Bejczy, 'Deeds without Value: Exploring a Weak Spot in Abelard's Ethics', *RTAM* 70 (2003) 11.

[28] Marenbon, *Philosophy*, 262; Saarinen, *Weakness of Will*, 51–60.

[29] *De spiritu et littera* XXXI.53, ed. and trans. A. Trapè and L. Volpi in *Sant'Agostino, Natura e grazia* I (Rome, 1981) 336, discussed by Sorabji, *Emotions and Peace of Mind* 335–6. Abelard appears to acknowledge this difficulty both at *Ethics*, ed. Luscombe, 16, 30–31; *Scito te ipsum* 1.10, ed. Ilgner, 11, 270–3 and at *Problema Heloissae* 20, PL 178, 708C, where he attempts to restrict the meaning of will at Romans 7:15 to approving of action: '"volo" dixit pro "fieri approbo"'.

[30] *Ethics*, ed. Luscombe, 32, 23ff.; *Scito te ipsum* 1.21, ed. Ilgner, 21, 556ff. See Augustine, *De sermone Domini in monte* I.12.34, ed. Mutzenbecher, 36, 781ff.

is everything, pleasure nothing, and assent remains obscure. Its obscurity derives from its postulated link with intellectual cognition, although an alternative explanation was at hand in the ancient idea of the 'pre-passions' (*praepassiones*). These unreflected emotions had been discussed by St Jerome and analysed, within living memory, by Anselm of Laon and his contemporaries.[31] There, at a stage prior to cognitive assent, Abelard might have located the slave's motivation. Instead he stresses 'the moment when we consent to what is unlawful' (*tunc vero consentimus ei, quod non licet*).[32] That the moment, the *tunc*, of choice or decision may depend on a background as various as the history or circumstances of moral agents, he recognises implicitly in the temporal and social details added to his models. But Abelard does not take the further step of acknowledging that context may be constitutive of ethical (mis-)deeds. Hence the ellipsis that makes an ambiguous act of homicide into murder and moral suicide. Prepared to allow for sins of the heart or the mind,[33] he never devoted to them the intense yet inadequate attention he gave to *consensus*.

Abelard did not have much of a moral psychology. Neglecting the contextual thought of the canonists and ignoring or rejecting the theory of the 'pre-passions' associated with the likes of Anselm of Laon, he preferred to stand alone. Yet his singularity, in this aspect of his ethics, is an illusion. Despite his urge to mark his distance from Augustine, he remained under that saint's shadow. And if the darkness which it cast on Abelard's notion of *consensus* did not prevent him from noting the plight of Heloise, it did limit his ability to empathise with her acratic state. Motivated irrationality was a problem he could grasp only in his own terms. Abelard's terms, in his second letter to her, are rational. The requests he makes of Heloise are, in his view, 'more reasonable'; and he writes not to justify his own position but to instruct and exhort.[34] *Doctrina* and *exhortatio* are classic definitions of spiritual guidance. He insists, once more, on the religious character of their relationship. In Abelard's *salutatio* to 'Christ's bride

---

[31] For a clear account, see Knuuttila, *Emotions*, 180.

[32] *Ethics*, ed. Luscombe, 14, 17; *Scito te ipsum* 1.9, ed. Ilgner, 227–8. Some allowance is made for *passio* (not *praepassio*) at *Ethics*, ed. Luscombe, 10, 2–4; *Scito te ipsum* 1.6, ed. Ilgner, 6, 136–8, but the point is not quite the same.

[33] *Problema Heloïssae* 24, PL 178 710C–D.

[34] 'Quibus quidem singulis rescribere decrevi non tam pro excusatione mea quam pro doctrina vel exhortatione tua, ut eo scilicet libentius petitionibus assentias nostris, quo eas *rationabilius* factas intellexeris…' *Ep.* v.1, ed. Pagani, 290. The comparative is Abelard's, but the adverb is Benedictine. See D. Knowles, 'The Rule of St. Benedict' in *Saints and Scholars: Twenty-Five Medieval Portraits* (Cambridge, 1962) 6.

from His servant',[35] the multiple paradoxes of Heloise's greeting to him are reduced to a single point. That point is pastoral. No ground is given in their debate about the parts they now play. And yet, far from clinging to the authoritarian role traditionally assigned to men in his position, Abelard, by his receptiveness to her assertions and reproaches, which he lists under four headings,[36] stations himself at the head of a contemporary avant-garde.

The old guard was outlined in Chapter 2. None of the accountants of the conscience trained by Burchard of Worms reckoned with being found at fault by a woman. Abelard does, when he counters the charges of neglect and of contempt made, or implied, by Heloise.[37] This was unprecedented in the penitential literature which forms a context of their correspondence. No confessor, on the available evidence, had felt the need to justify himself or to enter into real, rather than notional, dialogues with feminine sinners. The monologue was their chosen form, even when they purported to ask questions. Unlike Abelard, they were neither defensive nor apologetic; and their tone tended to be peremptory. After interrogation, short and sharp, they levelled their 'tarifs', confident that they would not be answered back.

It is against this background, emphasised by him and acknowledged by her, of spiritual guidance that a further aspect of the originality of the couple's correspondence can be appreciated. Abelard treats Heloise as an intellectual partner capable not only of understanding his *doctrina* and *exhortatio* but also of challenging them. For this too there was no model in the handbooks. Yet if he modifies a traditional role, she invents a new one. Unlike Ovid's heroines, Heloise also bears little resemblance to Mary Magdalene, despite the priory of the Paraclete founded, *c*.1142, at Sainte-Marie-Madeleine-en-Trainel.[38] Her uniqueness among sinful women is established by her scholarship. It is not the literary learning displayed in her classical quotations that is remarkable, but Heloise's command of Christian tradition which sets her apart. And nowhere is she more discriminating than in the choices she makes from the heritage of late antique thought on penance and related subjects.

---

[35] 'Sponsae Christi servus eiusdem', *Ep.* v.i, ed. Pagani, 290.
[36] *Ep.* v.i, ibid. See further Chapter 8.
[37] 'et tanto me amplius exaudias in tuis, quanto reprehensibilem minus invenies in meis, tantoque amplius verearis contemnere, quanto minus videris dignum reprehensione', *Ep.* v.i, ed. Pagani, 290.
[38] V. Saxer, *Le culte de Marie Madeleine en Occident* I (Auxerre, 1959) 117.

Heloise is a selective beneficiary of the Latin Fathers. Although they had been cited in the penitential literature of the early Middle Ages on the priority of contrition over physical affliction, long lists of 'tarifs' prescribing fasts and fines belied this theory. Sweeping aside the external details of mortification, she concentrates wholly on the internal sphere. There too she goes further than her contemporaries, who stressed the affective relationship between the sinner and God. Heloise alone dwells on the difficulties of penance with the aid of Saints Ambrose and Gregory the Great.[39] Both of the passages she cites were rarities.[40] Neither Gregory's strictures on those who rejoice when they should mourn in confession nor Ambrose's observations on those who have preserved their innocence being easier to find than true penitents were customarily quoted by early medieval writers on this subject.[41] They chose simpler texts, which generally amounted to recommendations of sincerity. Hypocrisy being the sin of which she accuses herself, Heloise singles out what others had ignored. More noteworthy, because less familiar to her readers than a verse from Ovid or a line from Lucan, are these passages from the Fathers which raise the problem of *fictio*.

Feigning in penance is regarded by Heloise with the same horror at religious inauthenticity felt by Bernard of Clairvaux. But he considers *fictio* from the standpoint of the sacerdotal prosecutor-cum-judge: she puts herself in the position of the defendant or, more accurately, of the accused. The accusation is levelled by what Gregory the Great called the 'internal judge' (*internus iudex*) – her rigorous, implacable conscience. It arraigns Heloise before the divine tribunal and the judgement of men. The charge to which she pleads guilty but of which she remains impenitent is conceived in terms of *Confessions* VIII. Heloise was not just inspired by Augustine's account of the struggle between the spirit and the flesh, modelled on St Paul's at Romans 7:14ff. Nor did she simply draw on the saint's portrayal of the self-division generated by a battle between errant will and imperative desire. These were themes that had been treated amply in other works of Christian literature. What set the eighth book of the *Confessions* apart from them was, Augustine's ambivalence. The saint who had prayed God to grant him continence and chastity, 'but not yet' (*sed noli modo,*

---

[39] See Chapter 2.
[40] ' … Gregorius: "sunt", inquit, "nonnulli, qui apertis vocibus culpas fatentur, sed tamen in confessione gemere nesciunt et lugenda gaudentes dicunt." … Ambrosius: "Facilius", inquit, "inveni qui innocentiam servaverunt, quam qui poenitentiam egerunt"', *Ep.* iv.8, ed. Pagani, 280–2.
[41] For context, cf. Anciaux, *Théologie*.

Confessions VIII.7.17), shaped Heloise's attitude towards 'physical desire' (*concupiscientia carnis*).[42]

Like him, she regards it as a 'mirror of an abiding, unhealed fissure of the soul'.[43] That fissure is cleaved by erotic nostalgia, which divides Heloise from penance, just as the sexual drive hindered Augustine's conversion and baptism. Baptism and penance demanded, and effected, purification of memory. Because Heloise's memories are impure, her thoughts are distracted from God. That predicament, familiar from the religious literature of late antiquity,[44] prevents her reconciliation and blocks her communication with Him. More distinctively Augustinian is the equivocal status which she attributes to the 'illusions' and 'phantoms' of sensuality that hold her in thrall.[45] That thrall is modelled on the Letter to the Romans 7:23, which raises the question of compulsive or involuntary behaviour.[46] Heloise leaves it open, registering a fault between her mental acts and her value-judgements on them. First she condemns her erotic fantasies as 'obscene' and 'filthy'. Then she commemorates them with epigrammatic elegance: 'When I should groan about what I have committed, I sigh instead about what I have omitted' (*Quae cum ingemiscere debeam de commissis, suspiro potius de omissis*).

Less the transgressions she has committed than the ones she has failed to perform are the objects of Heloise's regret. It is the spirit of the unconverted Augustine, whose 'long-standing girlfriends' of the flesh whispered seductively against forsaking 'this or that' (*Confessions* VIII.11.26), which animates her nostalgia. Heloise recalls all that Abelard had been anxious to put behind him in his reply to her first letter. And if she accepts the part of spiritual guide he chooses to play, it is at a price. That price is acknowledgement of his former role as her lover, extracted from him by her confession

---

[42] 'In tantum vero illae, quas pariter exercuimus, amantium voluptates dulces mihi fuerunt, ut nec displicere mihi nec vix a memoria labi possint. Quocumque loco me vertam, semper se oculis meis cum suis ingerunt desideriis nec etiam dormienti suis illusionibus parcunt. Inter ipsa missarum solemnia, ubi purior esse debet oratio, obscena earum voluptatum phantasmata ita sibi penitus miserrimam captivant animam, ut turpitudinibus illis magis quam orationi vacem. Quae cum ingemiscere debeam de commissis, suspiro potius de amissis', *Ep.* IV.9, ed. Pagani, 282.

[43] Brown, *The Body and Society*, 418.

[44] See R. Vernay, 'Distractions' in *Dictionnaire de spiritualité* III (Paris, 1957) 1347–63 and cf. M. Carruthers and J. Ziolkowski, *The Medieval Craft of Memory: An Anthology of Texts and Pictures* (Philadelphia, 2002).

[45] Cf. Augustine on Matthew 6:6: 'per ostium, id est per carnalem sensum, cogitationes nostras penetrant et turba variorum fantasmatum orantibus obstrepant', *De sermone Domini in monte* II.3.11, ed. Mutzenbacher, 102, 241–3.

[46] See Chapter 2.

on terms he could not deny, because they were standard in the penitential handbooks, which called them *circumstantiae*.[47] What? When? How? By whom? With whom? Not only the time, manner, and place of sin was taken into account but also the wealth or poverty, education or ignorance, and social position of penitents. Detail was required to specify the context in which transgressions had been committed; and Heloise is aware of this requirement when she alludes, with stinging understatement, to 'not only what *we* did but also the places and times at which *we* did it'.[48]

The sting derives from the first person plural. 'We' was not envisaged by the handbooks, none of which makes provision for a confessor being implicated in a penitent's avowal of sin. 'I' was the customary, if not invariable, form employed, because personal responsibility was deemed the essence of the sacrament by everyone except Heloise. The originality with which she alludes to the doctrine of the *circumstantiae* is as remarkable as it is unrecognised. Never before had a woman appealed in writing to the complicity of her confessor in the sins he was deputed to assess. So it is that, recurring to the theme of moral obligation that looms large in her first letter, Heloise again represents Abelard as both her witness and her judge.[49]

How to judge such a subtly insistent declaration of impenitence? Heloise's insistence is underlined by a repetitiveness untypical of her supple style. When, for example, she writes about her erotic fantasies, 'not even asleep do I have respite from them' (*nec dormiens etiam ab his quiescam*), she adds nothing to what she had described two sentences before: 'they do not spare me even when I am asleep' (*nec etiam dormienti ... parcunt*). Hammering home her anxiety, she voices fear of self-betrayal. A chance movement or an ill-judged word may give her peccant thoughts away.[50] To whom is unspecified, for surveillance by others is hardly the problem. It is a sense of inner imprisonment that anguishes Heloise in her captivity to sins of the mind.

The anguish has antecedents in a monastic tradition of thought-control. On that subject of spiritual discipline, no single figure in the Latin West exercised the authority of Evagrius of Pontus in the Greek East,[51] but

---

[47] Ibid.
[48] 'Non solum quae *egimus*, sed loca pariter et tempora in quibus haec *egimus*', *Ep.* IV.9, ed. Pagani, 282.
[49] 'tuo *examini* cuncta committo, tuo per omnia cedo *testimonio*', *Ep.* II.13, ibid., 250.
[50] 'Nonnumquam etiam ipso motu corporis animi mei cogitationes deprehenduntur, nec a verbis temperant improvisis', *Ep.* IV.9, ibid., 282.
[51] See Chapter 2.

strands of ascetic reflection about the sins of the mind were woven into a pattern that re-emerges in the fabric of Heloise's second letter by Isidore of Seville, who recommends, as an antidote to the 'viperous poison' of sinful thoughts, purity of prayer.[52] This is the standard by which she measures her inadequacy at mass 'where prayer should be more pure' (*ubi purior debet esse oratio*), and which was repeated by her near-contemporaries, such as Hugh of Saint-Victor.[53] Purity entailed freedom from the cares of the world and of the self in concentration on God. Distracted, distraught, and prey to erotic urges which she views with a combination of nostalgia and recoil, Heloise sees herself in an Isidorean mirror that magnifies the reflection of her impurity.

A milder perspective was offered by Augustine and his twelfth-century followers. Both distraction during prayer and 'desire in the heart' can be considered venial sins, argues the saint in *De natura et gratia*.[54] Full (or canonical) penance is not required for peccant thoughts.[55] Sins 'of weakness and inexpertise' are less grave than those 'of malice'.[56] It is on grounds of forethought and of intention that Augustine draws these distinctions, which represent some of the seeds that flowered into Abelard's anti-Augustinian theory of erotic desire as natural and necessary.[57] The singularity of his position on this issue has been exaggerated,[58] because it was not inconsistent with views held by highly placed members of the ecclesiastical establishment. Cardinal Pullen, for example, not only deemed concupiscence venial but even recommended, in the context of an otherwise virtuous life, a degree of indulgence towards acts of *libido* that arose from it.[59] And if Pullen had the ear of Pope Eugenius III, Bernard of Clairvaux, who bent it, could envisage purity of prayer by a sexual sinner.[60] His Biblical

---

[52] Ibid.   [53] *De modo orandi*, PL 176, 780A–B.

[54] *De natura et gratia* XXXVIII.45 in *Sant'Agostino, Natura e grazia* I, ed. A. Trapè and L. Volpi, 430–2.

[55] *Sermo* 98.5 in *Sant'Agostino, Discorsi II/2, (86–116) sul Nuovo Testamento*, ed. and trans. L. Carrozzi (Rome, 1983) 204–6, and see La Bonnardière, 'Pénitence et réconciliation des penitents I', 49 and n. 53 (with references to *De Trinitate*).

[56] Interestingly discussed by Vogel, 'Le péché et la penitence', 181ff.

[57] *Ethics*, ed. Luscombe, 14, 1–3; 20, 12ff.; 34, 27–30; *Scito te ipsum* 1.8, 13, 24, ed. Ilgner, 8, 210; 13, 324ff.; 23, 596ff. See further below.

[58] Lutterbach, *Sexualität*.

[59] *Sententiae* v.31, PL 186, 853D–854 and v.33, ibid., 854D.

[60] *Sermo* 107 (*Modus orandi Deum*) in *Opera* VI, 1, eds. J. Leclercq and H. Rochais (Rome, 1970) 379, 15ff., and see B. Stoeckle, '*Amor carnis – abusus amoris*: Das Verständnis von der Konkupiscenz bei Bernhard von Clairvaux und Aelred von Rielvaux' in *Analecta monastica: Textes et études sur la vie des moines au Moyen Âge*, eds. R. Grégoire et al., Studia Anselmiana 54 (Rome, 1965) 147–74. For a useful anthology of texts on this and related subjects, see

example was, of course, Mary Magdalene, with whom Heloise could not identify, for the harshness with which one tradition regarded sins of the mind prevented her from noting their veniality in the eyes of another.

Desire is less the cause than the symptom of her moral malaise. It does not originate in the flesh – which, as Augustine emphasises, is different from the body – but 'in a lasting distortion of the soul itself'.[61] If the diagnosis of her will warped by *concupiscentia carnis* is Pauline, as amplified by Augustine, the remedy is prescribed in her quotation of Romans 7:24–5. The divine grace which the Apostle extols has the effect of transforming Heloise's view of Abelard's castration from an unjust punishment or 'crime' into an intervention by a trusty doctor, who hurts in order to heal.[62] But if his unmanning liberated from him what St Paul calls 'the body of this death', Heloise remains the prisoner of an Augustinian pessimism about the capacities of human will and reason. Reason contributes nothing to her volte-face; she merely cites and glosses Scripture. Divine grace, for Heloise as for Augustine, is the only panacea against concupiscence. Commenting on the same passage of the Letter to the Romans, Abelard saw matters differently.

He, characteristically, equated 'the law of my mind', at Romans 7:23, with reason. It is reason that produces good, and concupiscence that leads to evil. As indebted to Augustine at this stage in the development of his ethical thought as Heloise in her second letter, Abelard parts company from her on the issue of 'captivity'. For him, it is neither involuntary nor compulsive. Captivity consists in obedience to sin not only imagined in thought but also executed by actions. It follows, on his interpretation of the letter to the Romans, that the prisoner of the flesh is a casualty of reason's defeat. And reason is defeated by consent to sensuality.[63] That is hardly the position of Heloise. She has not consented to *voluptas*. Her state is one for which no provision is made in Abelard's commentary on Romans. If he makes allowance, in *Scito te ipsum*, for the Augustinian categories of *suggestio* and *delectatio*,[64] carnal imaginings and pleasure, which he interprets, on the authority of St Paul (I Corinthians 10:13),[65] as temptations or trials

---

R. Imbach and I. Atucha, *Amours pluriels: Doctrines médiévales du rapport amoureux de Bernard de Clairvaux à Boccace* (Paris, 2006).

[61] Brown, *The Body and Society*, 418 – a sensitive and exact interpretation of Augustine's position.

[62] *Ep.* IV.9, ed. Pagani, 284.

[63] *Comm. in Rom.* III, 22ff. in *Petri Abaelardi Opera Theologica* I, ed. E. Buytaert, CCCM 11 (Turnhout, 1969) 209–10, 754–78 and cf. Abelard's solution to *Problema Heloissae* 14, PL 178, 697C–D.

[64] See above.   [65] Cf. *Ep.* v.26, ed. Pagani, 330.

which God never allows to become unbearable,[66] here too his attitude is different from hers. The blithe optimism with which Abelard views the problem of concupiscence stands in contrast to the bleak pessimism of Heloise, whose model of the conscience, powerless in the anguish of its motivated irrationality, has less in common with his than with that of the Cistercians.

One of them wrote, during her term of office at the Paraclete, a tripartite work entitled *De domo interiori*.[67] Misattributed to Bernard of Clairvaux but influenced by him, this little-known tract displays affinities with Heloise's second letter. Troubled by erotic fantasies, a monk is distracted from his devotions and cannot concentrate on prayer.[68] At nighttime, when he sleeps, spectres of past pleasure haunt and hold him in their thrall. It is of little use to plead that carnal lust is irresistible and that sin may be involuntary; his sense of guilt is not alleviated but heightened by being internal: *intus graviter pecco*.[69] The situation of Heloise, in short, described probably without knowledge of her letter, yet strikingly parallel to one of its central themes.[70]

The theme of desire, its temptations and its control, not only represents a dividing-line between the ethical sensibilities of Abelard and Heloise; it also marks a partial boundary between their exemplars of monastic culture. Hers was shaped by the darker, more ambivalent Augustine whose works she read in the self-critical light cast by Isidore and other censors of mental sin. Impervious to their influence and more confident of reason, Abelard looked elsewhere. He looked to the orthodox critics of Augustine's doctrine of concupiscence. And he did so in his capacity as a monastic thinker. From the *Collationes* of Evagrius' disciple John Cassian, Abelard drew his anti-Augustinian view of sexuality as implanted in mankind by God, in order to put us to tests which we are capable of overcoming.[71] Unlike Heloise but like Cassian, he did not consider desire to be central. Central was that 'collusion with the demonic world [which was] more basic to the monk's concern'.[72] This is the thought which is linked, in *Scito te ipsum*,

---

[66] *Ethics*, ed. Luscombe 34, 15; *Scito te ipsum* 1.22, ed. Ilgner, 22, 584ff.
[67] PL 184, 507ff. Cf. Bertola, *Il problema della coscienza*, 121ff., and P. Delhaye, 'Dans le sillage de saint Bernard: Trois petits traités *"De conscientia"'*, *Cîteaux in den Nederlanden* 5 (1954) 92–103.
[68] PL 184, 519B–521D.   [69] Ibid., 523C.
[70] For another parallel to Heloise's divergence from Abelard and affinities with the Cistercians, see *The Paraclete Statutes: Institutiones nostrae: Introduction, Edition, Commentary*, ed. C. Waddell, Cistercian Liturgy Series 20 (Kentucky, 1987).
[71] *Ethics*, ed. Luscombe, 34, 11ff.; *Scito te ipsum* 1.22, ed. Ilgner, 22, 580ff.
[72] See Brown, *The Body and Society*, 420–2.

with the naturalness of concupiscence. Those who read Abelard's work as
the manifesto of an ethical rationalist do not reflect on the significance of
the fact that, immediately after his own version of Cassian's thesis on sexuality, he goes on to treat 'the suggestions of demons.'[73] *Scito te ipsum* was
shaped in a monastic mould. The *Collationes* influenced both its structure
and its substance; and if it was composed after its author had left Saint-
Gildas, he did not forget Cassian's critique of Augustine.

Was the abbot Abelard beguiled by Cassian, and the abbess Heloise
bewitched by Augustine? The antithesis is too schematic, because both of
them were alert to divergences within the traditions of monastic thought
they had inherited. Those divergences were exploited by Heloise to establish
an independent position. If her position is influenced by the Augustinianism
of previous generations, she did not hesitate to revise and refine the saint's
ideas with the aid of Cassian. The process of revision is disclosed in finer
features of Heloise's Latinity. They derive from the niceness with which she
discriminates between concepts. A concept fundamental to her second letter, for instance, is chastity. This is the virtue others perceive in her, which
she distinguishes from 'cleanliness of the flesh'.[74] That quality is base, because
compatible with the hypocrisy attributed to herself by Heloise. Putting herself in a position described by St Jerome,[75] she draws from it radical conclusions. All or nothing is her attitude. Chastity is concentrated in the mind.

The mind that produced this idea was neither Augustine's nor Cassian's,
although both of them, as well as Jerome, contributed to her thought.
Heloise combined and refashioned their approaches with ethical imagination. Her imagination worked less mechanically than is suggested by the
positivists of source-criticism. They tell us, misleadingly, that she drew on an
aphorism from Augustine's *De bono coniugali*.[76] But Heloise cites only the
saint's predicate about the mental origin and location of virtue. Omitting
his subject 'continence', she substitutes for it the less positive, more slight-
ing expression 'cleanliness of the flesh', which stands in apposition to the

[73] *Ethics*, ed. Luscombe, 36, 16ff.; *Scito te ipsum* I.23, ed. Ilgner, 24, 623ff. On the interpreta-
tive tradition of Abelard, which ignores this factor in his thought, see the excellent study by
J. Marenbon, 'The Rediscovery of Abelard's Philosophy', *Journal of the History of Philosophy*
44 (2006) 331–51, especially 344–7 (on the ethics).

[74] '*Castam* me praedicant qui non deprehendunt hypocritam; *munditiam carnis* conferunt in
virtutem, cum non sit corporis sed animi virtus', *Ep.* IV.10, ed. Pagani, 284 with n. 41.

[75] See Chapter 2.

[76] '*Continentia* quippe non corporis sed animi virtus est', *De bono coniugali* XXI (25), ed. P. Walsh
(Oxford, 2001) 46.

chastity attributed to her. Why? *Continentia*, in the work by Augustine that Heloise read and recast, is a blanket-term used not only of celibacy but also of abstention from food and drink. Christ, who did not fast continually like John the Baptist,[77] was the supreme example of 'continence by disposition' as opposed to 'mental incontinence'.[78] Augustine even contrasts the 'chastity of continence' with 'marital chastity',[79] in his effort to reconcile marriage and virginity within the Church.[80] Noble though that effort was, clarity is sacrificed to his taste for tautology and to his promiscuity with synonyms. Cassian saw the problem. He solved it by erecting a hierarchy of virtues. At its summit stands chastity, which restores prelapsarian harmony between the spirit and the flesh.[81] That is why Cassian likens *castitas* to sanctity, the goal to be reached by the route of continence. Inferior to chastity, because susceptible to 'carnal revolts', continence still represents a positive, if imperfect good.[82] Even that is denied to herself by Heloise. Her hypercritical radicalism stations *munditia carnis* at a level lower than *continentia* and far below chastity.

Confining moral merit to the sphere of interiority, Heloise inverts Abelard's situation after Soissons. If, in the sequel to his condemnation, he believed that it was *fama*, manipulated by his enemies, which had condemned him, and *conscientia* which absolved him on grounds of his upright intentions, now it is *fama* that extols her, and *conscientia* that finds her guilty. The criteria remain the same, but the effect is the opposite. And the effect of this inversion is a paradox neither attested nor imaginable in Abelard's simpler (and perhaps saner) ideas on the conscience: the sincere hypocrisy identified in the first chapter. How can we, how could her contemporaries tell whether Heloise means what she says? it was then asked.

An answer is now available. They were not obliged to take her at her withering word, nor are we. One alternative to believing literally in Heloise's hypocrisy was offered by the hermeneutics of the conscience with which twelfth-century readers were familiar. Ambrose and Cassian, imitated and amplified by early scholastic theologians,[83] reckoned with a type of feigning known as 'pious' or 'religious simulation' (*pia/religiosa simulatio*) which, far

---

[77] *De bono coniugali* xxi (26), ibid., 48.   [78] *De bono coniugali* xxii (27), ibid., 52.
[79] *De bono coniugali* xxiii (28), ibid., 52.   [80] Brown, *The Body and Society*, 402.
[81] *Collationes* xii, especially 7–8, ed. Pichery 133ff.; and *Institutiones*, VI. 4 in *Jean Cassien, Institutions cénobitiques* ed. J. -C. Guy, SC 109 (Paris, 1965) 266.
[82] *Collationes* xii.10, ed. Pichery, 137.
[83] See Chapter 2 and A. Landgraf, 'Die Stellungnahme der Frühscholastik zur Lüge der alttestamentlichen Patriarchen', *Theologisch-praktische Quartalschrift* 92 (1939) 1–33, especially 18ff.; Landgraf, 'Definition und Sündhaftigkeit der Lüge nach der Lehre der Frühscholastik', *Zeitschrift für katholische Theologie* 63 (1939) 50–85, 157–80; and Colish 'Rethinking Lying', 161ff.

from being reprehensible, might even excuse lying in a higher cause. The higher cause espoused by Heloise in her first and second letters to Abelard is humility, most ambivalent of Christian virtues, which ranged from the *superbia sancta* recommended by Jerome to the arrogance *per humilitatem* criticized by Isidore.[84] Who was to know which was which? The confessor, in a sacrament that entailed sincerity, because his task was not inquisitorial. This made him vulnerable to both simulation and feigning; and the vulnerability was recognised by Robert Pullen when he admonished penitents not to exaggerate.[85]

The bluff common sense of the English cardinal is remote from Heloise's tormented scrupulousness. Yet her scrupulousness is more than tormented; it is also theatrical. Her self-accusations recall Aristotle's splendid simile (*Nicomachean Ethics* VII.4.2.2; 1147a 24) of the acratic as an actor reciting a part. Which part? Heloise assigns herself the role of hypocrite, on etymological authority,[86] in terms that dramatise her sense of alienation. One aspect of her self performs to applause: the other observes and condemns. The authentic Heloise, estranged from the image others have of her, is not the nun who dissembles chastity but the conscience which censures such pious posturing. So it is that she recreates Aristotle's likeness of the acratic to the actor, less as a paradox of rational choice than as a trope of moral psychology. This insight, achieved without knowledge of the *Nicomachean Ethics*, sets Heloise in a class apart from any previous writer on the subject in the Middle Ages. Then as now she has hardly been understood. Abelard was inclined to think that she was simply fishing for compliments. Aware of Cassian's criteria but referring to Jerome,[87] he warned her that, in appearing to shun praise, she might seem to court it on different grounds.

Those grounds are multiple. The first, and most important, cited by Abelard is Christ's declaration that the humble shall be exalted (*Qui se humiliaverit, exaltabitur*, Matthew 23:12, cf. Luke 18:4). Detecting the danger of an inversion, Heloise's husband insists on the literal sense of these words.[88] And he amplifies them with a classical quotation more pertinent than any he applies to himself in the *HC*. Abelard cites Virgil's delightful verse about Galatea wishing to be seen by her lover while fleeing from him (*Eclogue* III.5), before adducing Jerome's aphorism about seeking glory by

---

[84] On Jerome, see Chapter 2. Cf. Isidore, *Sententiae* III.19 and 24, ed. Cazier, 250, 260.

[85] 'Qui vere utiliterque confitetur is, prout res gesta est, persequatur, nec ultra quam res se habet turpitudinem suam exaggeret...', *Sententiae* VI.51, PL 186, 900D.

[86] See Chapters 1 and 2.   [87] Abelard, *Ep.* v.10, ed. Pagani, 304.

[88] Cf. Abelard's sermon for the Paraclete *in epiphania Domini* ed. De Santis, 196, 131ff.

seeming to spurn it.[89] The paradoxes of penance embodied by Heloise in her second letter are glossed as a form of *fictio*. On the part of Abelard, whose intellectualism rarely ventured beyond rational limits, at least in prose, and whose notion of feigning was seldom imaginative,[90] the attempt at empathy was remarkable. But the interpretation was hardly original. Heloise's spiritual guide has no new solution to the problem of her sincerity; he rehearses, elegantly and accurately, what tradition offered. Abelard could not tell whether Christ's words form the stage on which she acted out a charade of *fictio*. Nor perhaps could Heloise, lost in the labyrinth of her interiority.

&

A way out was precluded by her rejection of human judgement.[91] The reference, unstated but unmistakable, is to I Corinthians 4:2ff. Yet Heloise does not follow St Paul in subordinating her verdict to God's. She equates them, widening the accusation of hypocrisy from herself to the religious practices of her times. The polemic is reminiscent of Gregory VII.[92] That pope's distinction, inspired by his model and namesake Gregory the Great, between inner commitment and outward conformity of faith lies behind Heloise's attack; and it is no accident that Gregory VII was accustomed to drawing it in his broadsides against clerical unchastity.[93] Unchaste by standards even more rigorous than those of the pope, she deems her reputation for virtue a sign of others' vice. So it is that Heloise's reasons for self-criticism become the grounds on which she castigates them. Then, sensing that she has gone too far, she draws back.

As well she might. Even in an age noted for its cult of interiority, Heloise ran the risk of what Cardinal Pullen called exaggeration. Her intransigent position on the difference between religious appearance and reality diverged from the more lenient line taken by twelfth-century theologians. They did not regard motivation as *a priori* suspect, nor did their esteem for mental virtue entail contempt of actions. Holding 'external intention' on the part of those who approached the sacraments adequate to establish their validity, they recognised as legitimate the aim of 'doing what the Church does', without knowing what it was.[94] These were hardly generous concessions.

---

[89] See Chapter 2.   [90] See Chapters 3, 4, and 6.

[91] 'Religiosa hoc tempore iudicor, in quo iam parva pars religionis non est hypocrisis, ubi ille maximis extollitur laudibus, qui humanum non offendat iudicium', *Ep.* IV.10, ed. Pagani, 284.

[92] Cf. *Ep.* 54 in *The Epistolae vagantes of Pope Gregory the Seventh*, ed. H. Cowdrey (Oxford, 1972) 132.

[93] Cf. H. Cowdrey, *Pope Gregory VII, 1073–1085* (Oxford, 1998) 553.

[94] Landgraf, *Dogmengeschichte* IV, 2, 123ff.

Few alternatives to them existed in a period not yet acquainted with the procedures of the Inquisition, which Heloise's mistrust of her own motives unwittingly anticipates.

When this inquisitrix of the conscience declares that she is answerable solely to God, that declaration excludes everyone else. He alone can judge, on the criteria she adduces so harshly yet so vaguely, whether her denial of merit is true, false, or feigned. No correction is proposed, and the inconclusiveness recalls that of another thinker who 'aimed at recording … faults rather than at putting them right'.[95] Despite her volubility about her own failings, Heloise is reticent about why she criticises those of others. Her contemporaries cannot understand what she means by their hypocrisy because, offering no evidence of it, she appears to do no more than project her alleged defects onto them.[96] Affirming her autonomy from her environment, she stands in danger of moral isolation.

Recognising that danger, Heloise modifies her stance.[97] The modification is grudging. Indulgence does not come easily to her. Hedged about with reservations ('in some way', 'in one way or another', 'with whatever intention'), the acknowledgement is made that it may be better to avoid scandal 'by the example of outward deeds'. The argument was ancient and had been revived by St Anselm.[98] But his authority hardly explains Heloise's shift of ground. Why this concession to an exteriority treated with disdain? In the interests of the Church – bedevilled by hypocrites – to prevent the unfaithful blaspheming God's name – which has been blasphemed by her imprecations against divine injustice – and to maintain among the laity the reputation of the clergy – although it, on Heloise's former view, is worthless. Not a model of consistency, her position might have gained in coherence had she stuck to her injunction to loving God.[99] Yet it is not to

[95] B. McGuinness, *Young Ludwig: Wittgenstein's Life 1889–1921* (Oxford, 2005) 60.

[96] On the topical character of the accusation, see Constable, *Reformation* 34ff.

[97] 'Et hoc fortassis aliquo modo laudibile, et Deo acceptabile quoque modo videtur, si quis videlicet exterioris operis exemplo quacumque intentione non sit Ecclesiae scandalo, nec iam per ipsum apud infideles nomen Domini blasphemetur, nec apud carnales professionis suae ordo infametur', *Ep.* IV.II, ed. Pagani, 284–6.

[98] See Chapter 3.

[99] 'Et frustra utrumque geritur quod amore Dei non agitur. In omni autem (Deus scit) vitae meae statu te magis adhuc offendere quam Deum vereor, tibi placere amplius quam ipsi appeto. Tua me ad religionis habitum iussio, non divina traxit dilectio. Vide quam infelicem, et omnibus miserabiliorem ducam vitam, si tanta hic frustra sustineo, nihil habitura remunerationis in futuro. Diu te, sicut et multos, *simulatio mea fefellit, ut religioni deputares hypocrisim*; et ideo nostris te maxime commendas orationibus, quod a te expecto, a me postulas. Noli, obsecro, de me tanta presumere, ne mihi cesses orando subvenire; noli aestimare sanam, ne medicaminis subtrahas gratiam; noli non egentem credere, ne differas in necessitate subvenire;

Him but to Abelard that Heloise goes on to declare her love. The small matters of the Church and the infidels, the laity and the clergy are shelved as she reminds him, yet again, that she had taken the veil from fear of offending him, not awe of God. That echo of a reproach made in her first letter asserts a continuity between her present and her past. Unhappiness links them both. Now as then, Heloise lives a lie without reward in this world or hope of one in the next.

Moving words which, however, leave a number of questions unanswered. Why does all this amount to hypocrisy? What has it to do with simulation? Heloise's mode of assertion contradicts her case. Without hesitation or qualms she assumes the necessity and efficacy of the prayers she requests from Abelard. It is faith which leads this reluctant nun to doubt her vocational sincerity. Those doubts are not warranted by the authority on which Heloise draws at this point in her second letter: Augustine's exegesis of the Sermon on the Mount, a work that also exercised a formative influence on Abelard's *Scito te ipsum*. The saint offered no grounds for equating a religious life led for originally non-religious motives with simulation, nor did he confuse spiritual uncertainty with hypocrisy. His ideas were less complicated and more humane.

Augustine's no-nonsense concept of *fictio* is focused on the moral agent and his or her intentions: the feigners who are hypocrites and simulators seek praise by appearing to be what they are not.[100] Active in his exegesis, *fictio* becomes passive in Heloise's second letter. Her odd expression *ficta sui laus* refers to praise that is feigned in the sense of unfounded, because based on the mistaken admiration of others. Now, others may be mistaken but, on her own testimony, they are not being deceived. Her purpose is the opposite of simulation or hypocrisy, as defined by Augustine, whose categories she misappropriates in a further confusion of cause and effect. It is that confusion which leads Heloise to reject fame in terms which traduce the saint. When he argues that men should assess external facts and leave the secrets of the heart to divine judgement,[101] he does not seek to oppose, with her vehemence, inner truths to human misperceptions.

Suspicion of herself and of others now leading her conscience to identify with the God against whom she had railed, Heloise pronounces her anathema. When she warns Abelard that, by praising her, he incurs the stigma of

---

noli valitudinem putare, ne prius corruam quam sustentes labentem! Multis *ficta sui laus* nocuit et praesidium, quo indigebant, abstulit', *Ep.* IV.II, ed. Pagani, 286.
[100] See Chapter 2 above.   [101] Ibid.

the flatterer or the sin of the liar,[102] the assumption of inerrancy verges on Jerome's holy arrogance. That arrogance couched as a profession of humility, Heloise personifies paradox.[103] Her paradoxes are existential, her ethical identity compromised; and yet she maintains the sententiousness of the moralist. Nothing could be further from her purpose than the term 'personal' often used to describe her writing. The style of the *sententiae*, a leading vehicle of debate in the early twelfth century,[104] leaves its imprint on her works; and nowhere is it stamped more plainly than in her zest, peculiar to theologians, for making statements in the name of God, such as: 'In His judgement, things common to the elect and the reprobate obtain no merit.'[105] On what authority does Heloise advance this proposition? On none cited by her. The Biblical quotations (Jeremiah 17:9, Proverbs 14:12; 16:25 and Ecclesiastes 11:30) that follow offer no support to her theological ventriloquism.[106]

In the didactic tone of a teacher, Heloise speaks with the borrowed voice of God. Assertive rather than argumentative, she makes heavy use of Biblical quotation, but is light on reasoning. Even when her ideas are novel, there is a trace of traditionalism about the declaratory manner in which she presents them, harking back to the approach of an earlier generation. Far more than Abelard's, Heloise's style recalls that of Anselm of Laon. Established in the schools and devoid of the controversy that surrounded her husband's, it offered an air of familiarity to her attempt to create a role which was, when she began to play it, unprecedented on the intellectual scene. For Heloise, in her second letter, makes her début as a theologian. With one significant difference from the men who assumed that part. All of them maintained, rightly or wrongly, that they were in possession of their faculties. She denies being so, and that denial lends Heloise's writing a special status. It does not fit into recognised categories of speculative, mystical, and dialectical theology. And even when it is unmistakably moral, it needs to be considered in the light of her mental torment. This contributes

---

[102] 'Quiesce, obsecro, a laude mea, ne turpem adulationis notam et mendacii crimen incurras; aut si quod in me suspicaris bonum, ipsum laudatum vanitatis aura ventilet. Nemo medicinae peritus interiorem morbum ex exterioris habitus inspectione diiudicat', *Ep.* IV.11, ed. Pagani, 286.

[103] On the monastic character of this paradox, cf. Rupert of Deutz, *Super quaedam capitula Regulae divi Benedicti abbatis*: 'Mirum namque est in vilitate gloriari et ipsam humilitatem materiam facere superbiendi', PL 170, 520D.

[104] See Colish 'Systematic Theology'.

[105] 'Nulla quidquam meriti apud Deum obtinent quae reprobis aeque ut electis communia sunt', *Ep.* IV.12, ed. Pagani, 286.

[106] The thought, however, is a patristic commonplace. Cf. Gregory the Great, *Homilia in Evangelia*, 29, PL 76, 1216.

to rendering some of Heloise's positions dubious, others unsupported by argument or authority, and at least twice – in her despair of God's mercy and critique of divine justice – blasphemous. But who will repeat the condemnations she has anticipated? Motivated irrationality provides Heloise with an alibi, even when she errs.

Her errors are committed in a state of self-division represented as so radical that it can hardly be healed from within itself. The extremity of this condition is far from Augustine's delicate nuance: 'I was more in that which I approved of in myself than in that which I disapproved' (*Confessions* VIII.5.11). Alienated from herself, Heloise declares that she is estranged from God. Each of these declarations refers to the past or to a present depicted as continuous with it through uninterrupted suffering of pain. Painful recollection of the past is fundamental to St Paul's model of the conscience,[107] whose capacity to err he explains in terms of defective moral knowledge. It is in Pauline terms that Heloise's predicament can be understood. If, recalling her adversities and those of Abelard, she is led by 'the infirmity of a most anguished mind' to confuse ethical cause and effect, her self-accusations of hypocrisy and simulation, based on an inversion of Augustinian categories, also express a desire for the opposite. Sincerity and authenticity are Heloise's goals, towards which she advances in pyrotechnics of paradox.

The paradoxes of this religious acratic arise from the tensions between two aspects of herself. Those aspects are not the Roman or Romantic heroine and the involuntary nun. They are the conscience of Heloise which, in thrall to its memories, represents itself as desperate, impenitent, and blasphemous, and her intellect which, despite these emotions, retains both its lucidity and its faith. What else is it that enables her to believe, amid her *cris de coeur*, in the efficacy of her husband's prayers on her behalf? What other than St Paul's doctrine of grace reconciles her to Abelard's castration, once condemned as unjust? These are not the attitudes of an exponent of classical culture, defying the demands of Christianity. They are the attempts of an anguished conscience to break out of the prison of its past. A way of escape occurs to Heloise only when she addresses the future; and then her exit is abrupt. The 'cleanliness of the flesh' (*munditia carnis*) treated with contempt near the beginning of her letter suddenly

---

[107] See K. Stendahl, 'The Apostle Paul and the Introspective Conscience of the West', *Harvard Theological Review* 56 (1963) 199–215 and C. Pierce, *Conscience in the New Testament* (London, 1955) 99ff., 114ff., 126ff.

becomes, at its conclusion, outright 'incontinence' (*incontinentia*).[108] Why this heightening of censure? No reason is given; no alteration in her circumstances has been registered. Yet, at the point when it appears that any self-made stick will do to beat her, she rebuts the charge of ethical masochism: 'I do not seek the crown of victory, it is enough for me to avoid danger… In whatever corner of heaven God stations me, it will be sufficient.'[109]

Ostensibly addressed to Abelard, in order to dissuade him from urging her to heroism, these sentences are actually directed by Heloise to herself. For it is she, not he, who had driven herself into a moral maze from which there was no issue in this world. If, in the next, she imagines a heavenly reward which can only be assigned to her by the divine justice she has criticised so roundly, it follows that Heloise cannot have lost all hope in God's equity or mercy. The despair expressed in her state of motivated irrationality is overcome by the force of that faith which requested prayers from Abelard and accepted as providential his castration. That is why she does not close her debate with him by staging a conversion or by appealing to the rhetorical *deus ex machina* of aposiopesis.[110] Nothing is cut short by a believer who did not need to be converted. Reconciled with the God against whom she had railed, Heloise finds, in her imagined corner of heaven, an intimation of grace.

The present and the future are, in consequence, the themes of her third letter. Heloise's writing is no longer focused on the past. The loud voice of her conscience falls silent; and she addresses the 'sudden impulses of the passions' as issues for the mind.[111] In the reasoning mind, not the acratic will, she locates these emotions, whose power she acknowledges.

---

[108] *Ep.* IV.12, ed. Pagani, 288.
[109] 'Non quaero coronam victoriae; satis est mihi periculum evitare … Quocumque me angulo coeli Deus collocet, satis mihi faciet', *Ep.* IV.13, ibid. 288. Discussed by L. Georgianna '"In Any … Corner of Heaven": Heloise's Critique of Monastic Life' in Wheeler (ed.), *Listening to Heloise*, 204.
[110] For the contrary positions on this issue, cf. von Moos, *Abaelard und Heloise*, 9–48 and *Entre histoire et littérature* 3–43 with Dronke, *Women Writers*, 129ff.
[111] 'Suo specialiter, sua singulariter. Ne me forte in aliquo de inobedientia causari queas, verbis etiam immoderati doloris tuae frenum impositum est iussionis, ut ab his mihi saltem in scribendo temperem, a quibus in sermone non tam difficile quam impossibile est providere. Nihil enim minus in nostra est potestate quam animus eique magis obedire cogimur quam imperare possimus. Unde et cum nos eius affectiones stimulant, nemo earum subitos impulsus ita repulerit, ut non in effecta facile prorumpant et se per verba facilius effluant, quae promptiores animi passionum sunt notae secundum quod scriptum est: "Ex abundantia enim cordis os loquitur"', *Ep.* VI.1, ed. Pagani, 332.

Irrational judgements of the intellect, they can be partially controlled but not fully abolished, she argues with St Augustine.[112] If Stoic *apatheia* is an illusion, as Heloise implies, distance is marked both from Abelard's show of detachment and from his reluctance to take such factors into account. That distance, moral and philosophical, had already been signalled by her laconic *salutatio*. Proper names are omitted. And as the style of Heloise's writing changes, assertion is replaced by argument.

Argument about the emotions enables her to control them. Once their victim, she is now their mistress, restraining her hand in the hope that her mind will follow suit.[113] Here Heloise parts company from Augustine who uses the same image, at *Confessions* VIII.11.22, to evoke the monstrosity of self-division. Her self-division healed, she places her trust – qualified, but not as fragile as formerly – in the action of choice. Initiative and drive are conveyed by Heloise's simile of thoughts being hammered out of one another like nails. Worthy of Gregory the Great's teaching on mental control,[114] this likeness is the very opposite of her self-portrayal, in her second letter, as captive to sins of the mind. Obedience to Abelard's commands is coupled with insistence on the dignity of Heloise's agency. Taking charge of her present, she questions the rules on which it is based. The acratic, transformed with the aid of divine grace, has become the reformer.

Heloise does not become a reformer on Abelard's instruction. The *doctrina* and *exhortatio* which he offers have no direct connection with her request for a Rule. Notable, in the spiritual guidance of his second epistle, is, reluctance to tell her what to do. What Abelard does instead is, to compose his own confession, Augustinian in its tripartite structure of divine praise, self-accusation, and profession of faith.[115] Faith is professed and Christ praised by the substitution of Him for Abelard as the object of Heloise's devotion. Second to that purpose, but not secondary in the

---

[112] *De civitate Dei* XIV.9ff., *S. Aurelii Augustini De civitate Dei libri XI–XXII*, ed. Dombart and Kalb, CCSL 48 428, 92ff. with M. Colish, *The Stoic Tradition from Antiquity to the Early Middle Ages II: Stoicism in Christian Latin Thought through the Sixth Century* (Leiden, 1985) 142ff. and Nussbaum, *Upheavals of Thought*, 527ff.

[113] 'Revocabo itaque manum a scripto in quibus linguam a verbis temperare non valeo. Utinam sic animus dolentis parere promptus sit quemadmodum dextra scribentis! Aliquod tamen dolori remedium vales conferre, si non hunc omnino possis auferre. Ut enim insertum clavum alius expellit sic cogitatio nova priorem excludit, cum alias intentus animus priorum memoriam dimittere cogitur aut intermittere. Tanto vero amplius cogitatio quaelibet animum occupat et ab aliis deducit, quanto quod cogitatur honestius aestimatur et quo intendimus animum magis videtur necessarium', *Ep.* VI.1, ed. Pagani, 332–4.

[114] See *Moralia in Iob* II.52.82, ed. Adriaen, CCSL 143 109, 7–17 and A. Delchard, 'Examen de conscience', in *Dictionnaire de spiritualité* V, 2, 1812ff.

[115] See Ratzinger, 'Originalität und Überlieferung'.

dimensions of his work, comes the *mea culpa*. The *sic* of her accusations balanced by the *non* he points at himself, Abelard's criticisms of his own conduct demonstrate a penitential authenticity that balances the impenitence of Heloise.

Her nostalgic reminiscences are offset by his censures. Neither of them is inhibited about sex, real or imaginary; and Abelard recalls fornicating with Heloise in the refectory at Argenteuil.[116] He views that moment in Augustinian terms – as an instance not only of carnality but also of self-will – that serve to account for the revulsion with which he now alludes to physical love. Love (*amor*) is not the right word, Abelard claims, for what should be called *concupiscentia*.[117] Among the synonyms he lists (*libido, voluptas, intemperantia*) to describe this vice, *luxuria*, the term employed in the *HC*, never occurs. The vagueness of his former diction now clarified, Abelard admits the charge of lust levelled against him in Heloise's first letter and defers to the superior love of Christ. *Amor* stripped of its polyvalence and imprecision, love, in its strict and true sense, can be equated with *caritas*. And that is relevant to his views on past guilt.

Guilt is admitted in respect of erotic transgression, for which the responsibility is attributed by Abelard wholly to himself. Yet it was a *felix culpa* that made Heloise a 'partner both in fault and in grace' (*culpae particeps facta es et gratiae*).[118] This providential interpretation of their experience leads him partly to see her point. Just as Abelard forced Heloise, against her will and despite her weakness, to have sex with him (*te … ad consensum trahebam*),[119] so he, reluctant and compelled (*invitus … coactione mei*),[120] had suffered on her behalf. But this is hardly the ethical language of *Scito te ipsum*. Abelard did not learn from Heloise the terms in which he analysed assent to wrongful actions or described reluctant and acratic deeds; nor did he respond to all the assertions in her first letter. If he acknowledges that he had his way with her, using threats and blows, he ignores the idea of coerced consent when writing about matrimony. It is recognised as indissoluble only because it prevented Heloise from yielding to relatives' advice or carnal temptations after he became a monk.[121] The sacramentality of marriage, for Abelard, is instrumental at this point; of the theological or legal bonds created by *consensus* he breathes scarcely a word until the end of his letter.[122]

Instead he speaks, with a new tone of gentleness, words of comfort. Humility is expressed in the solicitude with which Abelard considers

---

[116] *Ep.* v.12, ed. Pagani, 308.　　[117] *Ep.* v.21, ibid., 322 and see above Chapter 4.
[118] *Ep.* v.17, ed. Pagani, 314 and 23, ibid., 324.
[119] *Ep.* v.15, ibid., 310.　　[120] *Ep.* v.21, ibid., 322.　　[121] *Ep.* v.17, ibid., 314.
[122] *Ep.* v.26, ibid., 328.

Heloise's plight. Desire, far from representing a cause of self-reproach, should be regarded as a challenge to which he is incapable of rising.[123] The dignity of women in their ordinariness, not their heroism, is the reason for their preeminence.[124] Eloquent, moving, and more 'feminist' than she, Abelard was less capable of addressing the subtler issues raised by Heloise. To the question implicit in her second letter – can one both be and seem humble? – he has no answer. The trauma of Soissons and its sequel inclined him to view ethical appearance and reality as contraries,[125] and this dichotomy led Abelard to identify *fictio* with the polar opposite of *sinceritas*. Less straightforward and more discerning in her perception of the similarities between them, Heloise recognised that uprightness and feigning are not so easy to tell apart. His polar opposites, for her, are Siamese twins. It is not only in her preference for a Cistercian form of observance over her husband's version of the Rule that she comes closer to the milieu of Clairvaux. If she styled herself the wife and handmaiden of Abelard, Heloise was also the spiritual daughter of St Bernard.

An impasse is reached, which is bypassed by her changing the subject and asking for advice about the Rule which she would decline to adopt.[126] More notable than the concerns shared by Abelard and Heloise are, the differences between them. Those differences – spiritual and stylistic, ethical and practical – arise not because there is any breach of civility in their exchange, but because it is conducted from moral standpoints which are scarcely commensurable. Equal to Heloise's insistence but not to her insights, Abelard was outmatched repeatedly in their duel of ideas. Against her rapier he deployed his truncheon, usually parrying her assaults but seldom striking the mark. He was on the defensive after the *HC*, she was on the attack; and speculation that he forged her letters can be sustained only by refusal to read them as they are. They are not a 'personal' correspondence of 'literary' character, but a real debate about ethical identity, set at a pitch of intellectual complexity unrivalled by their contemporaries and successors. And what this dialectic of the conscience has in common with the sometimes pretty, often pedantic, and invariably trivial love-letters of the thirteenth century that have been misattributed to the couple is, nothing.[127]

---

[123] *Ep.* v.24, ibid., 326.
[124] *Ep.* v.18, ibid., 316 with McLaughlin, 'Twelfth-Century "Feminism"'.
[125] See Chapter 5.   [126] *Ep.* vi.3ff., ed. Pagani, 334ff. See Waddell, *The Paraclete Statutes*
[127] For the date and character of the *epistolae duorum amantium*, see von Moos, *Abaelard und Heloise*, 199–214, 282–91.

Not even the verbal resemblances, few and feeble, that have been alleged to obtain between these works will sustain scrutiny; nor is their use of rhyme and rhythm comparable; nor do they display any conceptual affinity of significance.[128] Concepts count, as does their absence, in gauging an author's purpose. Ethical identity, for instance, that central concern of Abelard and Heloise, never figures in the *Epistolae duorum amantium*, because they performed a different role. Their role and function were better understood by the Cistercian bibliophile, John of Vepria,[129] than by many since him when, in the seventh decade of the fifteenth century, he abridged and transcribed these 'letters of two lovers', as he called them with no implication of realism, into a rhetorical anthology. There they belong, in the company of other models of epistolary eloquence, not in the corpus of Abelard's and Heloise's writings. Long on word-play and short on ideas, such simple texts are fitted for learning style at an elementary level. Little Latin and few brains are needed to imitate them.

Inimitable in the philosophical subtlety, theological finesse, and linguistic refinement with which they discussed who they were and should be, Abelard and Heloise transcended the conventions of epistolary form.[130] Formal criteria, which the *Epistolae duorum amantium* privilege over content, are secondary and subordinate to this contemplative couple's experiment in ethics. Their moral meditations are composed to an exacting standard, for a critical readership, in a distinct genre. The genre of self-examination which they developed far beyond its traditional limits should not be confused with fictive love-letters designed for the scholastic schoolroom, where the *Epistolae duorum amantium* played their modest part. The authentic works of Abelard and Heloise take the limelight in an earlier, more sophisticated, drama of thought.

---

[128] For a judiciously critical assessment, see J. Marenbon, 'Lost Love Letters? A Controversy in Retrospect', *International Journal for the History of the Classical Tradition* (forthcoming). On rhyme and rhythm, cf. P. Dronke and G. Orlandi, 'New Works by Abelard and Heloise', *Filologia mediolatina* 12 (2005) 123–77.

[129] See E. Könsgen (ed.), *Epistolae duorum amantium: Briefe Abaelards und Heloises?* Mittellateinische Studien und Texte 8 (Leyden, 1974) xxff.

[130] On the hybrid term *epistola*, see Chapter 6.

CHAPTER 8

The poetical conscience

The solemnity with which intellectuals discussed *fictio* during the second quarter of the twelfth century is alleviated only by a hint of humour in Abelard's autobiography, and even then his account of the inverted penance experienced by him and Heloise when their affair was discovered amounts to little more than a parenthesis.[1] The main thrust of the narrative is, to establish the authenticity of a monastic vocation that had begun, at Saint-Denis, as a form of feigning. On the margins of this central issue, a touch of irony might be directed at Cuno of Preneste when he 'repented' the act of injustice that had made him unpopular,[2] but the integrity of his own motivation was a truth at which Abelard allowed no one to laugh. Nor is there much that is comic in Heloise's self-accusations of insincerity. Despite a trace of black humour at her plight,[3] she regarded herself, in her first and second letters, with deadly seriousness, concluding, from her impenitence for her past sins, the *fictio* of her religious life in the present. Heloise did not do so because her conscience 'awoke'.[4] It turned on itself. The savage scrupulousness of that turn, which made few concessions to comedy and granted no quarter to feigning, was also embodied, during her lifetime and Abelard's, by that relentless enemy of mirth, St Bernard.

After his death in 1153, not everyone was willing to regard Bernard of Clairvaux with the earnestness he reserved for himself. Satire at his expense served as a reminder that the divinely inspired abbot was human.[5] An alteration in the tone and tenor of Latin literature is detectable in the third quarter of the twelfth century, as a new generation began to operate in an intellectual atmosphere that was less claustrophobic. Schism and its uprests

---

[1] See Chapter 4 above.   [2] See Chapter 5 above.   [3] See Chapter 6 above.
[4] *Pace* Chenu, 'L'Eveil'.
[5] 'Nonne abbas homo est?' in 'The Satirical Works of Berengar of Poitiers', ed. R. Thomson, *Mediaeval Studies* 42 (1980) 134 and cf. J. Berlioz, 'Saint Bernard dans la littérature satirique, de l'*Ysengrimus* aux *Balivernes des courtesans*' in *Vies et légendes de Saint Bernard: Création, diffusion, réception (xiie–xxe siècles)*, Commentarii Cistercienses (Cîteaux, 1993) 211–28.

contributed to the change. From 1159, for almost twenty years, there were two popes. Victor IV (1159–1164, the second antipope of that name), was supported by the Emperor Frederick Barbarossa, aided and abetted by his archchancellor, Rainald of Dassel, the archbishop-elect of Cologne. He was described by the rival, and ultimately victorious, candidate for the papacy, Alexander III (1159–1181), as the 'criminal, perfidious, and cruel author of schismatic error'.[6] The animus was not new. Since October 1157, when Alexander had encountered Rainald at Besançon, the two men had been natural opponents. The archchancellor detested and ridiculed the reforming movements in the Church which backed the former legate after his contested election to the papacy, among them the Cistercians.

Against them the imperial chancery of Barbarossa issued an edict, probably in 1161.[7] Cistercians who failed to submit to Victor IV were to be exiled. Although only a fragment of this document survives,[8] its language is revealing. What it reveals is, the familiarity of its author – Rainald himself or a notary in his entourage – with the discourses of the previous generation on penance, hypocrisy, and *fictio*. 'Beneath their tunics' (*sub tunicas*), the Cistercians are accused of shamming religiosity. Without vision in their planning (*ceca intentione*), malevolent in their motives (*malitioso studio*), they needed to be 'ground down with threefold abasement' (*necesse est [ut] triplici contritione conterantur*). These are not the clichés of polemic attested elsewhere in the debate between the empire and the papacy.[9] They are terms whose point and pertinence derive from their currency in the circles against which they are directed.

The language of penance appropriated by the Cistercians was employed to drive them from the Reich. It encompassed northern Italy, soon to be under the sway of the imperial forces. To them Milan fell on 1 March 1162. A month later Alexander III fled from Rome, and was not to return (temporarily) until November 1165. During the interval, the anti-Roman,

---

[6] 'illi viro scelerato, perfido et crudeli et huius schismatis erroris magistro Rainaldo', Letter of 16 May, 1166 to the archbishop of Reims, PL 200, 417D.

[7] Despite the hypothesis of T. Reuter, 'Das Edikt Friedrich Barbarossas gegen die Zisterzienser', *Mitteilungen des Instituts für österreichische Geschichtsforschung* 84 (1976) 328–36 in favour of a date after May 23, 1165, the arguments for 1161 remain cogent. See W. Ohnsorge, 'Eine Ebracher Briefsammlung', *Quellen und Forschungen aus italienischen Archiven und Bibliotheken* 20 (1929) 8–10.

[8] Reuter, 'Das Edikt', 336; J. Leclercq, 'Epîtres d'Alexandre III sur les Cisterciens', *Revue bénédictine* 64 (1954) 68ff.

[9] Cf. A. Höing, 'Die Trierer Stilübungen: Ein Denkmal der Frühzeit Kaiser Friedrich Barbarossas', *Archiv für Diplomatik, Schriftgeschichte, Siegel-und Wappenkunde* 1 (1955) 257–329 and ibid. 2 (1956) 125–249 and Godman, *The Silent Masters*, 218ff.

anti-reforming, and anti-monastic sympathies of Rainald of Dassel prevailed in the German sphere of dominance. There, at Pavia, he held court in the late autumn of 1163. And there, possibly in the last week of November, the most controversial patron of letters in the Latin West received an exercise in *fictio* composed by his Archpoet.

An Archpoet, imitating the pompous titles of the archchancellor and archbishop-elect, was a suspect figure, not only on account of his pseudonym. Falsehood, mendacity, and deception were taken to be the hallmarks of his medium.[10] Such was the mistrust attached to the name of poet that a mid-twelfth-century writer about the Trojan legend disclaimed it, on the grounds – voiced in verse – that: 'I make nothing up' (*nil fingo*).[11] *Fictio* in this negative sense was opposed to the truths of history.[12] Historians were supposed to report facts as accurately as penitents were meant to confess sins. At these pious platitudes of literalism sneered Rainald of Dassel, who had no qualms about plundering the relics of the Magi in Italy and establishing a lucrative cult of them at Cologne. His policy was based on inversion of the sacred and the profane. To this unscrupulous politician the Archpoet addressed the first comedy of versified confession in European literature.

A mask was needed to play a part that lent itself so readily to being interpreted as blasphemous. The theatricality of *fictio* had been recognised by its earlier analysts; and the classical connotations of acting or assumed identity implicit in the term *persona* had not been forgotten.[13] The Archpoet assumes the *persona* of a feigned penitent in verses which we may read, but cannot hear or see being performed. The dimension of performance, accompanied by wry expressions or humorous gestures, which enriched the significance of this work for its original audience, is lost. The loss is not irreparable, because other indications of drama are abundant. But it is worth recalling that the Archpoet's 'confession' was not only a written text. Delivered orally before the archbishop-elect of Cologne and his entourage, it takes its place in a medieval Latin tradition of declaimed

---

[10] See R. McKeon, 'Poetry and Philosophy in the Twelfth Century: The Renaissance of Rhetoric', in *Critics and Criticism: Ancient and Modern*, ed. R. S. Crane (Chicago, 1952) 297–318.

[11] 'Non ego sum, quoniam nil fingo, poeta vocandus', *Anonymi Historia Troyana Daretis Frigii* v.12, ed. J. Stohlmann, Beihefte zum *MlJb*, 1 (Ratingen, 1968) 267.

[12] See P. von Moos, '*Poeta* und *Historicus* im Mittelalter. Zum Mimesis – Problem am Beispiel einiger Urteile über Lucan', *Beiträge zur Geschichte der deutschen Sprache und Literatur* 98 (1976) 93–130.

[13] See M. Fuhrmann, 'Persona, ein römischer Rollenbegriff' in *Identität*, ed. D. Marquard and K. Stierle, Poetik und Hermeneutik (Munich, 1979) 83–106 and cf. M. Stevens, 'The Performing Self in Twelfth-Century Culture', *Viator* 8 (1978) 193–212.

verse which reaches back to the courts of Charlemagne and beyond.[14] If a legacy of recitation formed the background of this experiment, nothing prepared the Archpoet's hearers for his audacity on this occasion.

The occasion was public. Public confession of scandalous sins had been a feature of *paenitentia solemnis* since late antiquity. Nowhere was that penance more solemn than in the presence of a bishop.[15] But the episcopal status of Rainald in November 1163 was disputed; and the Archpoet covers up the controversy about his patron's position in terms both accurate and misleading. *Electus Coloniae* he is called once; *praesul,* three times.[16] 'Prelate' (*praesul*) is neutral, rather an honorific designation than a legal title. '(Archbishop)-elect' (*electe*) is more dubious because, from Rome's point of view, Rainald had forfeited the canonical prerogatives of that office when he was excommunicated by Alexander III during the spring.[17] The Archpoet is silent about this circumstance, which interpreters of his work have ignored. Yet the context is relevant to the meaning of his exercise in audacity without precedent or parallel. No one before nor anyone since 1163 addressed a verse-'confession' to a prelate separated from the Church.[18]

'Which Church?' Rainald of Dassel might have scoffed. 'The Church of Alexander III?', an enemy whose election he contested. 'Or the Church of Victor IV?', an antipope whom he had in his pocket. The realities of power, not the niceties of legalism, concerned this ecclesiastical man of the world, who waited to be consecrated archbishop until 20 October 1165, having been ordained priest only on 29 May of that year. In the perspective of inversion created by schism, orthodoxy and heterodoxy were hard to tell apart. The distinction between the laity and the clergy, long contested by opponents of reform in the German Reich,[19] was scarcely applicable to a prelate who behaved like nothing so much as a secular magnate. Rainald's personality and policy affected the Archpoet's writing.

---

[14] An example is edited and translated in P. Godman, *Poetry of the Carolingian Renaissance* (London, 1985) 150–63 (no. 15). On the genre, see D. Schaller, 'Vortrags – und Zirkulardichtung am Hof Karls des Grossen', *MlJb* 6 (1970) 14–36.

[15] Cf. Cardinal Pullen, *Sententiae* VIII.57: 'publica poenitentia episcopis cognoscitur attributa', PL 186, 907C.

[16] 'Confessio' 6, 1; 13, 4; 21, 1; 24, 1, ed. Watenphul and Krefeld, 74, 75, 76.

[17] See R. Benson, *The Bishop-Elect: A Study in Medieval Ecclesiastical Office* (Princeton, 1968).

[18] See Landgraf, *Dogmengeschichte* III, 2, 223–43.

[19] Cf. B. Schmeidler, 'Anti-asketische Äußerungen aus Deutschland im 11. und beginnenden 12. Jahrhundert' in *Kultur- und Universalgeschichte: Festschrift W. Götz* (Leipzig, 1979) 35–52; Godman, *The Silent Masters*, 218ff. and see further Godman, *The Ruin of the World: Rainald of Dassel and Latin Culture in the German Empire* (forthcoming).

What member of the archchancellor's entourage would have contemplated making a solemn avowal of his sins before a patron who had employed the diction of penance in an edict that banished meddling monks? Confession to this excommunicate ran the risk of mocking the sacrament. Quite so, reflected the Archpoet; and the risk was worth running as an opportunity for that mirth which the previous generation had excluded from its lugubrious soul-searchings on the theme of *fictio*. So it was that the most accomplished wit at Rainald's court seized on a public occasion to feign penance.

Fictio, not 'goliardic poetry' or *Vagantendichtung*, is the category to which this work belongs and which it transforms. The transformation is not effected by anything so naïve as a parody of Cistercian tracts on penance[20] or a celebration of wine, women, and song. No 'wandering poet' improvising scurrilous verse to earn his keep, this polished author was a member of Rainald's itinerant entourage. United in their hostility to Rome and reform, cultivated, canny, and malicious, he and his colleagues were led by an intellectual aware of the latest developments in Parisian theology and dialectic. A pedestrian parody was not to Rainald of Dassel's racy tastes. He had been trained in the analysis of ambiguity by Adam of Balsham at the Petit-Pont.[21] Now, in 1163 at Pavia, he needed the skills acquired in Paris to appreciate his Archpoet's 'confession'.

Its structure is dialectical; the *sic* of apparent affirmation being qualified by the *non* of implicit denial. This pattern of *fictio* had been noted, forty years earlier, by Bernard of Clairvaux.[22] His reflection and that of others during the second quarter of the twelfth century had established, by the third, a number of criteria for identifying the phenomenon. *Fictio* represented a code made up of linguistic signals, many of them emotive. Terms for the penitential emotions and their cognitive qualities were meant to indicate sincerity and authenticity. But the message might be distorted. Mistransmissions of the conscience were not easy to straighten out. If suspicion of feigning had grown apace, the instruments of control were scarcely sharper than they had been at the time of Gregory the Great.[23] In the twelfth century, as in the sixth, outside observers might be

[20] The opposite view, by F. Cairns, 'The Archpoet's Confession: Sources, Interpretation, and Historical Context', *MlJb* 15 (1986) 87–103, is criticised by P. Dronke, 'The Archpoet and the Classics' in *Latin Poetry and the Classical Tradition*, ed. Godman and Murray, 57–72.
[21] See L. Minio-Paluello, 'The *Ars disserendi* of Adam of Balsham "Parvipontanus"', *Mediaeval and Renaissance Studies* 3 (1954) 116–69.
[22] See Chapter 1.   [23] See Chapter 2.

mistrustful, but they still had to rely on the self-regulation of sinners. Into this vacuum of verifiability stepped the Archpoet. A master of penitential diction and practice, he did not make the mistake of what Cardinal Pullen called 'exaggeration'.[24] Less obviously, he sent signals which contradicted one another, to ironical effect. But the irony of the Archpoet is of a philosophical and theological sophistication unattested elsewhere in medieval literature.[25] Many have regarded him as a wag; some have taken him seriously; but no one appears to have seen him for what he is in this 'confession': a subtly anti-religious thinker.

The opening of the work takes the form of a soliloquy. Why does the author affect to speak alone and to himself when his 'confession' depends, in style and substance, on the presence of his patron? Because contrition ought to be as heartfelt as anger or anguish:

> Aestuans intrinsecus ira vehementi …
> Seething inwardly with violent wrath …[26]

If the language is originally Biblical,[27] it had acquired rich connotations by the twelfth century. The adverb 'inwardly' (*intrinsecus*), for example, was used to contrast the sphere of sincerity with the exterior world of appearances by theologians such as Cardinal Pullen in discussions of the conscience.[28] He and others advised against penitents being taken at their word. Words can deceive, which is just what the Archpoet intends to do by linking inwardness with the key concept of 'bitterness' (*amaritudo*):

> in amaritudine loquar mee menti.
> let me speak in bitterness to myself.[29]

The word 'bitterness' (*amaritudo*) of Job (10:1), glossed most influentially for the Latin West by Gregory the Great,[30] makes a brief appearance here, in the second verse of the work, not to recur until the very last line, where the punishment due to a self-confessed sinner is rejected as 'excessively bitter' (*nimis amarum*).[31] Feigning contrition at the beginning of his work, the Archpoet attempts to avert its punitive consequences at the end, in defiance of all the rules.

The rules prescribed self-examination. Parallels to the verses quoted above are numerous in works of twelfth-century spiritual literature. They

[24] See Chapter 7.
[25] Cf. D. Green, *Irony in the Medieval Romance* (Cambridge, 1979) and D. Knox, *Ironia: Medieval and Renaissance Ideas on Irony* (Leiden, 1989).
[26] x.1.1, ed. Watenphul and Krefeld, 73.   [27] Watenphul and Krefeld, ibid., compare Genesis 6:6.
[28] See Pullen, *Sententiae* v.29, PL 186, 852A.   [29] x.1.2, ed. Watenphul and Krefeld, 73.
[30] See Chapter 2 above.   [31] x.25.4, eds. Watenphul and Krefeld, 76. See further below.

include the opening of Hugh of Saint-Victor's *De arrha animae*.[32] This was the type of soliloquy with which the Archpoet's exordium will have been associated by his hearers. But Rainald and others cannot have failed to observe a basic difference, to which they were unaccustomed. Hugh wrote in prose, as was normal. For what purported to be soul-searching conducted in verse of this kind there was no precedent; and the innovation is highlighted by the discrepancy between form and content. The merriness of the disyllabic pure rhyme undercuts the solemnity of the declaration. If we are unable to recapture the expression of mock remorse with which this author probably recited his work before his patron, we are not reduced to speculation about its audial impact on Rainald. The jollity of the rhyming verses with which the Archpoet proclaims his anguish invites this schismatic prelate to smile.

The smile is one of complicity. Theoretically, Rainald of Dassel sits in judgement. Actually, he is encouraged to lean back in the easy-chair of authority and grin. Self-accusation, fundamental to penance, is about to be transformed into self-commendation. Self-commendation through confession of sins was a purpose shared by other feigned penitents. They, however, calculated on ingratiating themselves by a show of humility. There is nothing humble about the Archpoet: he vaunts his knowledge of the rules, before turning them on their heads. *Tergiversatio*, as Bernard of Clairvaux and Gratian labelled this phenomenon, was not regarded by them as funny. Their senses of humour did not extend to a sin equivalent to blasphemy; and that marks a fundamental difference between them and the outrageous Rainald. Yet *fictio* at his court was not permissible with the buffoonery of the Feast of Fools. Outrageous he could be, but he was also refined. The refinement of his patron is mirrored in the Archpoet's style.

That style appealed to medieval memories which resembled webs of association.[33] At the centre of these webs, finespun and flexible, stood the Bible. More than a text, Scripture represented, to Rainald of Dassel and his entourage, a living organism, revived every day in the liturgy. Liturgical worship conjured up Biblical associations which were reinforced

---

[32] 'loquar secreto animae meae … aperta conscientia soli verba conferemus', PL 176, 951C and cf. 967Cff. See further Bruno of Segni, *Expositio in Iob*, PL 164, 579D: 'confabulabor cum amaritudine animae meae' and Rupert of Deutz, *In S. Iob commentarius*, PL 168, 1011D: 'loquar in amaritudine animae meae, id est: confitebor peccata mea in tristitia poenitentiae'.

[33] Cf. Carruthers and Ziolkowski, *The Medieval Craft of Memory*.

by ritual language. Employed on occasions that varied from ceremonies in church to meals in the refectory,[34] this clerical *koinê* was disciplined by the authority of exegesis. And no exegete was more authoritative on the subject of penance than Gregory the Great. Gregory's is the thought, familiar to the Archpoet's audience from the much-studied *Moralia in Iob*,[35] that lies behind the next couplet:

> Unsubstantial and slight in my being,
> I am like a leaf played about by the wind.[36]

> factus de materia levis elementi,
> folio sum similis, de quo ludunt venti.

The leaf of Job 13:25 is interpreted by Gregory the Great as postlapsarian man, buffeted about by the winds of temptation.[37] The temptation of wrath (*ira*) to which he falls prey is succeeded by that of foolish merriment (*inepta laetitia*). Both are exemplified in the contrast between the Archpoet's angry declarations of penance and the humorously rhyming form in which they are couched. The medium undermining the message, his *persona* is further defined by Gregory the Great's strictures against those who laugh at what they should mourn.[38] These opposites are combined in a dialectic of *fictio*.

Fictio, in the Archpoet's 'confession', also arises from a tension between literal and implied meaning. The terms chosen are associative but exact. Not all of them are taken from the Book of Job or Gregory's exegesis of it; they are also complemented by references to the New Testament, as in the strophe that follows:

> Although it is the mark of a wise man
> to build the seat of his foundation on stone,
> I, a fool, am like a gliding river,
> never lingering under the same sky.[39]

---

[34] The Archpoet evokes this context when, in another poem (1.4.3–4, ed. Watenphul and Krefeld, 47), he imagines his reader falling asleep out of boredom and interrupting his recitation: 'ne dormitet lector pre tedio, / et "*tu autem*" dicat in medio'. The italicised phrase was used after a long reading in refectory following a course of fish or fowl: 'Et ad aliam ministrationem iterum legit lector tamdiu, quousque precipiat ei abbas, ut finiatur ... si autem longa fuerat lectio ... repetit ipsum [sermonem] et postea dicit: "*Tu autem*, Domine, miserere nobis".' *De convivio sive prandio atque cenis monachorum qualiter in monasteriis Romanae Ecclesiae constituta est consuetudo* in M. Andrieu (ed.), *Les ordines romani du Haut Moyen Âge* I. Spicilegium sacrum lovaniense 2 (Louvain, 1931) 13.

[35] See Chapter 2.   [36] x.1.3–4, ed. Watenphul and Krefeld, 73.

[37] *Moralia in Iob* xi.44.60, ed. Adriaen, CCSL 143A 619.

[38] See Chapter 2. Cf. Cardinal Pullen: 'qui de commissa [noxa] gaudet ... proprio de iudicio se condemnat', *Sententiae* v.30, PL 186, 852A.

[39] x.2, ed. Watenphul and Krefeld, 73.

Cum sit enim proprium viro sapienti
supra petram ponere sedem fundamenti,
stultus ego comparor fluvio labenti
sub eodem aere numquam permanenti.

'The seat of his foundation' (*sedes fundamenti*), or stable base, is an expression
warranted by neither of the Archpoet's Scriptural sources. Matthew 7:24 and
Luke 6:48 refer to building a house (*domum*) on stone, but only the second
mentions its foundation, which is hardly *Sitzfleisch*.[40] This is neither a medieval colloquialism nor one that would have made sense here if it were. The
reference is not anal but Biblical, and the style is mock-solemn. Modelled
on such constructions as St Matthew's *sedem maiestatis tuae* (25:31), the
genitive of place is as high-sounding as the subject is low. The subject is the
location, rather than the backside, of the Archpoet. It is unstable.

Instability was not a neutral concept for his audience. Rainald and his
entourage associated this Biblical text with a precept of monasticism. Monks
were meant to stay put in one place, obedient to the orders of their abbot:
the Archpoet revels in his wanderings, expressions of his aberrant character. If nature and inclination make him itinerant, this is not just a personal
or professional condition, but mankind's state after the Fall, according to
Gregory the Great in his interpretation of Job 14:2.[41] Gregorian is the idea
to which the last verse above refers, not without a malicious allusion to the
fool of Job 5:3 in the penultimate line. He 'takes root' (*firma radice*) but,
the saint declares, he is cursed, for he bases his love on life in this world,
rather than the next.[42] Of the next world, of the gloom and doom with
which fickle fools are menaced by this authority on penance, there are
few traces at the opening of the Archpoet's 'confession'. Its self-accusations
invert all that Gregory and his imitators took seriously.

Inversion is a characteristic of *fictio*. The pattern is now familiar to us.
Unfamiliar both to us and to the Archpoet's audience is, or was, his cheer-
fulness. It represents the contrary of what a penitent was supposed to feel.
What, then, are his real sentiments? Where does this sophist stand? The

---

[40] Dronke, 'The Archpoet and the Classics' 60n., referring to *fundamentum*. For the solemnity
of the reference to the stone or rock, and its identification with the Church, cf. the German
bishops' letter to Hadrian IV of 1158, Rahewin, *Gesta Frederici* III, 20, ed. F.-J. Schmale,
Bischof Otto von Freising und Rahewin, Die Taten Friedrichs oder richtiger Cronica, Ausgewählte
Quellen zur deutschen Geschichte des Mittelalters 17 (Berlin, 1965) 434, 20–1.

[41] *Moralia in Iob* XI.50.67, ed. Adriaen, CCSL 143A 624ff. Did the Archpoet's audience also
view him as an anti-type of those itinerant preachers of penance led by Robert of Arbrissel?
Cf. E. Werner, *Pauperes Christi: Studien zu sozial-religiösen Bewegungen im Zeitalter des
Reformpapstums* (Leipzig, 1956) 42ff. See further below.

[42] *Moralia in Iob* VI.6.7, ed. Adriaen, CCSL 143 288ff.

answer is, he does not. Movement, aimless and uncontrolled, is inherent in his anti-monastic pose:

> I am borne along like a ship without a sailor,
> like a wandering bird through airy ways.
> I am confined by neither chains nor key,
> I seek out my likes and keep wicked company.[43]

> Feror ego veluti sine nauta navis,
> ut per vias aeris vaga fertur avis.
> Non me tenent vincula, non me tenet clavis,
> quero mei similes et adiungor pravis.

The language is proverbial; the analogies are modelled on Wisdom 5:10; and the conventional character of the diction highlights the novelty with which an ancient doctrine is being transformed. The doctrine that self-accusation demonstrates sincerity had been taken to extremes by Heloise.[44] There, at the limit of paradox, Abelard had attempted to draw her back within the bounds of rationality.[45] Quoting Scripture, Virgil, and St Jerome, he had urged Heloise not to invert Christ's teaching about the exaltation of the humble or to seek praise by seeming to flee it. Now the Archpoet ignores that counsel of common sense, and trespasses into unexplored territory. Unlike Heloise, he is not lost in a labyrinth of interiority. He is deliberately constructing a moral maze. No way out of it was available to those who premised their soul-searchings on sincerity, for this feigned penitent goes on to celebrate the faults he is supposed to condemn. Gregory the Great taught that the 'internal judge' (*internus iudex*) was vigilant, but here he seems to have nodded off. In his slumbers, who can fathom the secrets of the Archpoet's conscience?

Did he have one, or is he conjuring up a mirage? This question is addressed in terms of taste. Bitterness (*amaritudo*), the cardinal term of penitential remorse at the beginning of the work, is now balanced by an ideal of sweetness (*dulcedo, suavitas*):

> Gravity of heart seems to me dreary,
> merriment is lovable and sweeter than honeycomb;
> all Venus' commands are sweet work;
> for she never dwells in craven hearts.[46]

> Mihi cordis gravitas res videtur gravis,
> iocus est amabilis dulciorque favis;
> quicquid Venus imperat, labor est suavis;
> que numquam in cordibus habitat ignavis.

[43] x.3, ed. Watenphul and Krefeld, 74.   [44] See Chapter 1.   [45] See Chapter 7.
[46] x.4, ed. Watenphul and Krefeld, 74.

The Archpoet assumes the role of the inverted moralist in this strophe. No longer self-accusatory, he waxes sententious. His subject remains the conscience, indicated by the Biblical metaphor of the heart. His heart, untroubled by the scruples of conscientious clerics, makes light of their criticisms. Ecclesiastical gravity cast as dreariness, the Christian virtue of chastity is countered by praise of the pagan goddess of love. It is Venus who transforms the 'wicked' (*pravis*) of the previous strophe into the 'valiant' (*non ... ignavi*) of the double negative in the last verse. The bitter negativity of moralism is offset by this apology of sweetness – a term that evoked, for the Archpoet's audience, moral opposites. *Dulcedo*, which signifies the gentleness of divine justice in the Bible,[47] also represented a cloying feature of sinfulness for Cardinal Pullen and St Bernard.[48]

Against them and their likes, the Archpoet uses one of their favourite terms of censure to defend his sins. Sweetness, so alien to the tastes of Rome or Clairvaux and so congenial to the palate of Rainald, serves as a motto for all that the moralists abhorred:

> I tread the primrose path, as young men do,
> enmeshing myself in vice, forgetful of virtue;
> keener on pleasure than on salvation,
> dead in the soul, I take care of my skin.[49]

> Vita lata gradior more iuventutis,
> inplico me viciis immemor virtutis;
> voluptatis avidus magis quam salutis,
> mortuus in anima curam gero cutis.

The 'wide gate and broad road' of Matthew 7:13 (*lata porta et spaciosa via*) are conflated into a single primrose path, which does not lead, as the Apostle claims, to destruction. It leads to pleasure. And if one of the casualties on that route is St Paul's condemnation of 'lovers of pleasure more than lovers of God' (*voluptatum amatores magis quam Dei*, II Timothy 3:4), the Archpoet gladly accepts the consequence. Putting himself in the position of the damned (*mortuus in anima*),[50] he recalls Bernard of

---

[47] See J. Ziegler, *Dulcedo Dei: Ein Beitrag zur Theologie der griechischen und lateinischen Bibel* (Münster, 1937) and C. Spicq, 'Bénignité, mansuétude, douceur, clémence', *Revue biblique* 54 (1947) 321–37.

[48] Cf. Pullen, *Sententiae* VI.52: 'nimirum quoniam dulcedine peccati Deum offendimus', PL 186, 962A and Bernard of Clairvaux, *Ad clericos de conversione* III.4 in *S. Bernardi Opera* IV, ed. J. Leclercq and H. Rochais (Rome, 1956) 75, 6–7. The model of both is Gregory the Great, *Moralia in Iob* XV.11.13, ed. Adriaen, CCSL 143A 756, 14–22.

[49] x.5, ed. Watenphul and Krefeld, 74.

[50] Cf. Augustine, *De civitate Dei* XIII.23, *S. Aurelii Augustini De civitate Dei libri XI–XXII*, ed. Dombart and Kalb, CCSL 48 406, 44ff.

Clairvaux's strictures against carnal vice and sartorial affectation which, according to that saint, are 'indicative of spiritual laxness. So much attention would not be paid to taking care of physical appearances unless the mind, unkempt of virtue, had been neglected.'[51]

Such were the antitheses of asceticism to which the Archpoet refers, pleading guilty to the charges levelled by Bernard and other censors of sin. 'Forgetful of virtue' (*immemor virtutis*), he is attentive to 'care of the body' (*cura corporis*). That expression had a special resonance in the language of the reformers. *Cura corporis* meant, for them, physical discipline.[52] The contrary is intended by the Archpoet: the sensual laxness, the carnal vanity which they deplored. Adopting the slogans of moralism, he reverses their meaning. And as he does so with an epigrammatic elegance which mocks that renunciation of corporeal care undertaken by penitents,[53] the basis of confession is undermined. It is undermined for the benefit of a connoisseur: Rainald of Dassel, who is described in the first verse below as 'most discerning' (*discretissime*). In possession of the *discretio* prized in monastic ethics,[54] he can be relied upon to discriminate between virtue and vice in ways no monk could or should:

> Most discerning prelate, I ask your pardon:
> I die the good death, I perish in sweet destruction;
> my heart is wounded by feminine charm
> and those whom I cannot touch, I lust at least in the heart.

> It is most difficult to overcome nature,
> to have pure thoughts while gazing at a girl,
> we young men cannot follow the hard law
> and pay no attention to smooth bodies.[55]

> Presul discretissime, veniam te precor:
> morte bona morior, dulci nece necor,
> meum pectus sauciat puellarum decor,
> et quas tactu nequeo, saltem corde mechor.

---

[51] ' … animi mollitiem indicant. Non tanto curaretur corporis cultus, nisi prius neglecta fuit mens inculta virtutibus', *Apologia* x.26 in *S. Bernardi Opera* III, ed. J. Leclercq and H. Rochais (Rome, 1967) 102, 23–5.

[52] See G. Zimmermann, *Ordensleben und Lebensstandard: Die cura corporis in den Ordensvorschriften des abendländischen Hochmittelalters*, Beiträge zur Geschichte des alten Mönchtums und des Benediktinerordens 32 (Münster, 1979).

[53] See J. Jungmann, *Die lateinischen Bußriten in ihrer geschichtlichen Entwicklung. Forschungen zur Geschichte des innerkirchlichen Lebens* 3, 4 (Innsbruck, 1934) 65ff.

[54] See Chapter 1.

[55] x.6–7, ed. Watenphul and Krefeld, 74.

Res est arduissima vincere naturam,
in aspectu virginis mentem esse puram;
iuvenes non possumus legem sequi duram
leviumque corporum non habere curam.

The naturalness of sexual desire was a theme reintroduced into medieval ethics by Abelard, drawing on St Augustine's critic, John Cassian;[56] and a degree of leniency towards both mental and physical sins of concupiscence is detectable even in the thought of such rigorists as Cardinal Pullen.[57] But none of them, orthodox or otherwise, set these views against Christ's teaching at Matthew 5:28.[58] The 'adultery in the heart' which Jesus condemns there is the sin which the Archpoet acknowledges here. The defender of sensuality has become its apologist against the 'hard law' of chastity. The spiritual origins and mental location of that virtue, expounded by Heloise,[59] are ignored as irrelevant to nature and youth. Ethical ideas of the previous generation superseded, different ones take their place. The 'hard law' (*lex dura*) – an expression regularly applied in Christian Latin to the severity of the Old Testament, as opposed to the mercifulness of the New – dismissed in these strophes is that of Jesus. Implicitly styling himself an antichrist, the Archpoet proclaims a revised gospel of 'sweetness'.[60]

This put Rainald of Dassel in a position unlike Abelard's when he received Heloise's confessional letters. Both of them, formally and figuratively, are cast as spiritual guides, deputed to judge *in loco Dei*. Neither of them could do so, for different reasons. Declining the God-like knowledge of Heloise's motivation attributed to him so ingeniously by her, Abelard expresses himself with reservations. His reservations, tempered by pastoral correctness and limited by a sensibility more straightforward than hers, lead him to voice hesitantly the suspicion of *fictio* which her self-accusations aroused. Suggestions, recommendations, and admonitions are addressed to Heloise but, throughout her correspondence with Abelard, she is treated with indulgence. Indulgence, for the Archpoet, is not enough. His unstated demand is for complicity on the part of his patron. Rainald of Dassel and he are linked by a bond that excludes others. Exclusion, however, does not mean secrecy. Sinfulness is proclaimed in a public context where the only

---

[56] See Chapters 4 and 7.   [57] See Chapter 7.
[58] This is the text cited by Abelard as an example of mental sin without action: *Problema Heloissae* 24, PL 178, 710C–D.
[59] See Chapter 7.
[60] On the figure of the erring prophet, to which the Archpoet alludes, see Abelard, *Sic et non*, prol.: 'Constat quippe et prophetas ipsos quandoque … per spiritum suum falsa protulisse … ', ed. Boyer and McKeon, 97, 195–7.

recipient who counts is, the judge. And judgement is to be passed, by this prelate separated from the Church, with matching irony, equal humour, and similar irreverence.

All these qualities, far from the solemnity with which *fictio* had been viewed by earlier writers on the subject, reveal much about the atmosphere of Rainald's court. Only there, in twelfth-century Europe, is spoof of a sacrament attested in such a refined form. Neither Thomas Becket – who began his career, like Rainald, by having more in common with secular magnates than with men of the Church – nor any other prelate in the Latin West aided and abetted writing of this kind. The saintly archbishop had in his service John of Salisbury;[61] the schismatic archbishop-elect employed the Archpoet. These two patrons of high culture, orthodox and heterodox, represent the poles between which oscillated Rome and the Reich. Small wonder that the supporter and ally of this feigned penitent was loathed by the rightful pope.

Popes are not invited to Pavia, where the Archpoet ignores the relics of Augustine, enshrined there for centuries, and concentrates on the less saintly presence of Venus:

> Who, when placed in fire, is not burnt?
> Who can be thought chaste while staying at Pavia,
> where Venus hunts young men with her finger,
> lures them with her eyes, preys on them with her looks?
>
> If you station Hippolytus at Pavia today,
> he will not be Hippolytus tomorrow:
> all roads lead to Venus' bedroom;
> among so many towers Alethia's is missing.[62]
>
> Quis in igne positus igne non uratur?
> Quis Papie demorans castus habeatur,
> ubi Venus digito iuvenes venatur,
> oculis illaqueat, facie predatur?
>
> Si ponas Ypolitum hodie Papie,
> non erit Ypolitus in sequenti die:
> Veneris in thalamos ducunt omnes vie;
> non est in tot turribus turris Alethie.

[61] On Becket and John of Salisbury, cf. Godman, *The Silent Masters*, 186ff.
[62] x.8–9, ed. Watenphul and Krefeld, 74.

The proverbial language of the third strophe becomes platitudinous here, but the change does not amount to a lapse of register. Presenting his outrageous claims as commonplace facts, the Archpoet couches assertion in the form of interrogation. If no one will quarrel with the proposition that fire burns, none should doubt that chastity, at Pavia, is impossible. Neither immorality nor weakness is the cause, but Venus, who dictates the rules. Voluntary action, like ethical choice, is out of the question, he implies. And as further issues that preoccupied twelfth-century thinkers are swept aside, *luxuria* is licensed on the grounds that the goddess is a predatory whore. All roads led not to Rome but to Venus' bedroom. The capital and symbol of moral reform supplanted by a figure of immortal vice, blame cannot be attributed to the young whose cause the Archpoet espouses. Fingers, eyes, face: every expression, each gesture beckons to sensuality.

Gestures and expressions were the 'signs of the soul' by which Bernard of Clairvaux and others detected *fictio*.[63] Now it is not the feigned penitent but the personified source of his sinfulness which pokes and points; and it is a fair guess that the humour of the recitation was enhanced by accompanying movements of the Archpoet's hands and eyes. No guessing is needed to appreciate his shift of register, from low to high. Higher than the platitudes manipulated in the eighth strophe is the allusion, in the ninth, to Hippolytus, archetype of sexual virtue, losing his chastity. Unmistakably Ovidian,[64] it recalls the sententiousness affected earlier. Once more the pose of the moralist is struck ironically. Never is the Archpoet more equivocal than when he affects to talk straight. Literal locations assume figurative significance: missing, among the many towers in the city, is that of truth (*turris Alethie*). Veracity is to be expected neither from Pavia nor from him. What this sophist asserts instead are, the truth-claims of lies.

A version of the Cretan paradox is constructed in the Archpoet's medium of mendacity. Lying about lies in verse, he banishes truth to a no man's land, where nothing is what it seems and all implies its opposite. The objective is, to counter the criticism of his detractors. They are anticipated by their target. Playing the role of the just man, as defined by Proverbs 18:17, the Archpoet accuses himself; and the seizure of initiative at this point enables him, later (20.3), to turn the tables on others. But the reason adduced for his fornication – its naturalness in youth – is inadequate to defend him

---

[63] See Chapter 1.   [64] Watenphul and Krefeld, 74 cite *Amores* II.4.32.

against their second charge, for gambling is a vice arguably less linked to age than sex. Addressing those who harp on his partiality for 'the game' (*ludus*), the Archpoet identifies, in such sinfulness, a mainspring of his art:

> Secondly I am blamed for gambling,
> but when I am skinned at the game,
> chilled outwardly, I sweat with mental heat,
> and, at that moment, I fashion finer verse.[65]

> Secundo redarguor etiam de ludo,
> sed cum ludus corpore me dimittit nudo,
> frigidus exterius mentis estu sudo;
> tunc versus et carmina meliora cudo.

Attention is now focused on critics who, 'secondly' (*secundo*) implies, have already been gossiping behind his back. This itemisation of charges mimics a technique employed at the beginning of Abelard's second letter to Heloise.[66] There he counts under four headings the reproaches she levelled against him. Such enumeration of error was common in theological and legal writing of the twelfth century, and it would become standard practice in the learned literature of high scholasticism, upon whose pedantry the humanists were to pour scorn. Less scorn than humour is the Archpoet's attitude, as he pretends to apply a systematic approach to his wayward life. The effect is, to cast his critics as more modern, but no less tedious, versions of the ecclesiastical accountants of the conscience depicted in the penitential handbooks of the early Middle Ages.[67]

Early, high, and late medieval sources on gambling are unanimous about its prohibition, categorical but unconvincing (because so often repeated that it cannot have been observed), for clerics.[68] The Archpoet, reduced to a nakedness incompatible with his order by losing at dice, presents himself as a figure of scandal, in breach of the rules of clerical deportment. But if he behaves like a layman, it would be mistaken to conclude that he is one. Few authors of the twelfth century laid such stress on the inaccessibility of their works to the unlearned laity:

> laymen do not understand the poet's craft.[69]

> laici non sapiunt ea, quae sunt vatis.

---

[65] x.10, ed. Watenphul and Krefeld, 74.   [66]*Ep.* v.i, ed. Pagani, 290.   [67] See Chapter 2.
[68] See W. Tauber, *Das Würfelspiel im Mittelalter und in der frühen Neuzeit: Eine kultur – und sprachgeschichtliche Darstellung*, Europäische Hochschulschriften 959 (Frankfurt am Main, 1987).
[69] iv.20.3, ed. Watenphul and Krefeld, 59.

At Cologne, where the Archpoet spent time in the service of the archbishop-elect, the distinctness of the two orders was a fact of daily life.[70] It is that fact, that distinction which the strophe above inverts. But if, in the *tergiversatio* of his riotousness, the Archpoet breaches prohibitions, he remains true to himself.

To himself? Who is this Proteus? His identity is affirmed in contradictions. Not only a violator of ecclesiastical decorum, he also represents the anti-type of an ideal. Nudity, the visible and tangible sign of the Archpoet's disgrace, was idealised in the twelfth century as a metaphor for imitation of Christ's humanity.[71] Unlike Christ in his practice of 'adultery in the heart', this sophist now styles himself the opposite of His imitators. For the Archpoet's nakedness is neither metaphorical nor voluntary; and if his gambling reduces him to pennilessness, it is not the poverty of religious devotion, but a source of poetic inspiration. Mentally heated and physically chilled, he modulates a merry variant on the penitential contrast between interiority and exteriority. And this *allegro* mocks proprieties cherished by others. Moral deterioration leading to literary improvement, the spoof-causality makes light of the notion, taken so seriously by Abelard and Heloise, that ethical conduct and intellectual endeavour should be in harmony;[72] while perhaps poking further fun at Ovid who, tongue-in-cheek at *Tristia* II.354, declares that his life is restrained and his muse jovial (*vita verecunda est, Musa iocosa mea*). Neither medieval concords nor ancient contrasts between behaviour and work satisfy the Archpoet. His original claim is that the wickedness of the one heightens the quality of the other.

In this symmetry between vice and art, the *sic et non*-method runs riot. The riot of thought appears tumultuous, but is controlled by dialectic. The Archpoet's dialectic aims to win over his patron by those inversions of the sacred and the profane for which Rainald of Dassel was notorious. Nothing – neither Biblical authority nor classical tradition – stands in the way of this purpose, just as the archchancellor brooked no opposition in having an anti-pope elected or in making Charlemagne a saint. Servant of

---

[70] See M. Bernards, 'Die Welt der Laien in der kölnischen Theologie des 12. Jahrhunderts' in *Die Kirche und ihre Ämte und Stände: Festgabe J. Kardinal Frings* (Cologne, 1960) 391–416. For the wider context, see G. Constable, *Three Studies in Medieval Religious and Social Thought: The Interpretation of Mary and Martha; The Ideal of the Imitation of Christ; The Orders of Society* (Cambridge, 1995) 289ff.

[71] Among the several studies of this topic, the best is G. Constable, '*Nudus nudum Christum sequi* and Parallel Formulas in the Twelfth Century' in *Continuity and Discontinuity in Church History: Essays Presented to G. Huntston Williams*, ed. F. Church (Leiden, 1979) 83–91. See further Constable, *Three Studies*, 199–217 and *Reformation*, 125, 153, 280.

[72] See Chapter 4.

a master for whom religion was an instrument of policy, the Archpoet feels free to stage his profane apotheosis:

> On the third heading I mention the pub,
> which I have never shunned and never shall,
> until I see the holy angels arriving,
> singing 'Eternal rest' for the dead.

> It is my intention to die in a pub,
> to have wines in reach at my last gasp.
> Then angelic choirs shall sing jubilantly:
> 'May God take mercy on this drinker!'[73]

> Tercio capitulo memoro tabernam.
> Illam nullo tempore sprevi neque spernam,
> donec sanctos angelos venientes cernam
> cantantes pro mortuis: 'Requiem eternam.'

> Meum est propositum in taberna mori,
> ut sint vina proxima morientis ori.
> Tunc cantabunt letius angelorum chori:
> 'Sit Deus propitius huic potatori!'

On the 'third heading' (*tercio capitulo*) of the pub, ecclesiastical legislation had been unsparing of prohibitions since at least the Carolingian age.[74] In the place where drunkenness, violence, and gambling were practised, clerics were forbidden to set foot. There, not by chance, the Archpoet stations his deathbed. And what a jolly scene is envisaged as he passes away! Angelic choruses first sing a requiem mass, then invoke a Biblical text. But it is not just the apostle's plea for divine mercy (*Deus propitius esto mihi peccatori*, Luke 18:13) which is transformed by the alteration of a single syllable (*potatori*) in the last word above. The Archpoet also recalls a specific context, familiar to every member of his audience, in which this chapter and verse were cited. Confessors were accustomed to quoting Luke 18:13 to penitents when they came to avow their sins.[75]

Avowing his sins with impenitence, the Archpoet thwarts expectations of remorse; and the hilarity may be heightened by a reminiscence of Ovid's *Liebestod* (*Amores* II.10. 35–8).[76] But the idea of dying during the act of love

[73] x.11–12, ed. Watenphul and Krefeld, 74–5.
[74] See R. Kaiser, *Trunkenheit und Gewalt im Mittelalter* (Cologne, 2002) 111ff., 143ff.
[75] See Burchard of Worms, 'Oratio sacerdotis dicenda ad paenitentiam venientibus: "Domine Deus omnipotens: *Propitius esto mihi peccatori*"' in *Decretum* xix.3 ('*Medicus*'), PL 140, 950A.
[76] Cited by Watenphul and Krefeld, and discussed by Dronke, 'The Archpoet and the Classics', 64–5.

(or drinking) is secondary. The primary purpose is, to shock. At the last moment in this world when a sinner was meant to undertake the atonement required for salvation in the next, the Archpoet, attended by the angels who, at Luke 15:10, rejoice at a penitent sinner,[77] remains defiant. Defiant of whom? Of those authorities, such as St Benedict, who abhorred excess in food and drink (*crapula*) as the contrary of Christianity.[78] Advocating the bottle, this feigned penitent severs his ties with the faithful. Such was the position of his patron. Rainald of Dassel is compared by him, in another work, with the vine of John 15:5, to which he stands in the relationship of a branch.[79] The analogy was interpreted as ecclesial communion by contemporary exegetes. Separate the branch, or the minister of the sacraments, from the vine, or the unity of the Church, and you have schism[80] – precisely the background against which the Archpoet's 'confession' was written. United in their laughter at bans on bibulousness, the schismatic prelate and his companion in cups defy the demands of orthodoxy.

Orthodoxy was not always abstinent, nor had Christ been a teetotaller. Christian tradition, however, tended to regard wine as a danger.[81] With clearly defined exceptions (such as cases of ill health or overwork), moderation in drinking was a common counsel given by moralists and reformers since St Benedict. The bibulousness extolled by the Archpoet represented a challenge to their sobriety, which was doubly difficult to answer in an atmosphere of court-intrigue:

> The soul's lantern is lit by goblets;
> the heart, imbued with nectar, soars up to heaven;
> to me wine from the pub has a sweeter taste
> than what the prelate's butler mixes with water.[82]

> Poculis accenditur animi lucerna;
> cor inbutum nectare volat ad superna.

---

[77] The allusion to Luke 15:10 is pointed out by Dronke, ibid. 75. Cf. Abelard, *Problema Heloissae* 11, PL 178, 693A.

[78] 'Nihil sic contrarium est homini Christiano, quomodo crapula', *Regula S. Benedicti* 39, ed. A. de Voguë, *La Règle de saint Benoît* II, SC182 (Paris, 1971) 578. For the influence of this precept in canon law, see Kaiser, *Trunkenheit und Gewalt*, 196ff.

[79] 'Ero palmes et tu vitis' II.94, ed. Watenphul and Krefeld, 56. Cf. John 15:5: 'ego sum vitis, vos palmites'.

[80] See Rupert of Deutz, *Commentaria in Evangelium Sancti Iohannis* XI, ed. R. Haacke, CCCM 9 (Turnhout, 1969) 650, 1937ff. and cf. Abelard, *Problema Heloissae* 6, PL 178, 686C.

[81] The fundamental authorities, Proverbs 20:1 and Ephesians 5:18, which equate *vinum* and *luxuria*, are both quoted by Abelard in his Christmas sermon for the Paraclete, ed. De Santis, 180, 203–4.

[82] x.13, ed. Watenphul and Krefeld, 75.

Mihi sapit dulcius vinum de taberna
quam quod aqua miscuit presulis pincerna.

Imagine the reaction of his critics when they heard this strophe being recited. Its effect was unsettling. The metaphors of illumination and exaltation in the first two verses are less Biblical than liturgical in flavour. They evoke the spiritual transports of the soul at contemplation of God which the liturgy sought to inspire in worshippers.[83] But the Archpoet worships wine, and the claim that it is a source of creativity is asserted as his sophistical truth. *In vino veritas*: the idea is not Christian. Here, more directly than in any other allusion to the Latin classics, he draws on Roman culture. Poetic inspiration by wine, a concept absent from the sombre heritage of the Latin Fathers and their medieval beneficiaries, recalls the convivial settings of ancient symposia.[84]

How convivial then was Rainald of Dassel's high table? Less so than the pub for this 'wine-bibber', this 'friend of publicans and sinners'. He gaily applies to himself the charges levelled against Jesus at Matthew 11:19 (*potator vini, publicanorum et peccatorum amicus*). The antitype of Christ accepts His invitation to rejoice, in contrast to John the Baptist's call to repent, on the irreverent grounds that, in the pub, the wine tastes sweeter. Sweetness, the prime value of the first part of this work, is missing from the prelate's symposia, because his butler has been diluting the vinous doses.[85] Why does he indulge in this underhand practice? Emphatically not because watered wine was recommended for women and monks.[86] Neither were present in Rainald's entourage, nor did such prim decorum suit his character. Was the butler implementing a policy of stinginess ordered by his master? Or was he acting on his own initiative? In either case, the meaning is clear: the Archpoet refers to what was an open secret at court. And in that malicious milieu, he turns not to his rivals but to their chief. A complicit wink, a knowing nod is implied by the last verse of this strophe. It represents the Archpoet and the archchancellor as a couple, inseparable in their singularity.

---

[83] Cf. A. Blaise, *Le vocabulaire latin des principaux thèmes liturgiques* (Turnhout, 1966) 280 (154) ff.; 451 (308).

[84] See J. Griffin, '*Regalis inter mensas laticemque Lyaeum*: Wine in Virgil and Others' and A. La Penna, 'Il vino di Orazio: nel *modus* e contro il *modus*' both in *In Vino Veritas*, ed. O. Murray and M. Tecusan (London, 1995) 283–95, 266–82.

[85] *Pincerna* is not used in its etymological sense, unrecorded by Isidore, of 'cupbearer' (πιγκέρνης), whose task it was to mix wine with water, but with the connotations of the crook at Genesis 40:1. See Jerome, *Hebraicae quaestiones in Genesim* in S. *Hieronymi presbyteri opera* 1.1, ed. P. De Lagarde, CCSL 72 (Turnhout, 1959) 46, 16–47, 1. I thank Dr R. Lokaj (Perugia/Rome) for discussion of this point.

[86] Kaiser, *Trunkenheit und Gewalt*, 211ff.

This partnership in provocation scoffs at those who condemn licentiousness, gambling, and drinking. Sins frowned on as grave by the moralists
are laughably venial for Rainald of Dassel and the Archpoet. In this jovial
complicity, the smiles or chuckles which the work draws from its chief
recipient serve to cement the unholy alliance between patron and author
and to drive a wedge into the ranks of the Archpoet's detractors. Portrayed
as ponderous, they cannot compete with his nimble wit for Rainald's
favour. Comedy becomes a vehicle of court-politics, and this agile courtier
deals a *coup de grâce* to his rivals:

> There are poets who avoid public places,
> seeking out dark and hidden recesses;
> they study fervently, stay up at night, and labour a lot,
> and at the end they are incapable of producing a masterpiece.
>
> The choruses of poets go without food and drink,
> avoiding public brawls and uproar in the marketplace,
> and, in order to create an immortal work,
> enslaved to labour, they die from diligence.[87]
>
> Loca vitant publica quidam poetarum,
> et secretas eligunt sedes latebrarum;
> student instant vigilant nec laborant parum
> et vix tandem reddere possunt opus clarum.
>
> Ieiunant et abstinent poetarum chori,
> vitant rixas publicas et tumultus fori
> et, ut opus faciant, quod non possit mori,
> moriuntur studio subditi labori.

Not only the writers idealised by Horace, who love the glades and flee
the city, are debunked in these strophes. The bucolic bores at whom fun
is poked here also resemble the feigned martyrs of abstinence whose life
led at death's door is sent up by Gregory the Great.[88] *Fictio* is the idea
which the Archpoet's syncretic imagination imposes on a classical *topos*. In
the contrast between his sparkling singularity and the choruses of diligent
drudges, neither virtue nor numbers compensate for lack of talent. An
inverse symmetry established between his effortless fertility and the arid
strivings of his rivals, he goes on to assert a direct correlation between the
quality of his verse and his wine-consumption:

[87] x.14–15, ed. Watenphul and Krefeld, 75. At 15, 3 I have adopted the reading *possit*, instead of
the editors' *possint*, and construe *quod* as relative.
[88] Watenphul and Krefeld, 75, compare Horace, *Ep.* ii.2.77. For Gregory the Great, see Chapter 2.

To each Nature gives his particular gift:
I could never write on an empty stomach;
a youngster could beat me when I'm hungry;
I hate hunger and thirst like a funeral.

To each Nature gives his particular gift:
while writing verse I drink good wine,
the purest contained in publicans' vessels:
such is the wine that creates eloquence.

The verse I write is proportionate to the wine I drink;
I can do nothing unless I've eaten;
what I compose on an empty stomach is utterly worthless;
after a glass I'm a better poet than Ovid.

The spirit of prophecy is never granted to me,
unless my stomach is first well and truly filled;
while Bacchus holds sway in my brain,
Phoebus sweeps into me and makes marvellous declarations.[89]

Unicuique proprium dat Natura munus:
ego nunquam potui scrivere ieiunus;
me ieiunum vincere posset puer unus;
sitim et ieiunium odi tamquam funus.

Unicuique proprium dat Natura donum:
ego versus faciens bibo vinum bonum,
et quod habent purius dolia cauponum:
tale vinum generat copiam sermonum.

Tales versus facio, quale vinum bibo;
nihil possum facere nisi sumpto cibo;
nihil valent penitus que ieiunus scribo;
Nasonem post calicem carmine preibo.

Mihi nunquam spiritus prophetie datur,
nisi prius fuerit venter bene satur;
dum in arce cerebri Bachus dominatur,
in me Phebus irruit et miranda fatur.

The natural urges that explained the Archpoet's licentiousness in previous strophes are elevated here to a personified force which fascinated

---

[89] x.16–19, ed. Watenphul and Krefeld, 75. At 19, 1 I have adopted the reading *prophetie*, instead of the editors' *poetrie*. On the prophetic stance of the Archpoet, see above and cf. Dronke, 'The Archpoet and the Classics', 68.

his contemporaries. In Nature, 'rediscovered' in the twelfth century,[90] they sought a philosophy, an explanation of how the world worked. He hits on a principle that justifies his sins. That principle has little to do with Roman elegy,[91] and much in common with medieval penance. Its language is inverted. Rejecting the fasts and abstinence which were standard 'tarifs' imposed on sinners, the Archpoet recalls other axioms of moralism. When, for example, he writes: 'To each Nature gives his particular gift' (*Unicuique proprium dat Natura munus/donum*, 16.1, 17.1), he is thinking in terms of the fortieth chapter of the Benedictine Rule, on moderation in drinking.[92] It opens by quoting St Paul: 'Every man has his proper gift of God' (*unusquisque proprium habet donum ex Deo*, I Corinthians 7:7). For God, Nature is substituted – not as the cosmic force of the philosophers, but as a counter-authority to Benedict's. The saint's caution on the issue of wine-consumption gives way to the Archpoet's 'proportionality'. That moribund cliché of penance, which signified matching punishments or 'tarifs' to sins or crimes,[93] is brought to life in these strophes. They do not excuse vulgar drunkenness or coarse gluttony. They claim that, because vintage wine produces first-rate verse, the relationship between drinking and creativity is 'proportionate' – bound to one another in a nexus, just and equitable, of cause and effect. And as he smirks at a penitential principle of rough justice, this mocker of moralism is confirmed by Nature in his prophetic status.

Here and later (21.3), the ambiguity of the Latin *vates*, meaning both 'poet' and 'seer', enables the prophet of vinous creativity to exalt his sins as the sources of his art. The wickedness of which he is accused may therefore be placed in inverted commata. What is the sense of *pravitas*, in the first verse below, when everything described as wicked by others is both natural and necessary? Ethical language stripped of its ordinary meaning, the moment has arrived to turn the tables on the Archpoet's accusers:

> Lo! I have betrayed my own 'wickedness',
> of which I am accused by your servants.

[90] See the excellent study of A. Speer, *Die entdeckte Natur: Untersuchungen zu Begründungsversuchen einer 'scientia naturalis' im 12 Jahrhundert* (Leiden, 1995).
[91] The opposite view, first proposed by Watenphul and Krefeld, 75, and repeated by Dronke, 'The Archpoet and the Classics', 66, is based on the resemblance of three words, none of them beyond the powers of what the Archpoet claims to be a fertile imagination. (With Propertius II.22.17: 'Uni cuique dedit vitium Natura creato', cf. 16.1 and 17.1). For a summary of the tradition of Propertius' elegies, see R. Tarrant in *Texts and Transmission: A Survey of the Latin Classics*, ed. L. Reynolds (Oxford, 1983) 324–6.
[92] See J. Hamacher, 'Die Vagantenbeichte und ihre Quellen', *MlJb* 18 (1983) 160–7.
[93] See Chapter 2. For the persistence of this cliché, cf. Peter the Chanter, *Summa de sacramentis*, ed. Dugauquier, 160, 164.

But none of them accuses himself,
although they want to play and enjoy this world.

Now, at this moment, in the presence of the blessed prelate,
according to the rule laid down by the Lord's command,
let him stone mercilessly the prophet,
who is not conscious of having committed sin!

Against myself I have spoken in self-knowledge,
and have spewed forth the poison I long harboured.
My old life displeases, I prefer the new:
man sees the face, but the heart is open to Jove.

Now I cherish virtue and loathe vice,
renewed in the soul, I am reborn in spirit;
like a newborn baby I feed on fresh milk;
with the effect that my heart shall no longer be a vessel of vanity.[94]

Ecce mee proditor 'pravitatis' fui,
de qua me redarguunt servientes tui.
Sed eorum nullus est accusator sui,
quamvis velint ludere seculoque frui.

Iam nunc in presentia presulis beati,
secundum dominici regulam mandati,
mittat in me lapidem neque parcat vati,
cuius non est animus conscius peccati!

Sum locutus contra me quicquid de me novi
et virus evomui quod tam diu fovi.
Vita vetus displicet, mores placent novi:
homo videt faciem, sed cor patet Iovi.

Iam virtutes diligo, viciis irascor,
renovatus animo spiritu renascor;
quasi modo genitus novo lacte pascor,
ne sit meum amplius vanitatis vas cor.

These strophes mark a turning-point in the development of *fictio* analysed
in previous chapters. In the first, Bernard of Clairvaux was observed
doubting the doctrine that self-accusation demonstrates sincerity.[95]
Doubts on that score multiplied rapidly during the second quarter of the
twelfth century, culminating in the anguished yet ambiguous declarations

---

[94] X.20–23, ed. Watenphul and Krefeld, 75–6.   [95] See Chapter 1.

of Heloise.[96] Now, in 1163, the Archpoet exploits ambiguity to its fullest potential. The charge of wickedness rebutted, a declaration of innocence is made; and the focus shifts to his self-appointed prosecutors. Their case collapses under the burden of their share in the guilt imputed to him. Having rendered them incapable of judging his motivation, he also disqualifies them from criticising his actions with Jesus's injunction that none but the sinless should cast stones (John 8:7).[97] The stone of symmetry which the Archpoet casts against his detractors is, *fictio*. They, rather than he, are put in the position of hypocrites. He claims not to feign but to assume a new identity, as a true penitent should. Yet the truth of the Archpoet's conversion is metaphorical. Poison spewed out in the figurative vomit of avowal,[98] the dedicated drinker claims to feed, like a newborn baby, on fresh milk.[99]

This has been taken literally: 'the Archpoet's confession tells us that the spirit of vitalistic renewal through natural exuberance and the Christian belief in metanoia and spiritual renewal were both alive and strong in … the twelfth century renaissance'.[100] The Archpoet's 'confession' tells us nothing of the kind, because the signals sent in its complex code raise ambiguity to the pitch of paradox. How does the inspiring wine, consumed in quantities prescribed by Nature, cohere with the metaphorical milk of regeneration? They do, and can, not cohere, for obduracy in vice is the source of the Archpoet's creativity. His 'spiritual renewal' displays no sign of grace.[101] Relapse into sin announced even before rebirth is proclaimed, this unregenerate sophist, interpreted along the Augustinian lines of twelfth-century theology, has rendered the sacrament void.[102] But the void is filled with the implicit meaning of a *fictio* which undermines almost every doctrine on which penance was based.

Every doctrine, that is, except one: the inscrutability of the conscience, which Abelard had asserted so idiosyncratically.[103] The Archpoet, no less

[96] See Chapter 7.

[97] For the link between this injunction and penance, cf. Abelard's solution to *Problema Heloissae* 8: 'Ipse primus in lapidandam dirigit lapidem, cum ei prius poenitentiam inspiret', PL 186, 690A.

[98] On the metaphor, see Chapter 3.

[99] On the antithesis wine–milk, cf. the pseudo-Bernardian *De conscientia*, PL 184, 556B, where wine is described as *asperum et insuave* and milk as *suavis*. See too Hebrews 5:12–13.

[100] G. Ladner, 'Terms and Ideas of Renewal' in *Renaissance and Renewal*, ed. Benson and Constable, 20.

[101] On this doctrine, see Z. Alszeghy, *Nova creatura: La nozione della grazia nei commentari medievali di s. Paolo*, Analecta Gregoriana 81 (Rome, 1956).

[102] See Chapter 2.   [103] See Chapter 5.

idiosyncratic, is more heterodox than the condemned heretic. Appealing to the ancient idea that men cannot judge the secrets of the heart, which they should leave to God,[104] he invokes Jove (22.4). This invocation does not obviously follow from the verse that precedes it (22.3). Why should a repudiation of past vice lead to an assertion of inscrutability in the present? Because the Archpoet plays with the expectations of his detractors. Ready to pounce on him, they are frustrated by his elusive eloquence. Its elusiveness consists not only in what is stated but also in what is left unsaid. Jove, Phoebus, Bacchus, Nature, Venus: the Christian deity is conspicuous by His absence.

Not naming God, the Archpoet pre-empts the charge of blasphemy, and reduces the Biblical metaphor of the conscience to a classical cliché. Access is denied to his heart in the very phrase that purports to guarantee its openness. Inscrutability is affirmed through irony. It lends support, from an unexpected quarter, to a thesis maintained in Søren Kierkegaard's doctoral dissertation. This 'ironic figure of speech' not only 'cancels itself', as Kierkegaard argues;[105] it also thwarts any attempt by the Archpoet's detractors to condemn him as a mocker of God. They are left speechless. Moral muteness prevails in the labyrinth of the conscience which he has built, and only a prelate as 'blessed' (*presulis beati* 21.1) as the schismatic Rainald can negotiate its recesses:

> Archbishop-elect of Cologne, take mercy on this penitent,
> grant pardon to him who seeks it,
> give penance to him who confesses his fault:
> I will do whatever you order willingly.

> The lion, king of beasts, spares his subjects,
> forgetting his wrath toward them,
> and you do the same, princes of the earth:
> what lacks sweetness is excessively bitter.[106]

> Electe Colonie, parce penitenti,
> fac misericordiam veniam petenti
> et da penitenciam culpam confitenti:
> feram quicquid iusseris animo libenti.

> Parcit enim subditis leo rex ferarum
> et est erga subditos immemor irarum,

---

[104] See Chapter 2.
[105] See S. Kierkegaard, *The Concept of Irony, with Continual Reference to Socrates*, ed. and trans. H. and E. Hong (Princeton, 1989) XIII, 323; 248.
[106] X.24–25, ed. Watenphul and Krefeld, 76.

et vos idem facite, principes terrarum:
quod caret dulcedine, nimis est amarum.

The 'king of the beasts' (*rex ferarum* 25.1) to whom the archbishop-elect is likened was known less for his mercifulness than for the cruelty and wrath described by St Augustine in his influential exegesis of Psalm 7:4.[107] Other connotations of the lion were diabolic,[108] as Alexander III would have been the first to agree in the case of Rainald of Dassel. His praise by the Archpoet is equivocal, and the equivocality is emphasised in the phrase 'princes of the earth' (*principes terrarum* 25.3) addressed to him in the *pluralis maiestatis*. It does not imply the presence of lay magnates,[109] but conveys a perception of how Rainald blurred boundaries that were meant to separate the secular and ecclesiastical aristocracy. From this 'prince of the earth' – a ruler over bodies, not souls, who was neither sacred nor profane but an incalculable combination of both – is requested the 'sweetness' (*dulcedine* 25.4) of divine mercy, in contrast to the 'excessive bitterness' (*nimis amarum* ibid.) of penance.[110] In that contrast is summed up the Archpoet's dialectic. Conventional in works of prescriptive moralism, such as Hugh of Saint-Victor's commentary on the Rule of St Augustine,[111] the antithesis 'bitterness' – 'sweetness' is unconventional here. Slanted by the term used, in the earlier part of the poem, as a motto of pleasure, it makes a mock request for sanctions into a real plea for complicity.

What is real, sincere, or authentic about the Archpoet's 'confession'? No category of twelfth-century thought was adequate to answer this question. The work cannot be counted among those 'pious lies' (*pia mendacia*) discussed by Cassian and reconsidered by others.[112] Impiety is one of its few unequivocal features. And how to distinguish between affecting impiety and committing blasphemy? A dividing-line hardly visible to Bernard of

---

[107] *S. Aurelii Augustini Enarrationes in Psalmos I–L* ed. Dekkers and Fraipont, CCSL 38, 38.
[108] For a succinct overview of the Biblical and iconographical ambiguity of the lion, see C. Frevel and M. Woelk, 'Löwe' in *Lexikon für Theologie und Kirche* VI, 1069–70.
[109] *Pace* Watenphul and Krefeld, 140.
[110] Note the nuance in the adverb. Excess was usually attributed to the sweetness of sin by moralists (cf. Cardinal Pullen, *Sententiae* VI.52, PL 186, 962A), for whom there could never be enough bitterness of remorse. The Archpoet reverses their procedure by attaching *nimis* to *amarum*. The reversal is anticipated by Bernard of Clairvaux's paradox of 'most sweet bitterness' (*amaritudo ... dulcissima*) in penance. See *S. Bernardi Opera* V, ed. J. Leclercq and H. Rochais (Rome, 1968) 373, 20–1.
[111] 'Sunt nonnulli, qui aliorum redarguunt culpas non tam ex charitate quam ex odii *amaritudine* ... Caveant ergo, ut neminem cum ira et indignatione, sed potius cum *dulcedine* et charitate redarguant', Hugh of St-Victor, *Expositio in Regulam S. Augustini* VII, PL176 404A.
[112] See Chapters 2 and 7.

Clairvaux,[113] it is thoroughly obscured by the Archpoet's irony. If 'irony is distinct from deceit, [in] that an ironical assertion is not an assertion',[114] nor does it lack consequences. Ironically claiming the moral high ground, this feigned penitent consigns his critics to shifting sands. There they flail about, perhaps trying to understand his 'confession' in terms of the 'jesting lies' (*iocosa mendacia*) which Augustine exempted from his strict conditions of truthfulness or in relation to theories of fallacy elaborated by logicians not notable for their sense of humour.[115] But the attempt is doomed to failure, for no one, in late antiquity or the Middle Ages, jested with such wit at a sacrament premised on veracity.[116] Formally, the rules of penance are maintained in this work: effectively, they are subverted; and the subversion is directed at one of the bases of the faith.[117] The verbal ingenuity of the Archpoet is not his only achievement. Another is the wealth of ideas with which he enriches the concept of *fictio*. Feigning penance at Pavia in 1163, this brilliant thinker created a new figure of spiritual sophistry.

[113] See Chapter 3.

[114] Williams, *Truth and Truthfulness*, 73.

[115] On Augustine, see Colish, 'Rethinking Lying', 157. On telling the truth in lies, see *Logica modernorum: A Contribution to the History of Early Terminist Logic I: On the Twelfth-Century Theories of Fallacy*, ed. L. De Rijk (Assen, 1962) 375, 18ff. For this problem and its inadequate solutions in scholastic theology, see A. Landgraf, 'Die Einschätzung der Scherzlüge in der Frühscholastik', *Theologisch-praktische Quartalschrift* 93 (1940) 3–11.

[116] How unprepared twelfth-century theories of *fictio* were to accommodate the Archpoet's practice is indicated by the following naïveté: 'non omne quod fingimus, mendacium est, sed quando id fingimus, quod nihil significat, tunc est mendacium. Cum autem fictio nostra refertur ad aliquam significationem, non est mendacium, sed aliqua figura veritatis', BAV Reg. lat. 223, 90v.

[117] On the related problem of sin as sacrament, see H. Weisweiler, 'Die Bußlehre Simons von Tournai', *Zeitschrift für katholische Theologie* 56 (1932) 190–230, especially 215ff.

Envoi: Spiritual sophistry

The spiritual sophistry of the Archpoet is the product of a particular time and place. Neither attested nor imaginable elsewhere in medieval Europe, his comedy of the conscience is written for the benefit of a schismatic patron and against the interests of rivals at court. But this exercise in feigned penance transcends the circumstances of its production and amounts to more than a jest. If the *fictio* is funny, its ironical dialectic of affirmation and denial subverts religious ideas taken seriously by the generation previous to the Archpoet's. And as he bends the rules of confession that demanded sincerity and authenticity, he addresses issues which were to remain on the ethical agenda.

High on a list revised in the twelfth century stood, throughout the later Middle Ages and the early modern period, the issues of a moral agent's intentions and of their assessment. Simulation of the sacraments continued to be debated.[1] Reference was made to the distinction, drawn by Gregory the Great and maintained by Gratian in his account of perjury and lies,[2] between the spirit in which a declaration was made and how it should be received. Dissimulation, equivocation, and irony were taken into account. *Fictio* was not forgotten; it made intermittent appearances in Western thought and literature after the twelfth century; and a number of these are significant. Yet they hardly form a tradition. Traditions may be discontinuous but the term, if it is to have meaning, implies a degree of repetition which this form of spiritual sophistry is too delicate, too subtle to bear.

---

[1] See Rosier, *La parole efficace*, 263ff., 288ff. and B. Hamm, 'Wollen und Nicht – Können als Thema der mittelalterlichen Bußseelsorge' in *Spätmittelalterliche Frömmigkeit zwischen Ideal und Praxis*, ed. B. Hamm and T. Lentes (Tübingen, 2001) 111–46. Cf. G. Müller, *Die Wahrhaftigkeitspflicht und die Problematik der Lüge* (Freiburg, 1962); M. Vincent-Cassy, 'Recherches sur le mensonge au moyen âge' in *Études sur la sensibilité au moyen âge* II (Paris, 1979) 165–73; and P. Zagorin, *Ways of Lying: Dissimulation, Persecution, and Conformity in Early Modern Europe* (Cambridge, Mass., 1990).

[2] M. David, 'Parjure et mensonge dans le Décret de Gratian', *Studia Gratiana* 3 (1955) 117–41.

Subtlety is not the same as fragility. *Fictio*, after the Archpoet, continued to sustain humour, ambiguity, and anguish in cases as diverse as the beginning of Boccaccio's *Decameron* in the fourteenth century and the interrogation of the Nazi conscience in the twentieth. These examples, outlined below, do not exhaust the fascination of a subject which ranges from the pyrotechnics of penance engineered by Villon in his *Testament* to coerced confession in the secular religion of Soviet totalitarianism.[3] But this is an *envoi*, not the further book that would be required to do justice to spiritual sophistry; and its purpose is to identify three of the descendants, indirect but worthy, of the Archpoet.

The first of them is a crook. If the character of ser Ciappelletto, the rogue-notary who becomes a saint in the *novella* that opens the *Decameron*, is based on a businessman from Prato,[4] his deeper affinities are with the Archpoet. Feigning penance in his deathbed-confession, Ciappelletto cuts his most dubious deal. Its terms are not simply comic. This *novella* has philosophical and theological implications,[5] undermining the principle that God knows the secrets of the heart invoked so piously by the narrator.[6] The subversion is directed less at divine omniscience than at human fallibility. The monk (*frate*) who hears Ciappelletto's confession is gullible. He believes everything that is told him by this obdurate sinner. So many times has Ciappelletto avowed his faults that this one will be easy work (*poca fatica*),[7] the *frate* is convinced. In a dialectic of inversion developed two hundred years previously, the monk's assumption of sincerity leads the feigned penitent to attempt the utmost inauthenticity. Believing himself to be irredeemable, ser Ciappelletto aims to be revered as a saint.

That goal is reached in a charade of scrupulousness. Ciappelletto blends his mixture of self-accusation and self-commendation shrewdly. If he is ashamed of telling the truth, that is because he fears to commit the

[3] See M. Burleigh, *Sacred Causes: The Clash of Religion and Politics, from the Great War to the War on Terror* (New York, 2007) 76ff. A less historicist approach than mine might also take account of the suggestive work by M. Kalderon, *Moral Fictionalism* (Oxford, 2005).
[4] See J. Benton, 'The Accounts of Cepperello da Prato for the Tax on Nouveaux Aquits in the Bailliage of Troyes' in *Order and Innovation in the Middle Ages: Essays in Honor of J. Strayer*, ed. W. Jordan *et al.* (Princeton, 1976) 453–7.
[5] See, best, K. Flasch, *Giovanni Boccaccio: Poesie nach der Pest* (Mainz, 1992), who does not draw the parallel, but argues convincingly for the philosophical-theological interest of the *Decameron*. (All references are to this edition.) Cf. further V. Branca, *Boccaccio medievale*, 5th edn (Florence, 1981) 3–24, 95–103; F. Fassò, *Saggi e ricerche di storia letteraria* (Milan, 1947) 31–90; and G. Almansi, *The Writer as Liar* (London, 1975) 25ff.
[6] *Decameron* 1.5, ed. Flasch, 272.   [7] *Decameron* 1.33, ibid., 286.

sin of vainglory.[8] It follows that his 'fault' is no fault at all, because the imputed blame derives from innocence. Deft but not new, Ciappelletto's *sic et non* of sophistry combines major claims to virtue with minor avowals of vice. Although he declares his assiduity in fasting, he admits that he has craved – not consumed – salads.[9] And in this pantomime of apparent affirmations and implied denials, a reversal of roles takes place. The *frate*, beaten into retreat by Ciappelletto's barrage of misleading confessions, himself occupies the position of a feigned penitent who defends his sins. When Ciappelletto pretends to own up to having 'sworn' (*bestemmiai*) at his mother in childhood, the credulous monk replies by excusing blasphemy as venial.[10]

Moral categories turned on their head, the subversion is complete when the crook achieves sanctity. But this *fictio* is not left at the level of spoof. An element of ambiguity is introduced, disguised as a pious platitude. Although inclined to believe that Ciappelletto went to hell, the narrator does not exclude redemption through true penance at his last gasp.[11] For the elegant audience of this 'poetry after the plague', there is no final word. The first *novella* of the *Decameron*, like the 'confession' of the Archpoet, closes by re-opening the enigma of the heart's secrets.

The secrets of the heart were specialities of the Roman Inquisition, which interrogated those suspected of ser Ciappelletto's sins – 'affected sanctity'[12] and feigned penance – with techniques modelled on classical rhetoric. Some of these techniques were refined in the sixteenth century, when the Holy Office thought itself confronted by heretics pretending to be orthodox. But, by the seventeenth, habits hardened in this bureaucracy of the conscience; and the inquisitors became less sensitive to finer distinctions. A literal mentality on the subject of *fictio* is attested in their historical archives.[13] Few will be exhilarated by the case of a fraud dressing up as a confessor or by a debate about the validity of penance performed in jest. The first case is that of a mere charlatan who has no claim to the title of sophist; the second demonstrates only the shortness of inquisitorial memory. For the authorities quoted in this debate are early modern theologians, not St Augustine, who had solved the problem thirteen hundred years earlier.[14]

---

[8] *Decameron* 1.37, ibid., 288.   [9] *Decameron* 1.41, ibid., 290.
[10] *Decameron* 1.72, ibid., 302.   [11] *Decameron* 1.89, ibid., 312.
[12] Cf. *Finzione e santità tra medioevo ed età moderna*, ed. G. Zarri (Turin, 1991) and M. Gotor, *I beati del papa: Santità, Inquisizione e obbedienza in età moderna* (Florence, 2002).
[13] Vatican, Archives of the Congregation for the Doctrine of the Faith, *Stanza Storica*, N 1 a–d; O 3, l. I thank my friend Monsignor A. Cifres for access to these documents.
[14] See Chapter 2.

Spiritual sophistry lacks a teleology; and the places where one might expect to find it sometimes yield meagre results. Richer pickings are to be had even from those whose acquaintance with Catholicism was passing, such as that temporary convert, Jean-Jacques Rousseau.[15] His bending of the rules of confession in his autobiography can be understood in terms of *fictio*. This medieval category enables us to approach, from a different angle, what has been taken to be the modern issue of Rousseau's sincerity.[16] It is summed up by Lionel Trilling when, paraphrasing Hegel, he refers to 'the simultaneous courting and transcendence of shame'.[17] Why one might seek to transcend shame is sufficiently obvious. How Rousseau courted it is illustrated by one of the most painful passages in his *Confessions*.[18] As a boy, he stole a ribbon, intending to make a present of it to his friend and fellow-servant, Marianne. This act of petty larceny, according to him, had momentous consequences. When confronted with the theft, he accused her, not out of malice (*méchanceté*), but because her name came to mind. This 'touching achievement of self-deception'[19] led Marianne to be dismissed without a reference. Before she left, she declared that she had believed Rousseau to be a good person, but that now she would not want to be in his place. Nor did he. Marianne's words lingered with him for the rest of his life.

Rousseau makes this ugly episode into his version of original sin. He interprets the tribulations of the next forty years as punishments for his mistreatment of Marianne. But he will not let his guilt alone. Rousseau worries at it relentlessly, asserting that his sufferings were inversely proportionate to the virtues of uprightness (*droiteur*) and honour with which he bore them. This spiritual sophist contrives both to admit moral wrong and to complain about ethical injustice. It is a symmetry reminiscent of Abelard; and it might tempt us to compare Rousseau with the Archpoet or ser Ciappelletto, had he not anticipated us and defined, inadvertently, his own variant on their *fictio*. When, in the phrase quoted as the second epigraph to this book, he depicts that exemplar of sceptical integrity, Michel de Montaigne, as 'the chief of those [who are] falsely sincere and

---

[15] From the vast bibliography on this subject, I single out only the three contributions from which I have learnt most: Trilling, *Sincerity and Authenticity*; Williams, *Truth and Truthfulness*; and J. Starobinski, *Jean-Jacques Rousseau: la transparence et l'obstacle* (Paris, 1971).

[16] See Williams, *Truth and Truthfulness*, 177 and notes.

[17] Trilling, *Sincerity and Authenticity*, 59.

[18] *Confessions*, II, ed. B. Gagnebin and M. Raymond, *Jean-Jacques Rousseau: Oeuvres complètes* I (Paris, 1959) 84–7.

[19] Williams, *Truth and Truthfulness*, 177.

intend to deceive by telling the truth',[20] Jean-Jacques Rousseau paints a self-portrait.

The truth, whole not partial, and his battle with it troubled the conscience of Albert Speer, Hitler's minister of armaments, after the Second World War.[21] At his trial in Nuremberg and for more than thirty years following it, the most intelligent member of the Nazi leadership ('the best we have', according to the Führer)[22] was a feigned penitent, in the medieval sense of one who confesses incompletely. He acknowledged coresponsibility for some of the crimes of National Socialism, but denied knowledge of the Holocaust. Not until April 1977, in an affidavit written at the request of the South African Board of Deputies, did Speer admit his complicity (*Billigung*) in the horrors perpetrated against the Jews.[23] The history of this moral metamorphosis has been written by that skilled inquisitrix of the conscience, Gitta Sereny.

What impresses, in Sereny's account of Speer's answer to her question of why he came clean in 1977, is, his inarticulateness. That expert in the evasive reply, who had never made the mistake of avoiding the issue of the Holocaust, spoke not only to her and others but also to himself with the muddle of honesty. His reason for not telling the complete truth earlier is explained convincingly by Sereny: 'If Speer had said as much at Nuremberg, he would have been hanged.'[24] Equally convincing is her view that his decision to stop feigning penance was taken by a conscience developed with 'the help of a Protestant chaplain, a Catholic monk, and a Jewish rabbi.' They assisted Albert Speer, near the end of his life, to assume a new ethical identity – to become what Sereny calls 'a different man'.[25] Can a process observed, and perhaps fostered, by her with a humane insight lacking in many of her male predecessors at the Holy Office be dismissed as a form of neurosis or masochism?[26] Or is there a lesson to be learnt here?

As taught by Gitta Sereny and implied by the twelfth century, it may be that the most effective interrogations of the heart's secrets are conducted not by the 'inner judge', acting alone, but with the aid of others, as intelligent as they are rare. Among the alternatives to this reciprocal trust count

[20] *Ébauches des Confessions*, ed. Raymond and Gagnebin, 1149–50.
[21] See G. Sereny, *Albert Speer: His Battle with Truth* (London, 1995).
[22] Ibid. 492 and see H. Trevor-Roper, *The Last Days of Hitler*, 7th edn (London, 1995) 215.
[23] 'Complicity' is my translation of *Billigung* in Speer's affidavit. Sereny renders this difficult word, perhaps too gently, as 'tacit acceptance'. Speer asked *Die Zeit*, three months later, to gloss *Billigung* as 'looking away' (Sereny's English: *Hinwegschauen* ?), adding that it amounted to the same thing. See Sereny, *Albert Speer*, 707–8.
[24] Ibid., 708.   [25] Ibid., 720.   [26] Cf. P. Bruckner, *La tyrannie de la pénitence* (Paris, 2006).

irony, equivocation, deception, lies, and that curious combination of them all, *fictio*. The spiritual sophists who have practised this elusive art are both comic and tragic; and, in their select company, one figure stands out. More beguiling than Boccaccio, less unrelenting than Rousseau, and with none of Speer's ambiguous anguish, the supreme, because the subtlest, exponent of *fictio* is the Archpoet.

Bibliography

PRIMARY SOURCES

MANUSCRIPTS

BAV. Barb. lat. 484
BAV. Ottob. lat. 175
BAV. Reg. lat. 223
BAV. Vat. lat. 1175 (I) and (II) (Raoul Ardens, *Speculum universale*)
BAV. Vat. lat. 1343 (*Sententiae Sidonis*)
Munich, Bayerische Staatsbibliothek clm. 168
Vatican, Archives of the Congregation for the Doctrine of the Faith (Holy Office),
Stanza Storica N 1, a-d; O, 3, l

PRINTED WORKS

Anonymous: *Anonymi Historia Troyana Daretis Frigii*, ed. J. Stohlmann, Beihefte
zum *MlJb* 1 (Ratingen, 1968)
Epistolae duorum amantium, ed. E. Könsgen, Mittellateinische Texte und
Studien 8 (Leyden, 1974)
Verba seniorum PL **73** 351–1062
Vita Burchardi episcopi, ed. G. Waitz, MGH *Scriptores* IV (Hanover, 1841)
Abelard, Peter: Autobiography and letters to Heloise, ed. I. Pagani, *Epistolario di
Abelardo ed Eloisa* (Turin, 2004); ed. J. Monfrin *Abélard: Historia calami-
tatum* (Paris, 1967)
Carmen ad Astralabium, ed. J. Rubingh-Bosscher (Groningen, 1987)
Collationes, ed. J. Marenbon and G. Orlandi (Oxford, 2001)
Commentaria in Epistolam Pauli ad Romanos, ed. E. Buytaert, CCCM 11
(Turnhout, 1969)
Expositio dominice orationis in diebus Rogationium que Letanie dicuntur, ed.
P. De Santis (Louvain, 2002)
Hymnus Paraclitensis, 2 vols., ed. J. Szövérffy (Albany, N.Y., 1975)
Letters, ed. E. Smits, *Peter Abelard: Letters IX–XIV* (Groningen, 1983)
Planctus: ed. P. Zumthor, *Abélard: Lamentations* (Paris, 1992)
Problemata Heloissae, PL **178** 677–730

Scito te ipsum: ed. D. Luscombe, *Peter Abelard's Ethics* (Oxford, 1971); ed. R. Ilgner, *Petri Abaelardi opera theologica* IV, CCCM 190 (Turnhout, 2001)

Sermons: PL **178** 379–610

Sermons for the Paraclete: ed. P. De Santis, *I sermoni di Abelardo per le monache del Paracleto*, Mediaevalia Lovaniensia Series 1/Studia 31 (Louvain, 2002)

Sic et non, ed. B. Boyer and R. McKeon (Chicago, 1976)

Theological works in progress: *Petri Abaelardi Opera Theologica* I, ed. E. Buytaert, CCCM 11 (Turnhout, 1969); II, ed. E Buytaert, CCCM 12 (Turnhout, 1969); III, ed. E. Buytaert and C. Mews, CCCM 13 (Turnhout, 1987), VI, ed. D. Luscombe, CCCM 14 (Turnhout, 2006)

Adam of Perseigne, *Epistolae*, PL **211** 583–694 and *Lettres*, ed. J. Bouvet, SC 66, Sér. mon. 4 (Paris, 1960)

Alan of Lille, *Sermo de Trinitate*, ed. M.-T. D'Alverny, *Alain de Lille: Textes inédits* (Paris, 1965)

　Liber poenitentialis, ed. J. Longère, 2 vols, Analecta mediaevalia namurcensia 17, 18 (Louvain, 1965)

Alcuin, *De virtutibus et vitiis*, PL **101** 919–46

Alexander III, Pope, *Epistolae*, PL **200** 62–1318

Ambrose, *De Cain et Abel*, ed. C. Schenkl, CSEL 32 (Vienna, 1896)

　De poenitentia, ed. R. Gryson, SC 179 (Paris, 1971)

Anselm of Aosta and Canterbury, St.: Letters, ed. F. Schmitt OSB, *S. Anselmi Cantuariensis Archiepiscopi Opera omnia* III (Edinburgh, 1956)

Anselm of Laon, *Sententiae*, ed. F. Bliemetzrieder, BPTMA 18, 2–3 (Münster, 1919)

Archpoet, *Die Gedichte des Archipoeta*, ed. H. Watenphul and H. Krefeld (Heidelberg, 1958)

Aristotle, *Nicomachean Ethics*, ed. I. Bywater (Oxford, 1894)

Augustine, St., *Confessiones: Augustine, Confessions: Introduction, Text, Commentary*, 3 vols., ed. J. O'Donnell (Oxford, 1992)

　De baptismo contra Donatistas, ed. M. Petschenig, CSEL 51 (Vienna, 1908)

　De bono coniugali, ed. P. Walsh (Oxford, 2001)

　De civitate Dei, ed. B. Dombart and A. Kalb, 2 vols., CCSL 47, 48 (Turnhout, 1955)

　De libero arbitrio, ed. W. Green in *S. Aurelii Augustini Opera* II, 2 CCSL 29 (Turnhout, 1970)

　De natura et gratia, ed. and trans. A. Trapè and L. Volpi in *Sant'Agostino, Natura e grazia* I (Rome, 1981)

　De opere monachorum, ed. J. Zycha, CSEL 41 (Vienna, 1900)

　De sancta virginitate, ed. J. Zycha, CSEL 41 (Vienna, 1990)

　De sermone Domini in monte, ed. A. Mutzenbecher, CCSL 35 (Turnhout, 1967)

　De spiritu et littera, ed. and trans. A. Trapè and L. Volpi in *Sant'Agostino, Natura e grazia* I (Rome, 1981)

　Enarrationes in Psalmos, ed. E. Dekkers and J. Fraipont, 3 vols., CCSL 38, 39, 40 (Turnhout, 1956)

　In Johannis Evangelium Tractatus, ed. R. Willems, CCSL 36 (Turnhout, 1954)

Letters: *S. Aurelii Augustini Hipponensis episcopi epistulae*, ed. A. Goldbacher, CSEL 44 (Vienna, 1904)

Sermones: Sant'Agostino. Discorsi. II/2 (86–116) sul Nuovo Testamento, tr. L. Carrozzi (Rome, 1983)

Sermones selecti duodeviginti, ed. C. Lambot, Stromata patristica et mediaevalia I (Utrecht, 1950)

Textus selecti de paenitentia, ed. B. Poschmann, Florilegium Patristicum 38 (Bonn, 1934)

Augustine, pseudo-, *De vera et falsa paenitentia*, PL **40** 1113–40

Benedict, St., *Regula*, ed. A. de Vogüé, *La Règle de saint Benoît*, 7 vols., SC 181–7 (Paris, 1971–1972)

Berengar of Poitiers, *Opera satirica*, ed. R. Thomson, *Mediaeval Studies* 42 (1980) 89–139

Bernard of Clairvaux, St., *S. Bernardi Opera*, ed. J. Leclercq, H. Rochais, and C. Talbot, 8 vols. (Rome, 1957–1977)

Bernard of Clairvaux, pseudo-, *De conscientia*, PL **184** 551–60

De domo interiori, PL **184** 507–55

Meditationes piissimae de cognitione humanae conditionis, PL **184** 485–507

Bible (Vulgate): *Biblia sacra iuxta vulgatam versionem*, ed. R. Weber, OSB, 2 vols. (Stuttgart, 1975)

Boccaccio, *Decameron* I, ed. and trans. K. Flasch, *Giovanni Boccaccio: Poesie nach der Pest* (Mainz, 1992)

Boethius, *Philosophiae consolatio*, ed. K. Büchner (Heidelberg, 1977)

Bonizo of Sutri, *Liber de vita christiana*, ed. F. Perels, Texte zur Geschichte des römischen und kanonischen Rechts im Mittelalter I (Berlin, 1930)

Bruno of Segni, *Expositio in Iob*, PL **164** 551–696

Burchard of Worms, *Medicus* (= *Decretum* xix), PL **140** 949–1014

Cassian, John, *Collationes*, ed. E. Pichery, 3 vols., SC 42, 54, 64 (Paris, 1955, 1958, 1959)

Institutiones ed. J.-C. Guy, SC 109 (Paris, 1965)

Cicero, *In Catilinam* in *Orationes* I, ed. A. Clark (Oxford, 1993)

De inventione, ed. E. Stroebel (Leipzig, 1925)

Damian, Peter, St.: Letters, ed. K. Reindel, *Die Briefe des Petrus Damiani*, MGH *Epistolae* III, 2 (Munich, 1989)

Dorotheus of Gaza, *Instructions*, eds. L. Regnault and J. De Preville, SC 92 (Paris, 1963).

Eadmer, *De S. Anselmi similitudinibus*, PL **159** 608–708,

Vita S. Anselmi, ed. R. Southern, *The Life of St. Anselm, Archbishop of Canterbury, by Eadmer*, (London, 1962)

Egbert of Schönau, *Sermones contra Catharos*, PL **195**, 11–93

Egbert, pseudo-, *Poenitentiale*, ed. H. Schmitz *Die Bußbücher und der Bußdisziplin der Kirche: Nach handschriftichen Quellen dargelegt* I (reprint Graz, 1958)

Evagrius of Antioch (translator of Athanasius), *Vita B. Antonii abbatis*, PL **73**, 125–70

Evagrius Ponticus, *Evagre le Pontique, Sur les pensées*, SC 438, ed. P. Géhin, C. Guillaumont, and A. Guillaumont (Paris, 1998)

Gratian, *Decretum*, ed. E. Friedberg, *Corpus Iuris Canonici* I (reprint Graz, 1959)

Gregory the Great, Pope and St, *In librum I Regum*, ed. P. Verbraken OSB, CCSL 144 (Turnhout, 1972)

   Moralia in Iob, ed. M. Adriaen, 3 vols., CCSL 143, 143A, 143B (Turnhout, 1979–1985)

Gregory VII, Pope and St., *The Epistolae vagantes of Pope Gregory the Seventh*, ed. H. Cowdrey (Oxford, 1972)

Gregory IX, Pope, *Decreta*, ed. E. Friedberg, *Corpus Iuris Canonici* II (reprint Graz, 1959)

Grosseteste, Robert St., 'Robert Grosseteste's Treatise on Confession, "Deus est"', ed. S. Wenzel, *Franciscan Studies* 30 (1970) 218–93

Guibert de Nogent, *Autobiographie*, ed. E.-R. Labande, Les classiques de l'histoire de France au Moyen Age 34 (Paris, 1981)

Heloise, Letters, ed. Pagani, *see* Abelard, Autobiography and Letters

   Problemata: *see* Abelard, *Problemata Heloissae*

'Hermas', *Pastor*, ed. R. Joly, SC 53 *bis* (Paris, 1968)

Hildebert of Lavardin, *De paenitentia* (*Sermo tertius in Quadragesima*), PL **171** 440–443

Hincmar of Reims, *De cavendis vitiis et virtutibus exercendis*, ed. D. Nachtmann, MGH Quellen zur Geistesgeschichte des Mittelalters 16 (Munich, 1998)

Horace, *Epistulae*, ed. D. Shackleton Bailey (Leipzig, 2001)

Hugh of St-Victor, *De arrha animae*, PL **176** 951–70

   De modo orandi, PL **176** 977–88

   De sacramentis PL **176** 174–618

   Expositio in Regulam s. Augustini PL **176**, 881–924

Isidore of Seville, *Etymologiae*, ed. W.M. Lindsay, 2 vols. (Oxford, 1911)

   Sententiae, ed. P. Cazier, *Isidorus Hispalensis Sententiae*, CCSL 111 (Turnhout, 1998)

Ivo of Chartres, *Decretum* XV PL **161** 47–1046

Jerome, St., *Dialogus contra Pelagianos*, PL **23** 517–613

   Epistolae, ed. J Hilberg, 2 vols., CSEL 54, 55 (Vienna, 1910, 1912)

   Hebraicae quaestiones in Genesim in S. *Hieronymi presbyteri opera* I, 1, ed. P. De Lagarde, CCSL 72 (Turnhout, 1959)

   In Esaiam in S. *Hieronymi Presbyteri Opera* I, 2, ed. M. Adriaen, CCSL 63 (Turnhout, 1963)

Juvenal, *Saturae*, ed. W. Clausen (Oxford, 1959)

Lanfranc of Bec, *De celanda confessione*, PL **150** 625–32

Leo the Great, Pope and St., *Epistolae*, PL **54** 593–1218

Logica modernorum: A Contribution to the History of Early Terminist Logic I: On the Twelfth-Century Theories of Fallacy, ed. L. De Rijk (Assen, 1962)

Lucan, *Bellum civile*, ed. A. Housman (Oxford, 1927)

'Master Simon', *Maître Simon et son groupe 'De sacramentis': Textes inédits*, ed. H. Weisweiler, Spicilegium sacrum lovaniense 12 (Louvain, 1937)

Oeuvres oratoires de maîtres parisiens au XIIe siècle, ed. J. Longère, 2 vols. (Paris, 1975)

Otto of Freising, *Gesta Frederici*, ed. F.-J. Schmale, *Bischof Otto von Freising und Rahewin, Die Taten Friedrichs oder richtiger Cronica*, Ausgewählte Quellen zur deutschen Geschichte des Mittelalters 17 (Berlin, 1965)

Ovid, *Amores, Ars amatoria, Remedia amoris*, ed. E.J. Kenney (Oxford, 1961)
  Heroides, Amores, trans. G. Showerman, revised G.P. Goold (Harvard, 1977)
  Metamorphoses, ed. R. Tarrant (Oxford, 2004)
  Tristia, ed. S. Owen (Oxford, 1915)

The Paraclete Statutes: Institutiones nostrae: Introduction, Edition, Commentary, ed. C. Waddell, Cistercian Liturgy Series 20 (Kentucky, 1987)

Peter of Celle, *De conscientia*, ed. J. Leclercq in *La spiritualité de Pierre de Celle* (Paris, 1946)

Peter the Chanter, *Summa de sacramentis et animae consiliis* ed. J.-A. Dugauquier, Analecta mediaevalia namurcensia 7 (Louvain, 1957)
  Verbum abbreviatum, PL **205** 23–370

Peter Lombard, *Sententiae in IV libros distinctae*, ed. I. Brady, 2 vols. (Grottaferrata, 1971–1981)

Peter the Venerable, *The Letters of Peter the Venerable*, ed. G. Constable, 2 vols. (Cambridge, Mass. 1967)

Pliny the Younger, *Epistularum Libri Decem*, ed. R. Mynors (Oxford 1963)

Plutarch, *De invidia et odio*, ed. S. Lanzi, Corpus Plutarchi Moralium 39 (Naples, 2004)
  De superstitione, ed. E. Lozza (Milan, 1980)

Propertius, *Carmina*, ed. E. Barber (Oxford, 1960)

Pullen, Robert Cardinal, *Sententiae*, PL **186** 639–1010

Rahewin, *Gesta Frederici*, see Otto of Friesing

Roland Bandinelli, *Die Sentenzen Rolands, nochmals Papstes Alexanders III*, ed. A. Gietl (Freiburg, 1891)

Rousseau, J.-J., *Confessions*, ed. B. Gagnebin and M. Raymond, *Jean-Jacques Rousseau Oeuvres complètes* I (Paris, 1959)

Rufinus, *Historia monachorum*, PL **21** 391–462

Rufinus decretalista, *Die Summa magistri Rufini*, ed. J. Schulte (Giessen, 1892)

Rupert of Deutz, *Commentaria in Evangelium Sancti Iohannis*, ed. R. Haacke, CCCM 9 (Turnhout, 1969)
  In S. Iob commentarius, PL **168** 961–1196
  Super quaedam capitula Regulae divi Benedicti abbatis, PL **170** 477–538

Russell, B., *Autobiography* (London, 2000)

Sacrorum conciliorum nova et amplissima collectio 21, ed. J. Mansi (Venice, 1726)

Seneca, *Epistolae morales*, ed. L. Reynolds, 2 vols. (Oxford, 1965)

Sereny, G., *Albert Speer: His Battle with Truth* (London, 1995)

Tertullian, *De poenitentia*, ed. C. Munier, SC 316 (Paris, 1984)

Theodulf of Orléans, *Carmina* in *MGH Poetae Latini Ævi Carolini* I, ed. E. Dümmler (Berlin, 1881)

Virgil, *Eclogues*, ed. R. Mynors (Oxford, 1983)

William of Saint-Thierry, *De natura et dignitate amoris*, ed. M.M. Davy, *Guillaume de Saint-Thierry, Deux traités de l'amour de Dieu: De la contemplation de Dieu: De la nature et de la dignité de l'amour* (Paris, 1953)
Wittgenstein, L., *Zettel*, eds. G. Anscombe and G. von Wright (Oxford, 1981)

SELECT BIBLIOGRAPHY OF SECONDARY LITERATURE

This bibliography lists studies quoted more than once and items of special interest.

Amory, F. 'Whited Sepulchres: The Semantic History of Hypocrisy to the High Middle Ages', *RTAM* **53** (1986) 5–39
Anciaux, P. *La théologie du sacrement de pénitence au XIIe siècle* (Louvain, 1949)
Andrieu, M. (ed.) *Les ordines romani du Haut Moyen Âge* I, Spicilegium sacrum Iovaniense 2 (Louvain, 1931)
Angenendt, A. *Geschichte der Religiosität im Mittelalter* (Darmstadt, 2000)
Arendt, H. 'Some Questions of Moral Philosophy' in *Responsibility and Judgment*, ed. J. Kohn (New York, 2003)
Austin, G. 'Jurisprudence in the Service of Pastoral Care: The *Decretum* of Burchard of Worms', *Speculum* **79** (2004) 929–59
Bautier, R.-H. 'Paris au temps d'Abélard' in *Abélard en son temps*, ed. J. Jolivet, Actes du 9e centenaire de la naissance de Pierre Abélard (14–19 mai 1979) (Paris, 1981) 54–77
Bejczy, I. 'Deeds without Value: Exploring a Weak Spot in Abelard's Ethics', *RTAM* **70** (2003) 1–21
  'Law and Ethics: Twelfth-Century Jurists on the Virtue of Justice', *Viator* **36** (2005) 197–216.
  'The Problem of Natural Virtue' in *Virtue and Ethics*, ed. Bejczy and Newhauser 133–54
Bertola, E., *Il problema della coscienza nella teologia monastica del XII secolo* (Milan, 1970)
Bezner, F. *Vela veritatis: Hermeneutik, Wissen und Sprache in der Intellectual History des 12. Jahrhunderts*, Studien und Texte zur Geistesgeschichte des Mittelalters 85 (Leiden, 2005)
Biller, P. and A. Minnis (eds.), *Handling Sin: Confession in the Middle Ages*, York Studies in Medieval Theology (York, 1998)
Blaise, A. *Le vocabulaire latin des principaux thèmes liturgiques* (Turnhout, 1966)
Boureau, A. 'La redécouverte de l'autonomie du corps: l'émergence du somnambule (XIIe–XIVe s.)', *Micrologus* **1** (1993) 27–42
Brown, P. *The Body and Society: Men, Women, and Sexual Renunciation in Early Christianity* (London, 1989)
Brundage, J. 'Concubinage and Marriage in Medieval Canon Law', *Journal of Medieval History* **1** (1975) 1–18
Bynum, C. Walker *Docere verbo et exemplo: An Aspect of Twelfth-Century Spirituality*, Harvard Theological Studies 31 (Missoula, 1979)
  Jesus as Mother: Studies in the Spirituality of the High Middle Ages (Berkeley, 1982)
  The Cambridge Companion to Abelard, ed. J. Brower and K. Guilfoy (Cambridge, 2004)

Carpin, A. *La confessione tra il xii e il xiii secolo: Teologia e prassi nella legislazione canonica medievale* (Bologna, 2006).

Carruthers, M. and Ziolkowski, J. *The Medieval Craft of Memory: An Anthology of Texts and Pictures* (Philadelphia, 2002)

Casagrande C. and S. Vecchio, *I peccati della lingua: Disciplina ed etica della parola nella cultura medievale* (Rome, 1987)

  I sette vizi capitali: Storia dei peccati nel Medioevo (Turin, 2000)

Chadwick H. 'Gewissen' in *RLAC* X (1978) 1025–107

Chenu, M.-D. *La théologie au XIIe siècle* (Paris, 1957)

  L'éveil de la conscience dans la civilisation médiévale, Conférence Albert le Grand 1968 (Montreal, 1969)

Clanchy, M. *Abelard: A Medieval Life* (Oxford, 1997)

Colish, M. 'St. Augustine's Rhetoric of Silence Revisited', *Augustinian Studies* **9** (1978) 15–18

  'The Stoic Theory of Lies and False Statements from Antiquity to Anselm' in *Archéologie du signe*, ed. L. Brind'Amour and E. Vance (Toronto, 1982) 17–38

  The Stoic Tradition from Antiquity to the Early Middle Ages II: Stoicism in Christian Latin Thought through the Sixth Century (Leiden, 1985)

  'Another Look at the School of Laon', *AHDLMA* **53** (1986) 7–22

  'Systematic Theology and Theological Renewal in the Twelfth Century', *Journal of Mediaeval and Renaissance Studies* **18** (1988) 135–56

  Peter Lombard 2 vols. (Leiden, 1994)

  'Rethinking Lying in the Twelfth Century' in *Virtue and Ethics* ed. Bejczy and Newhauser 155–74

Constable, G. '*Nudus nudum Christum sequi* and Parallel Formulas in the Twelfth Century' in *Continuity and Discontinuity in Church History: Essays Presented to G. Huntston Williams*, ed. F. Church (Leiden, 1979) 83–91

  'The Concern for Sincerity and Understanding in Liturgical Prayer, especially in the Twelfth Century' in *Classica et Mediaevalia: Studies in Honor of J. Szövérffy*, ed. I. Vaslef and H. Buschhausen (Washington, 1986) 17–30

  Three Studies in Medieval Religious and Social Thought: The Interpretation of Mary and Martha; The Ideal of the Imitation of Christ; The Orders of Society (Cambridge, 1995)

  The Reformation of the Twelfth Century (Cambridge, 1996)

  'Monastic Letter Writing in the Middle Ages', *Filologia mediolatina* **11** (2004) 1–24

Courcelle, P. *Les Confessions de saint Augustine dans la tradition littéraire* (Paris, 1963)

  Connais-toi toi-même: De Socrate à saint Bernard, 2 vols. (Paris, 1974)

Courtney, F. *Robert Cardinal Pullen: An English Theologian of the 12th Century*, Analecta Gregoriana 64 (Rome, 1954)

Cristiani, M. '*Ars artium*: La psicologia di Gregorio Magno' in *Le trasformazioni della cultura nella tarda antichità*, Atti del convegno tenuto a Catania 22 Sept. – 2 Oct. 1982 (Rome, 1988) 309–31

Dagens, C. *Saint Grégoire le Grand: Culture et expérience chrétiennes* (Paris, 1977)

Dahan, G. 'L'exégèse de l'histoire de Caïn et Abel du XIIe au XIVe siècle en Occident', *RTAM* **49** (1982) 21–89

Das Problem der Willensschwäche in der mittelalterlichen Philosophie. The Problem of Weakness of Will in Medieval Philosophy, ed. T. Hoffmann, J. Müller, and M. Perkams. Recherches de théologie et philosophie médiévales Bibliotheca 8 (Leuven, 2006)

De Jong, M. 'What was *Public* about Public Penance? *Paenitentia Publica* and Justice in the Carolingian World' in *La giustizia nell'alto medioevo 2*, 863–902.

Delchard, A. 'Examen de conscience' in *Dictionnaire de spiritualité* V, 2, 1812ff.

Delhaye, P. 'Le dossier anti-matrimonial de l'*Adversus Iovinianum* et son influence sur quelques écrits latins du XIIe siècle', *Mediaeval Studies* **13** (1951) 65–86

'Dans le sillage de saint Bernard: Trois petits traités *"De conscientia"*', *Cîteaux in den Nederlanden* **5** (1954) 92–103

Le problème de la conscience morale chez S. Bernard, Analecta medievalia namurcensia 9 (Louvain, 1957)

'*Grammatica* et *Ethica* au XIIe siècle', *RTAM* **25** (1958) 59–110

'Les idées morales de saint Isidore de Séville' *RTAM* **36** (1959) 17–49

Der Fehltritt. Vergehen und Versehen in der Vormoderne, ed. P. von Moos, Norm und Struktur (Cologne, 2001)

Dihle, A. *The Theory of the Will in Classical Antiquity*, Sather Classical Lectures 48 (Berkeley, 1982)

'Demut' in *RLAC* **III**, 735–78

Dingjan, F. OSB, *Discretio: Les origines patristiques et monastiques de la doctrine sur la prudence de saint Thomas d'Aquin* (Assen, 1967)

Dronke, P. *Women Writers of the Middle Ages: A Critical Study of Texts from Perpetua (†203) to Marguerite Porete (†1310)* (Cambridge, 1984)

'The Archpoet and the Classics' in *Latin Poetry and the Classical Tradition*, ed. Godman and Murray 57–72

Dronke, P. and G. Orlandi, 'New Works by Abelard and Heloise', *Filologia mediolatina* **12** (2005) 123–77

Düring, W. 'Discretio' in *RLAC* **III**, 1230–45.

Epstein, J. *Envy: The Seven Deadly Sins* (Oxford, 2003)

Faire croire. Modalités de la diffusion et de la réception des messages religieux du XIIe au XVe siècle, Collection de l'Ecole Française de Rome 76 (Rome, 1981)

Fälschung im Mittelalter, MGH Schriften 33, 1–6 (Hanover, 1988–1990)

Fuhrmann, M. 'Persona, ein römischer Rollenbegriff' in *Identität*, ed. D. Marquard and K. Stierle, Poetik und Hermeneutik (Munich, 1979) 83–106

Gaudemet, J. 'La définition romano-canonique du marriage' in *Speculum iuris et ecclesiarum* (Vienna, 1967) 107–14

'L'héritage de Grégoire le Grand chez les canonistes médiévaux' in *Gregorio Magno e il suo tempo* II, Studia ephemeridis 'Augustinianum' (Rome, 1991) 199–221

Gilson, E. *Heloïse et Abélard*, 3rd edn (Paris, 1964)

Godman, P. *Poetry of the Carolingian Renaissance* (London, 1985)

The Saint as Censor: Robert Bellarmine between Inquisition and Index, Studies in Medieval and Reformation Thought 80 (Leiden, 2000)

The Silent Masters: Latin Literature and its Censors in the High Middle Ages (Princeton, 2000)

Grellard, C. '*Fides sive credulitas*: Le problème de l'assentiment chez Abélard, entre logique et psychologie', *AHDLMA* **70** (2003) 7–25.

Gründel, J. *Die Lehre von den Umständen der menschlichen Handlung im Mittelalter* BGPTMA 39, 5 (Münster, 1963)

Hadot, I. *Seneca und die griechisch-römische Tradition der Seelenleitung* (Berlin, 1969)

Hadot, P. *Exercices spirituels et philosophie antique* (reprint Paris, 2002)

Hamacher, J. 'Die Vagantenbeichte und ihre Quellen', *MlJb* **18** (1983) 160–7

Häring, N. 'The Interaction between Canon Law and Sacramental Theology in the Twelfth Century' in *Proceedings of the Fourth International Congress of Canon Law*, ed. S. Kuttner (Vatican, 1976) 483–93

Heaney, S. *The Development of the Sacramentality of Marriage from Anselm of Laon to Thomas Aquinas*, Catholic University of America Studies in Sacred Theology 134 (Washington, 1963)

Hödl, L. *Die Geschichte der scholastischen Literatur und der Theologie der Schlüsselgewalt* I, BGPTMA 38, 4 (Münster, 1960)

Hoheisel, K. 'Schauspielerei und Heuchelei in antiken Beurteilungen' in *Secrecy and Concealment: Studies in the History of Mediterranean and Near Eastern Religions*, ed. H. Kippenberg and G. Stroumsa (Leiden, 1995) 177–90

Hoheisel, K., U. Wilckens, and A. Kehl, 'Heuchelei' in *RLAC* XIV, 1205–31

Honnefelder, L. '*Conscientia sive ratio*: Thomas von Aquin und die Entwicklung des Gewissensbegriffs' in *Mittelalterliche Komponenten des europäischen Bewusstseins*, ed. J. Szövérffy (Berlin, 1983) 8–19

Honoré, L. *Le secret de la confession: Étude historique-canonique* (Paris, 1924)

Hourlier, J. *Histoire du droit et des institutions de l'Eglise en Occident* X: *L'âge classique (1140–1378). Les religieux* (Paris, 1974)

Jaeger, H. 'L'examen de conscience dans les religions non-chrétiennes et avant le christianisme', *Numen* 6 (1959) 176–233

Jonsen A. and S. Toulmin, *The Abuse of Casuistry: A History of Moral Reasoning* (Berkely, 1988).

Judiç, B. 'Confession chez Grégoire le Grand, entre l'intériorité et l'extériorité: l'aveu de l' âme et l'aveu du corps' in *L'Aveu*, 169–90

Jungmann, J. *Die lateinischen Bußriten in ihrer geschichtlichen Entwicklung: Forschungen zur Geschichte des innerkirchlichen Lebens* (Innsbruck, 1934)

Kaiser, R. *Trunkenheit und Gewalt im Mittelalter* (Cologne, 2002)

Kantorowicz, E. 'Die Wiederkehr gelehrter Anachorese im Mittelalter' in *Selected Studies* (New York, 1965) 339–51

Kaster, R. *Emotion, Restraint, and Community in Ancient Rome* (Oxford, 2005)

Kierkegaard, S. *The Concept of Irony, with Continual Reference to Socrates*, ed. and trans. H. and E. Hong (Princeton, 1989)

Kittsteiner, H. *Die Entstehung des modernen Gewissens* (Frankfurt, 1992).

Knox, D. *Ironia: Medieval and Renaissance Ideas on Irony* (Leiden, 1989).

Knuuttila, S. *Emotions in Ancient and Medieval Philosophy* (Oxford, 2002)

Köhn, R. 'Dimensionen und Funktionen des Öffentlichen und Privaten in der mittelalterlichen Korrespondenz' in *Das Öffentliche und Private in der Vormoderne*, ed. G. Melville and P. von Moos, Norm und Struktur 10 (Cologne, 1998) 309–57.

Körntgen, L. 'Fortschreibung frühmittelalterlicher Bußpraxis: Burchards 'Liber corrector' und seine Quellen' in *Bischof Burchard von Worms 1000–1025*, ed. W. Hartmann (Mainz, 2000), 198–226

Kottje, R. *Die Bußbücher Halitgars von Cambrai und des Hrabanus Maurus: Ihre Überlieferung und ihre Quellen* (Berlin, 1980)

'Buße oder Strafe? ' Zur 'iustitia' in den Libri Poenitentiales' in *La giustizia nell'Alto Medioevo* **II**, 443–474

'Intentions – oder Tathaftung? Zum Verständnis der frühmittelalterlichen Bußbücher', *Zeitschrift der Savigny-Stiftung für Rechtsgeschichte* 122, Kanonistische Abteilung **91** (2005) 738–41

Kuttner, S., *Kanonistische Schuldlehre von Gratian bis auf die Dekretalen Gregors IX*, Studi e testi 64 (Vatican, 1935)

'Ecclesia de occultis non iudicat: Problemata ex doctrina poenali canonistarum et decretalistarum a Gratiano usque ad Gregorium P. P. IX', in *Acta congressus iuridici internationalis* III (Vatican, 1936) 225–46

L'Aveu: Antiquité et Moyen Âge, Collection de l'Ecole Française de Rome 88 (Rome, 1988)

La Bonnardière, A.-M. 'Pénitence et réconciliation des pénitents d'après saint Augustin', *Revue des études augustiniennes* **13** (1967) 31–53, 249–83; **14** (1968) 181–204

La giustizia nell'Alto Medioevo, Settimane del Centro Italiano di Studi sull'alto medioevo 44, 2 vols. (Spoleto, 1997)

Landgraf, A. 'Grundlagen für ein Verständnis der Bußlehre der Frühscholastik', *Zeitschrift für katholische Theologie* **51** (1927) 161–89

'Definition und Sündhaftigkeit der Lüge nach der Lehre der Frühscholastik', *Zeitschrift für katholische Theologie* **63** (1939) 50–85, 157–80

'Die Stellungnahme der Frühscholastik zur Lüge der alttestamentlichen Patriarchen', *Theologisch-praktische Quartalschrift* **92** (1939) 1–33

'Die Einschätzung der Scherzlüge in der Frühscholastik', *Theologisch-praktische Quartalschrift* **93** (1940) 3–11

Die Lüge des Vollkommenen und die Lüge aus Bescheidenheit im Urteil der Frühscholastik', *Divus Thomas* **19** (1942) 67–91

Dogmengeschichte der Frühscholastik, 8 vols. (Regensburg, 1955–1958)

Latin Poetry and the Classical Tradition: Essays in Medieval and Renaissance Literature, ed. P. Godman and O. Murray, (Oxford, 1990)

Leclercq, J. 'Un témoignage sur l'influence de Grégoire VII dans la réforme canoniale', *Studi Gregoriani* **6** (1959–1960) 173–227

Recueil d'études sur saint Bernard et ses écrits V, Storia e letteratura 182 (Rome, 1992)

Lloyd, A. 'Nosce te ipsum and Conscientia', *Archiv für Geschichte der Philosophie* **46** (1964) 188–200.

Luscombe, D. *The School of Peter Abelard: The Influence of Abelard's Thought in the Early Scholastic Period* (Cambridge, 1969)

Lutterbach, H. 'Intentions – oder Tathaftung? Zum Bußverständnis in den frühmittelalterlichen Bußbüchern', *Frühmittelalterliche Studien* **29** (1995) 120–43

Monachus factus est: Die Mönchwerdung im frühen Mittelalter, Beiträge zur Geschichte des alten Mönchtums und des Benediktinertums 44 (Münster, 1995)

Sexualität im Mittelalter: eine Kulturstudie anhand von Bußbüchern des 6. bis 12. Jahrhunderts (Cologne, 1999)

'Die Fastenbüße im Mittelalter' in *Frömmigkeit im Mittelater: Politisch-soziale Kontexte, visuelle Praxis, körperliche Ausdrucksformen*, ed. K. Schreiner (Munich, 2002) 399–437

Mansfield, M. *The Humiliation of Sinners: Public Penance in Thirteenth-Century France* (Ithaca, 1995)

Marenbon, J. *The Philosophy of Peter Abelard* (Cambridge, 1997)

'Life, Milieu, and Intellectual Contexts' in *The Cambridge Companion to Abelard*, 13–44

'Abélard: les exemples des philosophes et les philosophes comme exemples' in *Exempla docent: Les exemples des philosophes de l'Antiquité à la Renaissance*, Actes du colloque international 23–25 Oct. 2003, Université de Neuchâtel, ed. T. Richlin (Paris, 2006) 119–34

'The Rediscovery of Abelard's Philosophy', *Journal of the History of Philosophy* **44** (2006) 331–51

'Lost Love-Letters? A Controversy in Retrospect', *International Journal for the History of the Classical Tradition* (forthcoming)

Markus, R. *Saeculum: History and Society in the Theology of St. Augustine* (Cambridge, 1970)

Martin, J. 'Inventing Sincerity, Refashioning Prudence: the Discovery of the Individual in Renaissance Europe', *The American Historical Review* **102** (1997) 1309–42

Matter, E. 'Gregory the Great in the Twelfth Century: The *Glossa ordinaria*' in *Gregory the Great: A Symposium*, ed. J. Cavadini, Notre Dame Studies in Theology 2 (Notre Dame, 1995) 216–26

Mauro, L. 'Tra *publica damna* e *communis utilitas*: L'aspetto sociale della morale di Abelardo e i "libri paenitentiales"', *Medioevo* **13** (1987) 103–22

McKeon, R. 'Poetry and Philosophy in the Twelfth Century: The Renaissance of Rhetoric', in *Critics and Criticism: Ancient and Modern*, ed. R.-S. Crane (Chicago, 1952) 297–318

McLaughlin, M. 'Peter Abelard and the Dignity of Women: Twelfth-Century "Feminism" in Theory and Practice' in *Pierre Abélard – Pierre le Vénérable:*

Les courants philosophiques, littéraires, et artistiques en Occident au milieu du XIIe siècle, ed. J. Jolivet and R. Louis (Paris, 1975), 287–94

McNeill, J. 'Medicine for Sin as Prescribed in the Penitentials', *Church History* **I** (1932) 14–26

Merkel, H. 'Gotteslästerung' in *RLAC* **XI**, 1185–1201

Metz, R. 'Recherches sur la condition de la femme selon Gratien', *Studia Gratiana* **12** (1957) [= *Collectanea S. Kuttner* II) 377–96

Michaud-Quantin, P. *Sommes de casuistique et manuels de confession au Moyen Âge* (Louvain, 1962)

Miethke, J. 'Theologenprozesse in der ersten Phase ihrer institutionellen Ausbildung: die Verfahren gegen Peter Abelard und Gilbert von Poitiers', *Viator* **6** (1995) 87–116

Misch, G. *Geschichte der Autobiographie II, Das Mittelalter ii: Das Hochmittelalter im Anfang* (Frankfurt am Main, 1959)

Moos, von P. 'Gottschalks *O mi custos* – eine *Confessio*', *Frühmittelalterliche Studien* **4** (1970) 210ff.; ibid. **5** (1971) 317ff.

Consolatio: Studien zur mittellateinischen Trostliteratur über den Tod und zum Problem der christlichen Trauer, 4 vols. (Munich, 1971–1972)

Mittelalterforschung und Ideologiekritik: Der Gelehrtenstreit um Heloise (Munich, 1974)

'*Poeta* und *Historicus* im Mittelalter: Zum Mimesis – Problem am Beispiel einiger Urteile über Lucan', *Beiträge zur Geschichte der deutschen Sprache und Literatur* **98** (1976) 93–130

'Fehltritt, Fauxpas und Transgressionen in Mittelalter' in von Moos (ed.) *Der Fehltritt*, 1–96

Abaelard und Heloise: Gesammelte Studien zum Mittelalter I, ed. G. Melville, Geschichte: Forschung und Wissenschaft 14 (Münster, 2005)

Entre histoire et literature: Communication et culture au Moyen Âge (Florence, 2005)

Rhetorik, Kommunikation und Medialität: Gesammelte Studien zum Mittelalter II, ed. G. Melville, Geschichte: Forschung und Wissenschaft 15 (Berlin, 2006)

Öffentliches und Privates, Gemeinsames und Eigenes: Gesammelte Studien zum Mittelalter III, ed. G. Melville, Geschichte: Forschung und Wissenschaft 16 (Berlin, 2007)

Müller, G. *Die Wahrhaftigkeitspflicht und die Problematik der Lüge* (Freiburg, 1962)

Müller, J. 'Das Problem der Willensschwäche bei Petrus Abaelardus', in *Das Problem der Willensschwäche*, ed. Hoffmann *et al.*; 123–45.

Müller, M. *Die Lehre des heiligen Augustinus von der Paradiesehe und ihre Auswirkung in der Sexualethik des 12. und 13. Jahrhunderts bis Thomas von Aquin* (Regensburg, 1954)).

Murdoch, I. *The Sovereignty of Good* (London, 2001)

Murray, A. 'Confession as a Historical Source in the Thirteenth Century' in *The Writing of History in the Middle Ages: Essays Presented to R. Southern*, ed. R. Davis and M. Wallace-Hadrill (Oxford, 1981)

— 'Confession before 1215', *Transactions of the Royal Historical Society* **3** (1993) 51–81

— *Suicide in the Middle Ages* II: *The Curse on Self-Murder* (Oxford, 2000)

Muzzarelli, M. 'Teorie e forme di penitenza in fase di transizione' in *Dalla penitenza all'ascolto delle confessioni: il ruolo dei frati mendicanti*, Atti del XXIII convegno internazionale, Assisi, 12–14 Oct. 1995 (Spoleto, 1996) 33–58

Nagy, P. *Le don des larmes au Moyen Age: Un instrument spirituel en quête d'institution (Ve–XIIIe siècle)* (Paris, 2000)

Newhauser, R. 'Zur Zweideutigkeit in der Moraltheologie: Als Tugenden verkleidete Laster' in *Der Fehltritt*, 337–402

Newman, B. 'Authority, Authenticity, and the Repression of Heloise', *Journal of Medieval and Renaissance Studies* **22** (1992), 121–57, repr. in Newman, *From Virile Woman to Woman Christ: Studies in Medieval Religion and Literature* (Philadelphia, 1995) 46–75

Noonan, J. 'Power to Choose', *Viator* **4** (1973) 419–34

Nothdurft, K.-D, *Studien zum Einfluß Senecas auf die Philosophie und Theologie des zwölften Jahrhunderts* (Leiden, 1963)

Nussbaum, M. *Upheavals of Thought: The Intelligence of the Emotions* (Cambridge, 2001)

— *Hiding from Humanity: Disgust, Shame and Law* (Princeton, 2004)

Ohst, M. *Pflichtbeichte: Untersuchungen zum Bußwesen im hohen und späten Mittelalter*, Beiträge zur historischen Theologie 89 (Tübingen, 1995)

Ott, L. *Untersuchungen zur theologischen Briefliteratur der Frühscholastik*, BGPTMA 34 (Münster, 1937)

Pane e acqua: Peccati e penitenza nel Medioevo. Il penitenziale di Burcardo di Worms, ed. and trans. G. Ricasso, G. Piana, and G. Motta (Novara, 1986)

Payer, P. 'The Humanism of the Penitentials and the Continuity of the Penitential Tradition', *Mediaeval Studies* **46** (1984) 340–51

Pears, D. *Motivated Irrationality* (Oxford, 1984)

— *Paradox and Platitude in Wittgenstein's Philosophy* (Oxford, 2006)

Perkams, M. *Liebe als Zentralbegriff der Ethik nach Peter Abelard* BGPTMA 58 (Münster, 2001)

Pétré, H. *Caritas: Étude sur le vocabulaire latin de la charité chrétienne* (Louvain, 1948)

Pettazzoni, R. 'La confession des péchés dans l'histoire générale des religions' in *Mélanges F. Cumont*, Annuaire de l'Institut de philologie et d'histoire orientales et slaves 4 (Brussels, 1936) 893–901

Pierce, C. *Conscience in the New Testament* (London, 1955)

Platelle, H. 'Le problème du scandale: les nouvelles modes masculines au XIe et au XIIe siècle', *Revue belge de philologie et d'histoire* **53** (1975) 1071–96

Pollmann, K. 'The Splitting of Morality in *Matthew* 23 and its Exegetical Consequences' in Pollman (ed.), *Double Standards in the Ancient and Medieval World* (Göttingen, 2000) 263–86
'Hypocrisy and the History of Salvation: Medieval Interpretations of Matthew 23', *Wiener Studien* **114** (2001) 469–82

Poschmann, B. *Die abendländischen Kirchenbüße im Frühmittelater* (Breslau, 1930)

Rahner, H. *Symbole der Kirche: Die Ekklesiologie der Väter* (Salzburg, 1964)

Ratzinger, J., Cardinal (Benedict XVI) 'Originalität und Überlieferung in Augustinus Begriff der *Confessio*', *Revue des études augustiniennes* **3** (1957) 375–92
'Conscience and Truth' in *Benedict XVI and Cardinal Newman* (Oxford, 2005)

Renaissance and Renewal in the Twelfth Century, ed. R. Benson and G. Constable (Oxford, 1982)

Rigg, G. 'Golias and Other Pseudonyms', *Studi Medievali*, 3rd ser., 18 (1977) 65–105

Romer, J. *Die Theologie der Sünde und der Buße beim heiligen Ambrosius* (St Gallen, 1968)

Rosier-Catach, I. *La parole efficace: Signe, rituel, sacré* (Paris, 2004)

Rusconi, R. *L'ordine dei peccati: La confessione tra Medioevo ed età moderna* (Bologna, 2002)

Saarinen, R. *Weakness of the Will in Medieval Thought from Augustine to Buridan*, Studien und Texte zur Geistesgeschichte des Mittelalters 44 (Leiden, 1994)

Sauer, E. 'Christus medicus: Christus als Arzt und seine Nachfolger im frühen Christentum', *Trierer Theologische Zeitschrift* **101** (1992) 101–23

Saxer, V., *Le culte de Marie Madeleine en Occident*, 2 vols. (Auxerre, 1959)

Schmidt, P. 'The Quotation in Goliardic Poetry: The Feast of Fools and the Goliardic Strophe *cum auctoritate*' in *Latin Poetry and the Classical Tradition*, ed. Godman and Murray, 39–56

Schmitt, J.-C. *La Raison des gestes dans l'Occident médiéval* (Paris, 1990)

Schmitz, G. 'Schuld und Strafe: Eine unbekannte Stellungnahme das Rathramnus von Corbie zur Kindestötung', *Deutsches Archiv* **38** (1982) 363–87

Schmitz, H. *Die Bußbücher und die Bußdisziplin der Kirche: Nach handschriftlichen Quellen dargelegt* I (reprint Graz, 1958)

Schwartz, E. 'Der verfluchtete Feigebaum' in *Zum Neuen Testament und zum frühen Christentum. Gesammelte Schriften* V (Berlin, 1963) 42–7

Severus, von E. 'Gebet' in *RLAC* VIII, 1134–1258

Solomon, R. *Not Passion's Slave: Emotions and Choice* (Oxford, 2003)

Sorabji, R. *Emotion and Peace of Mind: From Stoic Agitation to Christian Temptation* (Oxford, 2000)
Self: Ancient and Modern Insights about Individuality, Life, and Death (Oxford, 2006)

Southern, R. *St. Anselm and his Biographer: A Study of Monastic Life and Thought 1059–c.1130* (Cambridge, 1966)
Saint Anselm: A Portrait in a Landscape (Cambridge, 1991)

Scholastic Humanism and the Unification of Europe I: *Foundations* (Oxford, 1995)

Speer, A. *Die entdeckte Natur: Untersuchungen zu Begründungsversuchen einer 'scientia naturalis' im 12 Jahrhundert* (Leiden, 1995)

Speyer, W. 'Fluch' in *RLAC* VIII, 1253–88

Spicq, C. 'Bénignité, mansuétude, douceur, clémence', *Revue biblique* **55** (1947) 321–37

Stelzenberger, J. *Conscientia bei Augustinus: Studie zur Geschichte der Moraltheologie* (Paderborn, 1959)

Stendahl, K. 'The Apostle Paul and the Introspective Conscience of the West', *Harvard Theological Review* **56** (1963) 199–215

Steinen, von den W. *Menschen in Mittelalter: Gesammelte Forschungen, Betrachtungen, Bilder*, ed. P. von Moos (Berne, 1967)

Stevens, M. 'The Performing Self in Twelfth-Century Culture', *Viator* **8** (1978) 193–212

Straw, C. *Gregory the Great: Perfection in Imperfection* (Berkeley, 1988)

Suchomski, J. *'Delectatio' und 'Utilitas': ein Beitrag zum Verständnis mittelalterlicher komischer Literatur* (Berne, 1975)

Tauber, W. *Das Würfelspiel im Mittelalter und in der frühen Neuzeit: Eine kultur – und sprachgeschichtliche Darstellung*, Europäische Hochschulschriften 959 (Frankfurt am Main, 1987).

Taylor, G. *Pride, Shame, and Guilt* (Oxford, 1985)
    Deadly Vices (Oxford, 2006)

Teetaert, A. *La confession aux laïques dans l'Eglise latine depuis le VIIIe jusqu'au XIVe siècle* (Bruges, 1926)

Thomas, Y. *'Fictio legis*: L'empire de la fiction romaine et ses limites médiévales', *Droits: Revue française de théorie juridique* **21** (1995) 17–63

Töpfer, B. *Urzustand und Sündenfall in der mittelalterlichen Gesellschafts – und Staatstheorie*, Monographien zur Geschichte des Mittelalters 45 (Stuttgart, 1999)

Trilling, L. *Sincerity and Authenticity* (Cambridge, Mass., 1971)

Troncarelli, F. 'L'attribuzione, il testo, il falso' in *Lo spazio letterario nel Medioevo: Il Medioevo Latino I: La produzione del testo* (Rome, 1993) 373–90

Ullmann, W. 'Cardinal Roland and the Incident at Besançon', *Miscellanea Historiae Pontificiae* **18** (1954) 107–25

Ulrich, A. *Kain und Abel in der Kunst: Untersuchungen zur Ikonographie und Auslegungsgeschichte* (Bamberg, 1981)

Vaccari, P. 'La tradizione canonica del *debitum* coniugale e la posizione di Graziano', *Studia Gratiana* **1** (1953) 535–47

Vecchio, S. 'Segreti e bugie: I *peccata occulta*', *Micrologus* **14** (2006) 41–58

Vernay, R. 'Distractions' in *Dictionnaire de spiritualité* 3 (Paris, 1957) 1347–63

Vincent-Cassy, M. 'Recherches sur le mensonge au moyen âge' in *Études sur la sensibilité au moyen âge* II (Paris, 1979) 165–73

Virtue and Ethics in the Twelfth Century, ed. I. Bejczy and R. Newhauser (Leiden, 2005)

Vogel, C. 'La discipline pénitentielle en Gaule des origines jusqu'au IXe siècle', *Revue de sciences religeuses* **30** (1956) 1–26, 157–86

Le péché et la pénitence: Aperçu sur l' évolution historique de la discipline péniten-tielle dans l'Eglise latine, Bibliothèque de théologie II, Théologie morale 8, *Pastorale du Péché*, ed. P. Delhaye *et al.* (Tournai, 1961)

Vorgrimler, H. *Buße und Krankensalbung*, Handbuch der Dogmengeschichte 4, 3 (Freiburg, 1978)

Wasselnyck, R. 'Les compilations des *Moralia in Iob* du VIIe au XIIe siècle', *RTAM* **29** (1962) 5–32

'L'influence de l'exégèse de Saint Grégoire le Grand sur les commentaires bib-liques médiévaux (VIIe–XIIe siècles)', *RTAM* **32** (1965) 157–204

'La présence de saint Grégoire le Grand dans les ouvrages de morale du XIIe siècle', *RTAM* **35** (1968) 197–240

Wasserschleben, F. *Die Bußordnungen der abendländischen Kirche* (reprint Graz, 1958)

Weingart, R. 'Peter Abelard's Contribution to Medieval Sacramentology', *RTAM* **34** (1967) 159–78

The Logic of Divine Love: A Critical Analysis of the Soteriology of Peter Abelard (Oxford, 1970)

Weisweiler, H. 'Die Bußlehre Simons von Tournai', *Zeitschrift für katholische Theologie* **56** (1932) 190–230

Wheeler, B. (ed.) *Listening to Heloise: The Voice of a Twelfth-Century Woman* (London, 2000)

Williams, B. *Shame and Necessity*, Sather Classical Lectures 57 (Berkeley, 1993)

Truth and Truthfulness: An Essay in Genealogy (Princeton, 2002)

Winroth, A. *The Making of Gratian's Decretum*, Cambridge Studies in Medieval Life and Thought 49 (Cambridge, 2000)

Ziegler, J. *Dulcedo Dei: Ein Beitrag zur Theologie der griechischen und lateinischen Bibel* (Münster, 1937)

Ziementz, H. *Ehe nach der Lehre der Frühscholastik: Eine moralgeschichtliche Untersuchung zur Anthropologie und Theologie der Ehe in der Schule Anselms von Laon und Wilhelms von Champeaux, bei Hugo von St. Viktor, Walter von Mortagne und Petrus Lombardus*, Moraltheologische Studien, Historische Abteilung 1 (Düsseldorf, 1973)

Zimmermann, G. *Ordensleben und Lebensstandard: Die cura corporis in den Ordensvorschriften des abendländischen Hochmittelalters*, Beiträge zur Geschichte des alten Mönchtums und des Benediktenerordens 32 (Münster, 1979)

Ziolkowski, J. 'Lost and Not Yet Found: Heloise, Abelard and the *Epistolae duorum amantium*', *The Journal of Medieval Latin* **14** (2004) 171–202

Index of quotations

General index

abbots, role and authority of 4, 8, 67, 128
Abelard, Peter
    as abbot of Saint-Gildas 9ff, 113ff
    as Don Quixote 71ff, 110
    as Narcissus 85ff
    attitude to love 83ff, 128ff
    attitudes to marriage 86ff, 122ff, 162
    castration of 90ff, 114, 117
    concept of equity 104, 131
    condemnation of 103ff
    ethical theory of 64–65, 97, 104ff, 116ff, 136ff
    'feminism' of 163
    humility of 67, 118, 162ff
    integrity of 117ff
    irony of 87, 101, 109
    moral psychology of 139f, 144
    on the virtues of pagans 90
    pride of 83ff
    rhetoric of 75, 101
    solipsism of 68, 83, 95
    stupidity of 81, 83, 90
    tactlessness of 110ff
abstinence, feigned 31ff
    from wine 183ff
accountancy, of the conscience 35ff
acting, as analogy 34
    literal 34
actions
    intended 136ff, 140ff
    unintended 94, 136ff, 140ff
Adam 24
Adam, of Perseigne 61–62
Adam, abbot of Saint-Denis 98ff, 111
affectus 69ff
ἀκρασία 24ff, 35, 139ff, 154
Alan, of Lille 61
Alberic, of Reims 80, 100
Alexander III, Pope 14, 60, 160ff, 168
amaritudo, as remorse 33, 57, 105, 117, 174, 191
ambiguity 7ff, 147ff
Ambrose, St 22–24, 103ff

amicus, of *HC* 68, 90, 95, 116
amor 84ff, 126, 128, 161ff
Anacletus II, antipope 44
Anselm, of Aosta and Canterbury, St 48ff, 156
Anselm, of Laon 51ff, 60, 77ff, 98, 100, 123, 144, 158
antiquitas 78
antithesis, and antithetical thought 92ff, 103ff, 137
Antony, St 107
aphrodisiacs 40
arcana cordis 3, 53, 104, 130, 141, 194ff
Archpoet 11ff, 167ff
Ardens, R. 61
Argenteuil, nunnery 114
Aristotle 24, 35, 154
Astralabe, son of Abelard and Heloise 87ff, 132ff
Athanasius, St; creed of 101
Athens 110
atonement 106, 139
Augustine, St 17, 24ff
    ambivalence of 10, 146ff
    and confession 10, 24ff
    and continence 146, 152ff
    and *fictio* 26ff, 157
    and hypocrisy 27, 157
    and monks 28
    and pride 27
    and sacraments 27ff
    and sexuality 147ff
    and truthfulness 28
    ethical identity of 24ff
    exegesis of 26ff, 50, 157
    imitation of 48ff, 67ff, 157
Augustine, pseudo- 45ff
authenticity of Abelard's and Heloise's works, 163ff
    religious/spiritual 1ff, 47, 164
autobiography, Latin 68, 69, 76

Bacchus 186ff
baptism 21, 41, 56, 59
Bandinelli, R. 60
Bede, the Venerable 110

CAMBRIDGE STUDIES IN MEDIEVAL LITERATURE